Literacy practices: Investigating literacy in social contexts

Mike Baynham

Longman
London and New York

Longman Group Limited,
Longman House, Burnt Mill,
Harlow, Essex CM20 2JE, England
and Associated Companies throughout the world.

*Published in the United States of America
By Longman Publishing, New York*

First published 1995

ISBN 0 582 087090 CSD
ISBN 0 582 087082 PPR

British Library Cataloguing-in-Publication Data

A catalogue record for this book is
available from the British Library

Library of Congress Cataloging-in-Publication Data
Baynham, Mike, 1950–
    Literacy practices / Mike Baynham.
      p. cm.—(Language in social life series)
    Includes bibliographical references and index.
    ISBN 0–582–08709–0.—ISBN 0–582–08708–2 (pbk.)
    1. Written communication. 2. Literacy. I. Title. II. Series.
P211.B36 1994
302.2'244—dc20   93–39308
                                                        CIP

Set by 5V in 10/12pt Palatino
Produced by Longman Singapore Publishers (Pte) Ltd.
Printed in Singapore

Contents

Author's Acknowledgements

The first draft of this book was written in Sydney and I am grateful to Su Dovey for letting me use a sunny room with a view over Bondi to write in.

The second draft was written while I was a Visiting Fellow in the Department of English, Media and Drama at the Institute of Education, University of London in 1993. I am grateful to Gunther Kress, Cathy Wallace and Euan Reid for their hospitality.

I would also like to thank those who read and commented on parts of the manuscript at various stages: Ken Cruickshank, Sheilagh Kelly, Gunther Kress, Alison Lee, Helen Lobanga Masing, Janet Maybin.

I am grateful for the opportunity to try out some of the material presented in this book in seminars at the University of Technology, Sydney, the Literacy research group at Lancaster University, the Mass Observation Archive at the University of Sussex, the Institute of Education, University of London and with MA students at Thames Valley University.

The tyre-changing activity in Chapter six is based on an idea developed by Hermine Scheeres.

I would also like to thank my friends, colleagues and students from the Moroccan Community in London who first made me curious about the diversity of literacy practices.

Under Chris Candlin's editorship I learnt a great deal about writing and the teaching of writing.

Lastly I would like to acknowledge with gratitude the support of my family.

Publisher's Acknowledgements

We are grateful to the following for permission to reproduce copyright material:

Australian Government Publishing Service for extracts from the articles 'A migrant women's learning centre' by Miriam Faine and 'An open learning centre inside a steelworks' by Margrit Stocker in *Good Practice in Adult Literacy*, No 8, June 1990, Department of Employment Education and Training; The British Association for Applied Linguistics for the article 'The Oral dimension of a Literary event: a letter from the DHSS' by Mike Baynham in T. Bloor and J. Norrish (ed.) *Written Language* (London CILT/BAAL, 1986), pp 98–113; the author, Ita Buttrose for an extract from 'Ita's Page' in *Woman's Day*, November, 1987; Cambridge University Press for the article 'Code-switching and mode-switching, Community interpreters and mediators of literacy' by Mike Baynham in B. Sweet (ed.) *Crosscultural Approaches to Literacy*, pp 294–314; Deakin University for the article 'Just like farmlands and goldmines: workplace literacies in era of longterm unemployment' by Baynham & Wickert in *Collection of Original Essays for Curriculum for the Workplace* (Unit EEE604: Curriculum & Competencies); Education Links for text from the article 'Getting Constituted and Getting Funded' by Mike Baynham in *Education Links* No 39, pp 19–22; the author, Annie Lampe for an extract from her article 'Insurers overstated AIDS by 100pc' in *Sydney Morning Herald*; IPC Magazines for 'Golden Banana Cake' recipe from *Woman's Realm* 9.2.93; Oxford University Press for an adapted extract from *English Language Teaching Journal*, Vol 37, No 4 (October 1983); the author's agents/Penguin Books Ltd for extracts from *Kes: A Kestral for a Knave* by Barry Hines (Michael Joseph, 1968) copyright © Barry Hines, 1968. Reproduced by permission of Michael Joseph Ltd; Research and Practice in Adult Literacy for the article 'Literacy Research in the UK: Adult and School Perspectives' by Mike Baynham in J. McCaffery & B. Street (Eds.) *RaPAL Bulletin*, 1988; TAFE for extracts from *Literary Program Management Curriculum*, Department of Employment Vocational Education, Training and Industrial Relations; Lancaster University for Figure 1.3 *Partnership in the Study of Literacy*; Longman Group UK Limited for Figure 4.1 from page 153 of *Bilingualism in Education: Aspects of Theory, Research and Practice* by J. Cummins and M. Swain; Eileen Chau to use Transcription 9 of her unpublished MA in TESOL thesis as Figure 4.2; The Roads and Traffic Authority of New South Wales, Australia (RTA) for Figure 5.2, being two pages of the *Road Users' Handbook*.

We have been unable to find the copyright holders of 'Door Trouble' tip in *Practical Householder*, March 1993, and an extract by Mahbubar Rahman in *Classrooms of Resistance* by J. Searle and would appreciate any information which would enable us to do so.

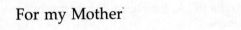

For my Mother

ONE

Defining literacy: models, myths and metaphors

THE SCOPE OF LITERACY PRACTICES

This book draws on ideas from linguistics and anthropology, and educational and social theory. It draws on both research and practical experience in the literacy development of adults. It is organized around some basic premises, which can be stated as follows:

- literacy has developed and is shaped to serve social purposes in creating and exchanging meaning;
- literacy is best understood in its contexts of use;
- literacy is ideological: like all uses of language it is not neutral, but shapes and is shaped by deeply held ideological positions, which can be either implicit or explicit;
- literacy needs to be understood in terms of social power;
- literacy can be critical.

WHY LITERACY PRACTICES?

Investigating literacy as practice involves investigating literacy as 'concrete human activity', not just what people do with literacy, but also what they make of what they do, the values they place on it and the ideologies that surround it. Practice provides a way of linking the cognitive with the social, opening up the possibility of an integrated approach to the study of literacy in use.

The other necessary dimension in the study of literacy is linguistic. Where does the concept of practice fit in relation to language? I will argue in this book that it is not enough to study the objective 'evidence' of language in the shape of spoken and written texts (the 'product' dimension). It is not even enough to study the 'process' dimension of what people do with spoken and written language in context. We also need a further dimension of language as social practice to deal with the ways that language operates to reproduce and maintain institutions and power bases as well as the ways that discourses and ideologies operate through language.

Becoming aware through language of how social practice operates and, in particular, how language operates as social practice is a key component of critical language education (cf. Fairclough 1989, 1992a).

IF LITERACY CAN BE CRITICAL, WHAT IS CRITICAL LITERACY?

If literacy can be defined as the uses of reading and writing to achieve social purposes in contexts of use, what makes literacy critical? In this book I will be arguing for what could be called a 'critical functional' approach to literacy.

An approach to literacy which is functional but not critical would involve, for example, literacy instruction which taught participants to achieve their social purposes, in terms of giving them access to relevant uses of literacy, but did so uncritically, accepting dominant means of communication on their own terms as something given and natural.

Critical literacy doesn't accept the natural status of dominant institutions and discourses but calls them into question. In fact, the notion of the question is a useful one in understanding the idea of critique (which is not of course the same as the everyday use of 'critical'/'criticism' as finding fault with someone or something). Critique is to do with finding out how something works, not taking things as given, but looking below the surface, asking questions like:

- Why does this exist/happen?
- What is its purpose?
- Whose interests does it serve?
- Whose interests does it frustrate?
- How does it operate?
- Need it operate like this or could it be done differently and better?

Literacy work isn't necessarily critical in itself, but it can be a powerful tool for developing critical thinking just because language is powerful as social practice. Institutions and social organizations are sustained and reproduced through language; language is what introduces the human subject into social orders. Critical literacy work can be the opportunity to develop control over the production of text (the dimensions of product and process). But it can also develop a critical awareness of social purpose and whose interests are being served by it.

DEFINING TERMS: A THEORETICAL FRAMEWORK FOR THE BOOK

Another important emphasis of this book is on literacy in use. To understand literacy in use, we need to take the following concepts into account in a framework for understanding literacy:

1 *social contexts*: literacy acquisition and use takes place in context and unless we take into account the influences of context on literacy practices, we are ignoring an important dimension for the understanding of literacy. The importance of context is stressed by writers like Street (1984) from anthropology, Levine (1986) from sociology, Heath (1983) from ethnography of communication, as well as by educational theorists like Freire (1973, 1985).

2 *situated interactions*: literacy acquisition and use takes place in situated interactions. The effect of the dominantly psychological and textual emphasis of earlier literacy studies was to neglect the importance of social interaction in context in our understanding of literacy. Writers like Cook-Gumperz (1986) and Heath (1983) have re-emphasized the importance of the social interactional aspects of literacy acquisition and use.

3 *acquisition processes*: we still don't know enough, despite decades of research about the ways in which children and adults become literate. Detailed ethnographic studies of literacy acquisition in process may hold the key to unlocking how these processes work. Stubbs (1987) writes of 'a whole theory of transitions through which children have to pass in the education system' (p. 23). Emphasis by researchers such as Meek (1991) and Cook-Gumperz (1986) on the social construction of literacy acquisition may provide the basis for making grounded hypotheses about the processes of literacy acquisition in children and in adults. Here we have a need for more studies and more richly interpreted data.

4 *readers/writers/participating others*: studies of literacy in context (for example, Heath 1983; Wagner *et al.* 1986; Shuman
   1986, 1993; Street 1993) emphasize that literacy tasks are
   often jointly achieved and that the social dimension of literacy
   practices is ignored by the textual/psychological model of the
   solitary writer struggling to create meanings via written text
   which can be re-created by the solitary reader. We need studies
   of readers reading and writers writing, but also we need
   studies of the ways in which reading and writing purposes
   can be collaboratively achieved.

5 *text production and interpretation*: this refers to the processes
   by which texts are created, recreated and interpreted by
   readers and writers. We need to know more about how these
   processes work and to draw on cross-disciplinary work from
   areas like literary theory, with rich theories of reading and
   writing.

6 *texts*: an adequate theory of literacy has to include a theory
   of texts, both in terms of the types of organization of written
   texts,the relationship of written texts to spoken language and
   the embedding of texts in contexts of use The genre theorists
   (Martin 1986; Kress 1989) have developed approaches to
   the study of written texts that promise useful outcomes in
   practical literacy work. Underpinning this work is the need
   to understand the relationship between spoken and written
   language and the embedding of both in an educationally useful theory of language (cf. Halliday 1985b and Stubbs 1986).

7 *media*: the availability and role of different media for doing
   literacy work is a key area. A classic historical moment is
   the invention of printing (cf. Eisenstein 1979); currently the
   growth and influence of word-processing technologies and
   technologies such as faxing and teleconferencing must be
   considered an important dimension in a conceptual framework
   for understanding literacy in use.
   Literacy need not just apply to language-based literacies. It
   is possible to extend the concept of literacy metaphorically
   and talk of visual literacy, computer literacy, even cultural
   literacy.

8 *ideologies*: an ideology is a collection of ideas, beliefs and
   attitudes which, taken together, make up a world view or
   political position. An ideology can be explicit or implicit.
   Ideologies tend to 'naturalize' themselves: to behave as if

they were the obvious, natural common-sense perspective. The term 'hegemony' is often used for ideological positions which have achieved such a position of power that they are taken for granted as the natural, obvious order of things. A number of theorists (for example, Kress and Hodge 1979, and Kress 1989) have written about the ways that ideologies can operate in texts. Street (1984 and elsewhere) emphasizes that literacy itself can be articulated through different ideological positions (Street's ideological and autonomous models of literacy will be reviewed in Chapter 2). Ideologies are articulated in discourse.

9 *discourses*: the term 'discourse' can have a number of meanings. As it is used in linguistics it refers to the organization of language, both spoken and written, beyond the level of the sentence, into extended stretches: conversations, letters, lectures, medical interviews, television interviews, newspaper articles, for example. Another meaning of discourse, for example as in the work of Kress, deriving from the work of Foucault (1972, 1980), refers to the 'systematically-organized sets of statements which give expression to the meanings and values of an institution' (Kress 1989: 7), which define and determine what can or cannot be said. Discourses, in Foucault's sense, articulate ideological positions. Uses of literacy are not neutral, technical channels of communication, but are informed by deeply seated ideological positions, some explicit, some implicit. The relative dominance of certain genres of written language is 'naturalized' within the education system.

10 *institutions*: an institution can be defined as any social organization with a power base. If the concept of discourse favours the role of language in social organization, the concept of institution is more sociologically grounded. Schooling, the law, medicine are institutions. In Chapter 4 we look at the library both as an institution and as a discourse.

DEFINING LITERACY

'SHARON S. IS ILLITERATE'
                (among the graffiti in a West London playground)

The graffito quoted above already gives an indication that 'literacy' itself is a loaded word, with a cluster of associations and ideologies attached to it, a word that can be critiqued, a 'generative theme', in Freire's terms. What we need to do is to 'problematize' literacy, to show that it is not something that can be neatly and easily defined, that any definition is likely to be contested.

Even from this brief example, we see how literacy defines itself, as it so often does, through its opposite, 'illiterate'. How it is that the literate/illiterate opposition can be used to frame a playground insult, and, by extension, how literacy can function as a way of labelling, sorting and grading people. In Chapter 3 we will explore the consequences of being sorted into the 'have-not' group. Instead of the objective notion of defining literacy, with which I start this section, it quickly becomes clear that literacy defines us, as a powerful sorter and grader of persons.

'Literacy' is not the same thing to everyone, but a whole complex of ideological positions, which taken together can be read as the educational 'debate' on literacy. On the basis of these ideological positions, explicit or implicit, policies are formulated, programmes are planned and classes are organized and taught. The adult learners who come along to start a literacy group also come along with their own ideas and expectations about what literacy is and should be about, their own literacy ideologies. Sometimes these ideologies are in conflict with the ideologies and expectations of the teacher. (The case study later in this chapter of a community-based Arabic language programme provides an example of such a conflict in ideologies and expectations around educational practices.)

Activity

One way to gather information about ideological differences in definitions of literacy is by collecting references to literacy and associated terms like 'educational standards' in the media. Editorials and opinion columns are a good source of highly ideological statements on literacy/illiteracy, as well as literacy levels, the 'decline in standards' and other issues.

CATEGORIZATION AND STIGMA

If literacy/illiteracy defines and categorizes people, being sorted into the 'have-not' box carries with it the stigma of being defined by a lack. It creates what Freire calls 'a culture of silence'. There is no necessary outward sign that someone has difficulties with reading and writing. It is well documented that adults with literacy difficulties develop networks and strategies to cope with their reading and writing demands (cf. Fingeret 1983), and we will look at the role of social networks in literacy practices in Chapter 2. Literacy 'problems' have a kind of invisibility. The self-image of individuals and societies requires 'healthy' literacy levels: if you can't read and write you keep quiet about it.

FROM LITERACY 'PROBLEMS' TO PROBLEMATIZING LITERACY

If literacy/illiteracy categorizes people into educational haves and have-nots, it also attaches a problem label to those defined as literacy have-nots. It is an easy extension from X *has* a problem to X *is* a problem, and literacy is thus conveniently tagged as an individual problem with individual solutions, a deficit that can be topped up. The collocation of 'literacy' and 'problem' reveals the underlying concept of a lack within an individual, which can be topped up or remedied by instruction.

DEFINING LITERACY IN CONTEXTS OF USE

Vignette

> I am sitting in the waiting area of a South London Labour Exchange, waiting to speak to the manager about the literacy project where I work. While I wait, a woman in a nearby cubicle is signing on as available to work. She explains to the interviewer that her children are now all at school and she is now looking for a job. She works through the form hesitantly and the interviewer begins to help her with it, spelling out words for her, explaining what questions mean. When the form is complete, she shyly comments that she was never much good at school. The interviewer replies that these forms would tie anyone up.

The interviewer here shifts the focus away from the individual and her self-blame, 'I was never much good at school', onto the general difficulty of form-filling, thus establishing solidarity with the interviewee. This small vignette of literacy in practice moves us a stage further towards our definition of literacy. The earlier section of this chapter points to the fact that definitions of literacy are always *ideological*; in other words, the definition of literacy is shaped by ideological perspectives on what literacy is, how it should be taught, who should have access to it. Definitions of literacy must be *context-sensitive*: that is, they must be sensitive to the social purposes, demands and processes within which they are constructed.

FUNCTIONAL LITERACY OR CRITICAL LITERACY?

The heading of this section implies an either/or relationship between functional and critical literacy. As I argued earlier, it is more useful to think of the relationship as a complementary or additive one: the functional dimension addressing issues of social purpose in contexts of use, the critical dimension providing a meta-level of critical awareness, both linguistic and social.

Literacy has been the focus of a whole series of attempts at definition and re-definition, particularly associated with Unesco:

> A person is literate when he *(sic)* has acquired the essential knowledge
> and skills which enable him to engage in all those activities in
> which literacy is required for effective functioning in his group
> and community, and whose attainments in reading, writing and
> arithmetic make it possible for him to continue to use these skills
> towards his own and the community's development.
>
> (Unesco 1962, cited in Oxenham 1980: 87)

Unesco's definitions of literacy illustrate some of the problems associated with the work of generating definitions of social practices that are complex, multi-faceted and ideologically loaded. Street, for example, has critiqued the linkage between literacy and development that is implied in this definition. The 'definition', with its apparent closure, is simply a current stage in a continually evolving debate about a range of educational and social practices on which the label 'literacy' conveniently hangs. Not only that, but the definition will always be subjected to the pull of conflicting interests. What unifies the series of Unesco definitions of literacy is their functional perspective. Indeed, the term 'functional literacy' emerges as a powerful construct in defining literacy in terms of its social purposes, the demands made on individuals within a given society, to function within that society, to participate and to achieve their own goals.

So where does the critical literacy dimension come in? We have already introduced it above in talking of the shift from literacy-as-a-problem to problematizing literacy. If literacy demonstrates the operations of powerful social processes, such as the sorting and categorizing into educational haves and have-nots discussed above, it follows that educational practices designed to develop literacy should have that layer of critical self-awareness. This is particularly the case in literacy work with adults, who may well have been the victims of literacy in their schooling. A critical literacy theme here is the way that schooling creates educational failure.

If literacy is not a given which can be reduced to a set of discrete skills, then it follows that a literacy pedagogy cannot treat its object as a given but must problematize it, developing the dimension of critical reflection, which, within the Freirean definition of praxis (action and reflection) must complement action.

Activity

Here is a current definition of literacy from the Australian Council for Adult Literacy. How does it compare with the Unesco definition quoted above? To what extent does it incorporate both functional and critical criteria for literacy? Is it a 'context-sensitive' definition and, if so, in what ways?

Literacy involves the integration of listening, speaking, reading, writing and critical thinking; it incorporates numeracy. It includes the cultural knowledge which enables a speaker, writer or reader to recognise and use language appropriate to different social situations. For an advanced technological society such as Australia, the goal is an active literacy which allows people to use language to enhance their capacity to think, create and question, in order to participate effectively in society.

FROM DEFINITIONS OF LITERACY TO LITERACY DISCOURSES

It should be clear by now that there are difficulties associated with achieving handy, portable definitions of complex constructs like literacy. For each definition of literacy we can unpack a discourse, defined by Kress in the following way:

> Discourses are systematically organized sets of statements which
> give expression to the meanings and values of an institution. Beyond
> that, they define, describe and delimit what it is possible to say
> and not possible to say (and by extension – what it is possible
> to do or not to do) with respect to the area of concern of that
> institution, whether marginally or centrally. A discourse provides
> a set of possible statements about a given area, and organises and
> gives structure to the manner in which a particular topic, object,
> process is to be talked about. In that it provides descriptions, rules,
> permissions and prohibitions of social and individual action.
>
> (Kress 1989: 7)

When the Back to Basics movement argues that standards have
dropped in schools due to modern teaching methods and the way
to ensure a return to high levels of literacy is to reinstate traditional
methods of teaching the basics in the school system, a discourse
is being articulated which claims and re-orders social space, treats
some things as given, others as not.

Some of the 'systematically organized sets of statements' underlying the Back to Basics position would be:

- standards of literacy have dropped in recent years;
- this fact is connected to the decline of formal teaching of
  'the basics';
- progressive teaching methods are to blame – for example, the
  'whole language' approaches to reading;
- if teachers return to formal instruction of the three Rs, standards
  will improve.

Competing and conflicting discourses may try to account for the
same phenomena in different and incompatible ways. Cope and
Kalantzis (1990) have shown how this operates in traditional/
progressive and post-progressive pedagogies. The problems of
definition are markers of underlying discourses, consciously or
unconsciously articulated. For example, the basic premises which
I stated for this book earlier in the chapter are an attempt to make
explicit my own stance on literacy, to articulate 'a systematically
organized set of statements' about the scope of a definition of
literacy:

- literacy has developed and is shaped to serve social purposes
  in creating and exchanging meaning;
- literacy is best understood in its contexts of use;

- literacy is ideological: like all uses of language it is not neutral, but shapes and is shaped by deeply held ideological positions, which can be either implicit or explicit;
- literacy needs to be understood in terms of social power;
- literacy can be critical.

Activity

The following article on literacy (Figure 1.1) contains a number of perspectives: the perspective of the writer, Ita Buttrose; the perspective articulated by the spokesperson of the Adult Literacy Information Office, Kate Johnson; and the perspective articulated by Constance Thomas.

What differences do you find in the way that these perspectives construct the 'literacy problem'? Can you identify any of the 'systematically organized sets of statements', as Kress calls them, which would articulate the position on literacy taken by the different contributors? Does Ita Buttrose use her authorial power to support a particular perspective?

A critical reader of literacy practices needs to be able to interpret the discourse perspectives implicit or explicit in text like newspaper articles, policy documents or curriculum materials, and the aim of this chapter is to suggest critical readings of definitions of literacy that may present themselves as given or unproblematic.

DEFINITIONS FROM THE INSIDE

Saturday evening – late

After the session we had a couple of drinks at the Lee Centre and then a couple of the girls went to the off licence for a few more drinks then returned to my bedroom to read a book between the six of us. We read a page each as the book went round, each of us helping the others. First of all I had my doubts about reading the book, but when I had help I couldn't let go of it. We were all pretty slow but yet again we all understood because we all had the same problem. We read the book, eventually got through it about 12.15 and we all thoroughly enjoyed it. It was one of the best parts of the weekend.

    (from 'A weekend diary: diary of a student research weekend',by Debbie; (Research and Practice in Adult Literacy Bulletin 1989: 15)

Ita's page

What's wrong with the way we are teaching our children basic English?

ARE YOU aware that some 15 to 20 per cent of all Australians are either illiterate or semi-illiterate ... which means that something like one million of us can't read well enough to understand basic instructions, classified advertisements, employment notices or simple education forms?

In fact the Adult Literacy Information Office in New South Wales estimates that some six to 10 per cent of Australians don't read or write as part of their daily lives.

The true extent of the problem is unknown because people with reading difficulties often successfully hide them, saying they've forgotten their glasses or hurt their arms so badly that they are unable to fill in a form. So someone else does it for them.

Kate Johnson, a resource officer with the information office, believes the problem has always been with us.

"A survey carried out in 1944 on people applying to enter the Army showed a 20 per cent illiteracy rate," she said.

Kate says the problem occurs because of missed schooling when children are between the ages of five and eight. "They may miss schools because of illness, or hidden defects like poor sight or hearing, or they may attend many schools because of the demands of their parents' careers.

"If children haven't acquired reading and writing skills by the age of nine, they never pick them up and the problem remains undetected."

I find it difficult to accept Kate's argument. While some children may miss schooling for a variety of reasons, I can't believe that the majority of the 15 to 20 per cent of adults with literacy problems have them as a result of missing school at this young age.

And while a 20 per cent illiteracy rate may have existed in 1944,

there is no satisfactory reason why we should accept such a high figure in 1987.

After all, we have teachers with better skills and resources (or so we're continually told by both the Federal and State Governments), smaller classes, plus a stricter enforcement of the regulations that require children to attend school. The situation should be getting better.

The seriousness of the problem is highlighted by the knowledge that Adult Basic Education is the fastest growing area in TAFE Colleges throughout New South Wales.

Constance Thomas, director and founder of the Language Foundation of Australia, says the major cause of our growing illiteracy is the way young people are taught to read and write, coupled with the poor understanding of language shown in a child's early years at home.

"Modern methods of teaching are all wrong. Instead of learning that 'a' is pronounced 'a' and 'b' as 'b' children are shown whole words and told to memorise them.

"They aren't taught the breakdown of words until much later. This is the reason for the growing number of bad spellers!"

"The language isn't being taught. Children just pick it up. And because they learn by sight they don't understand it. There's evidence of people having learned by sight everywhere - in signwriting and so on. The right letters are there but often they're in the wrong order.

"Very few people people understand how to use the apostrophe. If they see a word which ends in 's' they feel it has to have an apostrophe before it."

The sight-word method used in

our schools today is called Look Say, and Constance says that wherever it has been introduced, remedial classes have later become necessary.

"It began in Germany a generation ago and within 10 years there was a need for remedial classes. Australia followed America and the remedial empire in both countries is vast, because children have been unable to learn by the Look Say method.

Everyone knows we have a problem with our education methods but it seems no-one wants to do anything about it. Education ministers and their bureaucrats keep telling us "Australia has the best education system in the world" yet letters to the editor in newspapers throughout the nation indicate enormous concern on the part of some teachers, parents, business people and students themselves.

Everyone knows we have a problem with our education methods

"Nobody wants to knock anybody else," Constance said.

Constance's awareness of Australia's alarming illiteracy problems began because her own sons were having reading troubles. She helped set up the Language Foundation.

"I often look at teachers' spelling and some of it just terrifies me. I remember one who spelled 'excellent' as 'exulent'," she said.

When Prime Minister Hawke stated recently that his government would strive to make sure no child in Australia lived in poverty, I applauded. I hope he has similar plans to do something about the great many youngsters affected by poverty of the mind. They need help, too.   **WD**

Figure 1.1

Earlier in this chapter, I suggested that it is as important to recognize how literacy defines, categorizes and sorts people as it is to achieve a working definition of literacy. This recognition incorporates the awareness of social power into any attempt to define literacy. The anonymous victim of the graffito quoted at the beginning of this chapter is the victim of a label that sorts and excludes. Definitions of literacy tend to be definitions from the outside (us defining them) although there is a growing tradition of publishing (cf. Gregory 1991); that is, making public the definitions from the inside generated by adult literacy learners who define and re-define themselves, breaking out of the 'culture of silence'.

In the above extract we can see how acquiring literacy for Debbie is a process of re-definition, from the competitive world of schooling to the cooperative domain of the reading circle, from the expectation of failure to the experience of success. The practice of reading aloud, which is often recalled as an experience of humiliation and failure in early schooling, is turned around and becomes a way of sharing reading. Definitions of literacy from the inside document and describe such change processes.

MODELS OF LITERACY/ILLITERACY: THE WORLD IN THE HEAD

In an often-quoted phrase, Freire writes that 'reading the world always precedes reading the word'. He is using the word 'reading' in an interesting and important way. Reading here does not just mean *decoding* the printed marks on the page but also *interpreting*. Reading in this sense involves getting meaning from a text and is an active work of decoding and interpretation on the part of the reader. In this striking phrase, Freire argues that we can decode and interpret the world in the same way that we decode and interpret written text, that critical reading can precede getting meaning from written text. He is also making the point that you literally can't read without involving previous world knowledge.

An important concept here is that of the *mental model* or *schema*. The concept of schema was first introduced by the psychologist Bartlett (1932) and has been used productively in psycholinguistics, discourse analysis, reading theory (Carrell and Eisterhold 1988), artificial intelligence and cognitive science

(Minsky 1975). For an account of its use in linguistically based discourse analysis, see Brown and Yule (1983). Organizing knowledge in schemata makes it more retrievable than, for example, lists of information with no particular organizing principle.

The 'world in the head' is organized as a set of mental representations of how things are in the world and how they are/should be organized. We have mental models or schemata for everyday activities like visiting a restaurant, what is likely to happen in a classroom. These involve both linguistic and social knowledge and create a structured set of expectations about how social life is conducted. Models and schemata can also provide ways of interpreting social behaviour, not just about everyday social situations, but also in conceptualizing more abstract concerns – for example, why people can't read and write as adults. Mental models or schemata are the psycholinguistic correlates of discourses and ideologies: they create the set of structured expectations about how the world is or should be, what is to be expected, taken for granted, given. It is through mental models and schemata that we naturalize the social world.

If models and schemata, the world in the head, have a decisive influence on how we read our world, what current models are available for reading the literacy/illiteracy construct?

We have already come across a very influential one, the *deficit model*, itself critiqued in Freire's work. Deficit-model thinking constructs the literacy learner as an empty vessel, a jug that needs filling with knowledge.

Kress writes about the colonising tendency of discourses:

> Discourses tend towards exhaustiveness and inclusiveness; that is they attempt to account not only for an area of immediate concern to an institution, but attempt to account for increasingly wider areas of concern. . . . A discourse colonises the social world imperialistically, from the point of view of one institution.
>
> (Kress 1989: 6)

Deficit thinking, as a discourse, colonizes other social domains: a literacy 'deficit' may be taken to imply a deficit in spoken language, a deficit in child-rearing practices (parents not reading to children, not having books in the house, not doing educationally orientated play activities with their children). Deficit thinking may generalize across whole social groups and collude with racist discourses or it may lay the blame at the door of the individual.

The medical model is a powerful metaphor which treats the lack of literacy as a medical condition that certain individuals suffer from. The use of the term 'diagnosis' and the concept of diagnostic testing, the construction of illiteracy as an affliction that people suffer from, the over 'diagnosis' of dyslexia, all imply a medical model of 'illiteracy'.

We have already mentioned the Back to Basics model, which is really a critique of educational practices, particularly progressivist schooling. A typical formulation of this position would be: If English was better taught in the schools, these people would have learnt to read and write years ago.

The *skills development model* treats the acquisition of literacy as the acquisition of a series of discrete skills.

The *therapeutic model* sees literacy development within a psychological framework as a way of working though problems.

The *personal empowerment model* sees the development of literacy as a process of developing confidence and personal power, not just in the area of literacy but also in other life areas.

The *social empowerment model* moves beyond the goal of personal empowerment and links literacy development with social change. Theorists like Freire (1973, 1985), Shor (1986, 1992) and Lankshear (1987) advocate social empowerment models of literacy development.

Functional models of literacy emphasize social purpose and context. The aim is to provide the learner with the abilities to fit in and achieve within the social framework as it currently exists.

Critical models of literacy, while also emphasizing social purpose and context, do not take these purposes and contexts as given, but subject them to critical analysis as part of the educational process.

It is clear that this range of models does not represent a set of discrete options and that it is possible to have mixes and blends of a number of them. For example, critical literacy and functional literacy do not need to be either/or options. Deficit-model thinking may also typically express the lack of literacy in terms of an individualized medical condition. The line between personal and social empowerment may be hard to draw.

Activity

> The following case studies (see Figure 1.2) describe different literacy
> programmes. What are the models of literacy underpinning them?
> Are they, for example, conceptualizing literacy as skills development,
> personal or social empowerment, or perhaps a mix of more than one
> model of literacy?

LITERACY FROM A CROSS-DISCIPLINARY PERSPECTIVE

Levine describes the 'complex amalgam of psychological, linguistic and social processes' that make up literacy. It follows from this
that investigating literacy has to involve cross-disciplinary work.
No particular discipline can or should be seen as dominant in
this. Barton and Ivanic (1988) express the relationship between
different disciplines and the necessity for research partnerships
in Figure 1.3.

In this section, I will try to outline the necessary connections
to be made between a linguistic perspective on literacy and a
perspective that emphasizes literacy as social practice. I will argue
in doing so that literacy is primarily a socio-political construct
and that the corresponding term in linguistics is a theory of
spoken and written language (cf. Halliday 1985b; Stubbs 1986,
1987 and so on).

Some of the contradictions involved in defining literacy can be
illustrated by the following collocations, typical in considering
literacy at the level of educational policy. We find 'the language
and literacy policy' for a particular state or country, language
and literacy units or centres abound. What is the implication
of collocating language with literacy? Does it mean that literacy
is not language or that for language we should gloss (spoken)
language? It is clear that the commonplace collocation of language
and literacy raises problems of definition from another angle and
that these issues of definition are commonly elided, even at the
level of policy where they ought perhaps to be explicit.

What does it mean, then, to say that literacy is a socio-political
construct as much as a linguistic one and that the linguistic
correlate of the literacy construct is a theory of spoken and written
language? First, it emphasizes the interaction of linguistic and
socio-political factors in the construction of literacy, implying the
kind of collaborative investigations across disciplines suggested

A migrant women's learning centre

Miriam Faine describes an innovative delivery by a Melbourne TAFE College

Collingwood Migrant Women's Learning Centre was set up with the help of Commonwealth ESL funding in 1984 by Collingwood College of TAFE. It began late in 1985 and ran with meagre funding but a great deal of community support from a shopfront in Smith Street, a main road in a depressed inner-city area.

Some of the classes were ESL/literacy classes. However, there were many other classes that provided a place where the women were able to make practical items – such as the sewing class, which was taught in English. Being able to take something home helped the women justify their attendance at a class to their family and it also allowed them to explore their own potential and have pride in their work. The women were encouraged to read and write during these different activities and later invited to share their skills with other classes by becoming tutors for new students.

New students come to the centre either as referrals from agencies, through friends or after hearing about it on radio 3EA. The women are highly motivated and committed, many coming from far away to attend classes, but at the same time their domestic and family responsibilities remain their priority and attendance patterns naturally reflect this.

The reasons for low literacy and general education among immigrant women differ from those for Anglo-Celtic women. In rural cultures females from poor families have a 'use-by date' and whilst the males are often encouraged to learn, compete and succeed, the girls are discouraged from pursuing formal education beyond primary level. Rather they are taught domestic skills that are highly valued and necessary for marriage. One reason for illiteracy amongst younger Indo-Chinese women is war in their countries.

These women sometimes have very low self-esteem, seeing themselves as stupid, saying it is their own fault and feeling very guilty at being unable to read and/or write. Other women suppress their anger at the unfairness that leaves them uneducated while their children are very often university graduates. Many are desperate to learn, to gain general knowledge as well as literacy, to be an 'educated person.' It is important to be gentle with these women, and look at what skills they do have in order to raise awareness and pride in their ability and potential. At the same time it is necessary to be extremely careful not to de-stabilise them or risk losing their family support.

Some students begin to take risks and increasingly share their experiences on a number of topics. Women's issues become a dominant part of classes and both written materials and art works demonstrate these issues. Over twenty nationalities are represented at the centre and a great bond of women's solidarity emerges as they pursue more classes together. The centre has been involved in a number of community projects including the creation of six beautiful appliqué panels reflecting women in their own countries of origin.

Changes in funding guidelines and the increased emphasis on vocational

Figure 1.2a Case Study One

outcomes in TAFE threatened the MWLC's future in 1988. It was saved by a massive community campaign but had to move into an annexe on the main college site. The centre now has guaranteed recurrent funding as well as a number of special projects. The curriculum also became more of a conventional TAFE ESL curriculum offering intensive courses for the more typically educated new arrivals, as well as increased ESL/literacy for the Mediterranean arrivals of the 50's and 60's.

In 1990 the centre has a full-time permanent coordinator for the first time, as well as the prospect of permanent teacher appointments. We are re-thinking our curriculum and focusing very specifically on:

- complementing (rather than duplicating) other ESL and literacy provision.

- acknowledging the need for specific educational access for bilingual women who have been denied this basic right

- offering courses that reflect women's needs and issues

- offering outreach ESL classes in our local community that help access women gradually into further education and training

- widening the curriculum to include non-traditional areas such as computing and maths/numeracy (we have just about been knocked over by the response!).

Currently we offer:

- an intensive course for newly-arrived women with 11 years or more education, focusing on preparing women for retraining or employment and including a brief practical work placement

- a DEET-funded course offering vocational training in areas like catering, hotel room attendant and basic keyboard skills to sole parents and other labour-market-disadvantaged women; a high proportion of these women have social or personal problems and most have had little or no access to general education

- a less intensive course offering English language/literacy skills to women whose primary concern is to 'catch up'; again many of these women have disadvantaged backgrounds in their own country or are victims of war or social unrest

- the above course can be supplemented by basic education subjects like numeracy/maths, general science, computing and typing, and practical skills like dressmaking and horticulture; more will be added. We are interested in suitable accreditation for these so women can progress to units 1 and 2 of VCE (Victorian Certificate of Education), or other TAFE courses

- part-time ESL literacy courses at three levels offering articulation from complete-novices-level to pre- VCE

- community ESL classes in conjunction with tenants' associations on local housing commission estates, and distance education for out-workers who are unable to attend other classes.

There is a growing involvement in projects relating to ESL/literacy needs and award restructuring/ workplace education in employment areas traditionally filled by female migrants, such as hospital domestic work.

More information: Miriam Faine, Northern Metropolitan College of TAFE, 03419 6666 ext. 316

Figure 1.2a Case Study One continued

An open learning centre inside a steelworks

Margrit Stocker outlines an industry innovation at BHP Port Kembla

BHP's Slab and Plate Products Division (SPPD) near Wollongong has approximately 9,500 employees. Approximately two-thirds are 'wages' and fifty three percent of this group have a non-English-speaking background.

In line with the recent industry restructuring, strict demarcation is disappearing and the number of job classifications is being drastically reduced.

In order to assist in the training/retraining of employees as a result of this industry restructuring, and the Steel Industry Development Agreement which is presently being implemented, SPPD is providing considerable in-house training plus using outside providers for skills and knowledge development. As well as this, it is also being innovative – and providing a literacy and numeracy based model both for its other divisions and industry generally – in setting up an on-site open learning centre for use by employees at all levels.

Why an open learning centre?

The need for the centre should be put into context.

Due to the high proportion of employees of non-English-speaking background the Adult Migrant Education service (AMES) has been operating within the plant for the last fifteen years. Attendance at AMES classes has been within employees' work time.

In one area of the works, a language audit was conducted in late 1989 and the results from this could be viewed as a microcosm of the needs throughout the plant.

The audit showed approximately 50% of all employees at wages level in this area would experience difficulties if faced with retraining based on reading and writing.

If these figures were extrapolated across the whole of the Port Kembla works, the problem could be enormous and would present an undeniable challenge to management who have a strong commitment to equality for all.

In November 1989 SPPD employed the writer as coordinator of the open learning centre to establish an on-site support framework for employees having, or likely to have, problems with literacy and numeracy associated with retraining. The coordinator acts as facilitator between the needs of particular individuals or business units and the various education providers that can cater to these needs.

BHP OPEN LEARNING CENTRE: types of programs

The following table shows the broad range of programs available through the Open Learning Centre:
Note: All courses must have course

- aims
- objectives
- outline/curriculum
- assessment

and must be adapted to meet the individual needs and differences of employees.

BUFFER PROGRAMS
Designed for employees who for any reason do not have the appropriate entry requirements for a course to be undertaken. In this instance a base line of these employees' skills and/or knowledge is compared to that required in the proposed course. A buffer program is then designed to bridge this gap in terms of skills and/or knowledge.

SUPPORT PROGRAMS
For any employee enrolled in a training/educational course who needs assistance with that course in order to maximise his/her performance and realise his/her true potential.
e.g. an employee may experience difficulty in
an area of maths not previously learnt – metrics for an older person
                                        – imperial for a younger person
understanding written assignments.

INNOVATIVE PROGRAMS
Here programs are designed for a specific need in a particular work area. This type of program is particularly pertinent following a skills audit and provides appropriate educational programs to meet the needs of groups of employees in particular circumstances.

Figure 1.2b Case Study Two

The service provided by AMES will now be incorporated within the responsibilities of the open learning centre along with other providers such as TAFE, City Mission, Trade Union Training Authority (TUTA), Workers' Educational Association (WEA) and the University of Wollongong.

The types of programs conducted by these providers in the open learning centre are summarised in the table (left).

Plans are currently being drawn up for a building for the open learning centre and construction should be completed before International Literacy Year is over.

In the interim classes are held as close to the employees' specific workplace as possible for the following reasons:

   it provides a positive role model for other employees

   it shows education is part of work and is not separate from it

   it maximises work-release time.

Once the centre is built, it will provide a wide range of courses for employees (and in the longer term, their families) to attend in their own time, whilst the on-site work programs will also continue so as to continue to support the needs of the workforce in the workplace.

Within each of these broad bands, many courses can be established to meet specific individual or group needs. Programs will change to meet the changing needs of employees/business units.

Funding

SPPD had prepared a budget for the expected cost, but a successful submission to the Education Training Foundation has resulted in funding of up to $200,000 being made available. This is to be used in conjunction with teaching programs and the surveys required to provide a firm basis for these.

What are the implications for educational providers?

These workplace groups can create some new avenues for exploration for the providers of programs. Often the staff have never worked in heavy industry, so there needs to be staff development carried out to allow the teachers to better understand the present position of the employee, the type of working conditions they experience and the type and range of skills needed. This type of background information then allows the teacher to more quickly hone in at the appropriate level.

Conclusion

BHP is very interested in the concentration on literacy and numeracy as a basis of the open learning centre here at Slab & Plate Products Division.

As a division, we are learning as we go as the field is very new.

For educational providers it gives another dimension to their expertise and experience.

For the employee it gives an opportunity to advance.

Above all, I see our workplace literacy and numeracy program as a means of getting to the root of learning problems and not just dealing superficially with the symptoms.

More information: Margrit Stocker, BHP Open Learning Centre, Port Kembla, 042 75 3924

Figure 1.2b Case Study Two continued

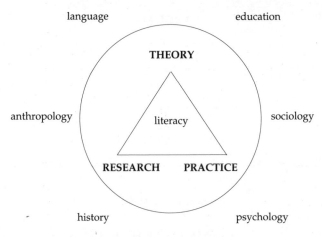

Figure 1.3 Partnerships in the study of literacy

by Barton and Ivanič. Secondly, it demands a theory of language which can make connections with socio-political context in an effective way. These issues will be raised in more detail in the following chapters, but in this introductory chapter it is worth spending some time introducing the theoretical perspective on language which can underpin an understanding of literacy in its contexts of use. In doing so I draw on the work in critical discourse analysis of Fairclough (1989) and Kress (1989).

A THEORY OF LANGUAGE IN CONTEXT

This theory of language (see Figure 1.4) comprises three major components, which are represented as embedded or nested one within the other. The outer layer is *language as social practice*, incorporating ideologies and discourses and institutions in the way described by Kress earlier in this chapter. The next layer, *language as social process*, incorporates the ways that language is interactionally accomplished in contexts of situation, and the concept of genre is relevant here, defined by Martin and Rothery (1980, 1981) as staged, goal-orientated social process.

Discourses and ideologies (the layer of social practice) do not exist in a vacuum, but are expressed or realized in social process, whether in spoken or written (or for that matter visual) mode.

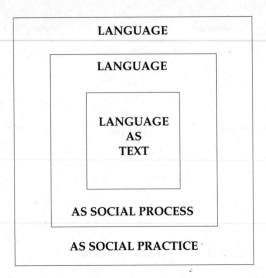

Figure 1.4 A model of language in social context

The innermost core of the model is *language as text*, in which we work back into the core lexico-grammatical and phonological systems of the language in the areas that have traditionally been the preserve of linguistic analysis.

An illustration of the language model

The following illustrates how a linguistic item can function on the level of text, social process and social practice. Take the word 'Out' uttered in the context of a cricket match. On the phonological level it functions as a string of sounds with a typical intonation pattern. It functions as a single item on the lexico-grammatical level and is a complete text on the textual level. As social process it is a linguistic move in the activity type 'cricket match' which typically involves both verbal and non-verbal action. It is difficult to imagine a cricket match without the somewhat laconic verbal repertoire of players and umpire ('Howzat!' 'Out!' 'Not out!' 'Over!'), or the written language component of scoring. The social process layer captures the ways in which social activity is achieved through language.

A cricket match may be broadcast on the radio or television, in which case a running commentary will accompany it; it may be reported in the newspaper, with a description of the highlights of the match and any other relevant information. The word 'Out!' may equally crop up in the newspaper report in a dramatized narrative of a highlight of the match.

The cricket match itself, the way it might be reported and commented on in the media, are all part of social process, the layer of language most immediately accessible to language users. Few spectators or participants in a cricket match will pause to consider the fact that the word 'Out' is quite difficult to categorize grammatically. The layer of text is not foregrounded in day-to-day awareness of language.

So what about the layer of language as social practice? How can we conceive of the cricket match as social practice? To do so would involve problematizing the cricket match and sport in general, to try and reveal the ways that sport functions institutionally, the ideological positions that are implied: are there gender issues; is one sport seen as the domain of women, the other of men? To what extent is sport seen as a metaphor for other social activities ('playing the game', 'the level playing field')? How are individuals socialized into the norms, attitudes and values of a sporting culture? These are the kinds of questions that might be worth asking of the game of cricket as social practice. In doing so we would be problematizing, engaging in a critical activity.

In terms of accessibility to everyday understandings, the layer of social process is clearly more accessible than language as text or language as social process. Much of the everyday metalanguage used in ordinary conversation (cf. Stubbs 1983) illustrates this. A very typical and recurrent means for a speaker to negotiate a way out of conversational difficulty is to make explicit in a metacommunicative way what they are trying to do with language:

I'm not asking you, I'm telling you.
I only asked.
I was only joking.

Such evidence indicates that language users typically focus on and conceive of language as 'doing things with words', as purposeful social process. It is less easy to focus on and conceive of the core of textual organization (grammar and language as form) and possibly even less easy to identify ideological positions in discourses (the layer of language as social practice). Writers on language and ideology like Fairclough have shown how powerful social forces operate to 'naturalize' dominant discourses, to make them appear normal, everyday, part of the natural scheme of things.

In the case of cricket, the dominant discourse makes it a man's game, so that women cricketers have a hard time claiming their right to play the game. A critical approach would ask: why is cricket taken to be a male sport? The basic critical question is 'why?'.

This discussion brings us back to the question of critical literacy and enables us to expand the definition of critical literacy in terms of the language theory outlined above. Critical literacy necessarily implies operating on the level of language as social practice; it involves identifying what is problematic, not accepting the taken for granted version. It involves asking 'why?'.

It also follows that, like social practice, critical literacy does not exist in a vacuum but is expressed or realized in social process. A critical literacy that attempted to operate only on the level of social practice would be, in Freire's terms, mere verbalism, since it would not carry with it the orientation towards action which is the other component of Freire's praxis.

A focus on the layer of social process is a focus on the active, purposeful 'doing things with words' dimension of language, so what are the implications for literacy pedagogy of the emphasis on social process? It depends on whether the focus is on literacy as social process alone or whether there is also a dimension emphasizing literacy as social practice. In the former, the purposeful activity with language typical of social process would be treated as given, unproblematic, it would be naturalized. This would be typical of a functional model of literacy, whose aims would be to equip literacy learners to function within current contexts without questioning them. In the latter, the dimension of literacy as social practice would produce a critical pedagogy, recognizing that, while a key goal of literacy education is to empower learners to use language effectively in a range of relevant contexts (literacy as social process), an equally important goal is to control these uses of language critically and knowledgeably.

LITERACY IN COMPLEX URBAN MULTI-LINGUAL SETTINGS: THE CONTEXT OF THIS BOOK

Given the emphasis I have placed on the interaction of text and context in this book, it is worth situating it both within its political and theoretical context and its scope of reference. Theoretically, the book explores the interface between language-based approaches to literacy education and those derived from critical social theory and anthropology. The concept of *practice* is the key mediating construct. The model of language presented earlier in this chapter demonstrates from the linguistic end of the spectrum how this interface can be achieved.

As will become clear in following chapters, literacy makes sense as situated social practice more than as a universal category, transferable into any context. So it is worth making explicit the scope of social contexts to which this book will refer.

The authors of the Linguistic Minorities Project (1985) describe the setting of their research as 'a multilingual setting characterized by immigrant bilingualism'. Similarly, in this book, the setting presupposed is of the large multi-lingual cities of industrialized countries; the focus is on adult rather than 'schooled' literacy – although, to the extent that adults have been through the school system and been shaped and formed by it, the influence of schooled literacy will impinge on the book continually, most particularly in Chapter 3.

So the book does not focus, for example, on situations undergoing revolutionary social change – as does Lankshear (1987) for example – but on the contextual complexities of the industrialized economies and the impact and necessity of critical literacy to make sense of the demands of these contexts.   The economies of these industrialized cities attracting a workforce from abroad, as well as housing populations of refugees, contain microcosms of communities adapting from rurally based economies (cf. Kalantzis *et al.* 1989) and therefore a diversity of literacy practices in the context of the dominance of literacy practices in English. The following sketch from Burnaby and Bell illustrates some of the possible permutations in the case of an individual.

Tsab is a man of 35 who came to Canada as a refugee. His home was in the mountains of Laos and he belonged to the Hmong group. The Hmong language has no formalized writing system although, in

recent years, work has been done on writing Hmong in the roman
alphabet and the Lao script. Tsab's village was a farming community
with no local school. All his learning was acquired orally from older
adults in the village, and he and his fellow villagers never had to use
print in their daily lives.

As the war in Laos progressed, he and his family were forced
down from the mountains into refugee camps. Tsab was too old
to be eligible for the school in the camps although he did pick up
a fair command of spoken Lao, the language used in the schools.
Later he was moved to a refugee camp in Thailand where he learned
some Thai.

When Tsab was finally resettled in Canada, he was able to speak
three languages but still had no exposure to literacy. With his proven
facility for languages Tsab was confident that he could learn English
and do well in Canada. He made rapid progress in spoken English
but now realizes that this is not sufficient to get him a well-paying
job because he will need literacy skills. He is in an ESL class which
reflects his oral abilities but is lagging badly behind the rest of the
class in written work.

(Burnaby and Bell, *ESL and Adult Literacy: The Canadian Situation,*
Ontario Institute for Studies in Education, undated)

In the case study that follows, the diversity of literacy practices in complex urban settings is illustrated with data from the
literacies of the Moroccan community in London.

Case study: literacy practices in a multi-lingual setting

The Linguistic Minorities Project, whose research is written up
in LMP (1985), included a range of questions on literacy in
their surveys, designed to bring out the functional distribution
of literacies in a multi-lingual society and to examine the role
of the so-called 'mother-tongue' teaching initiatives in trans-
mitting literacy in languages other than English, both within
the school and in supplementary schooling. Marilyn Martin-
Jones writes:

Urban Britain of the 1980s has become a multilingual, multiliteracy
society. The communicative repertoires and language resources
of different linguistic communities in Britain include a range
of written languages, alphabets and scripts, yet it is still only
literacy in English that is recognised as having any value in British
society.

(1984: 426)

The report of the LMP, in its section on mother tongue teaching provision, notes that 'although there are great differences in the aims and origins of MT classes in the various languages, one of their main common functions is certainly the introduction of literacy' (LMP 1985: 227). In this case study we will look at the transmission of literacy in Arabic to children of the Moroccan community in West London.

There are a number of strands in the question of 'Arabic school for the children' in the Moroccan community in London. First is the involvement of parents and community organizations in the struggle to set up facilities on a voluntary basis, against considerable odds. Second is the involvement of institutions outside the immediate networks of the community: the local authority, Islamic organizations in the United Kingdom, the Moroccan embassy (who had, at the time of writing, after years of negotiation, sent three teachers to work with the community in London). Third is the question of conflicting views, or 'ideologies', as to what kind of education should be provided.

An example of ideological conflict over literacy education in Arabic

A small example of a summer holiday scheme aimed at teaching Arabic language and culture to Moroccan children can illustrate this. The scheme was planned and run by Moroccan and English professional workers and Moroccan students over in London doing courses. The funding body, guided by its policies on what are appropriate out-of-school activities for young children, gave the money on condition that there was a sizeable component of play activities over and above formal schooling activities. Parents, perhaps less inhibited about commenting on a more home-grown educational initiative than they are about intervening in the school, commented that they would have liked their children to be doing more formal learning and less time-wasting play. To understand the dynamics of this contention and the expectations of the parents, it is useful to look at the school as a site for the transmission of literacy in Morocco.

LITERACY PRACTICES IN MOROCCO
The Morocco Literacy Project, a joint project of the Literacy Research Centre at the University of Pennsylvania and the

Mohammed V University in Rabat, has carried out a study of the functions and social distribution of literacy in Morocco using a three-part framework for the study of literacy in complex societies (cf. Wagner *et al.* 1986; Wagner 1994). First, they look at the functions of literacy 'in context', secondly, they look at the 'institutions of transmission', notably materials and artefacts of literate activity. In this case study, we are interested in the school as a site for the transmission of literacy.

The traditional form of initial education in Morocco, as throughout the Islamic world, was the Qur'anic school. There is a very vivid account of traditional Qur'anic schooling in Egypt in the autobiography of Taha Hussein (1981) and a discussion of 'maktab literacy' in Iran in Street (1984). The traditional Qur'anic school would concentrate entirely on the acquisition and study of the text of the Qur'an. The memorization of the Qur'an was achieved by rote learning, starting the younger children with the shorter 'surahs' and moving through the longer ones. The emphasis is on faultless reproduction of a sacred text, whose linguistic form literally incorporates the word of God, with – in terms of initial acquisition, at any rate – no particular emphasis on understanding a text which is anyway of a conceptual and linguistic complexity far beyond the understanding of the young children who memorize it. The learning cycle associated with memorizing the Qur'an involves reciting after a model, copying, learning by heart, testing.

This emphasis on recitation by heart is encoded in the language to the extent that the word for 'read', 'qara'a', has a meaning of 'recite by heart'. The practice of retaining words by heart is encoded in religious observances from the very beginning of the Qur'anic revelation, when the Prophet, who did not read or write, received the revelation in the form of written text:

> And Gabriel came to me when I was asleep with an embroidered cloth and there was writing on it and he said to me 'read' and I replied 'I can't read'. Thereupon he throttled me until I thought death was coming. Then he released me and said 'read' and I replied again, 'I can't read'. Thereupon he throttled me again until I though death was coming. Then he released me and said again 'read' and I replied, 'I don't know how to read', and Gabriel said (revealing the first words of the Qur'an), 'read in the name of thy

Lord who created humans from a clot of blood, read and thy Lord
is the most generous, who teaches by means of the pen and teaches
humans what they do not know.' And Mohammed said, 'I read it
and when I awoke from my sleep, it was written in my heart, like
in a book.'

(Translation based on the account in Ibn Hisham's *Sirat an-Nabi*,
Cairo, 1346 A.H.)

So we see that the equivalence of literacy and recitation by heart
is inscribed both linguistically and in religious revelation.

Wagner *et al.* describe the ways in which the contemporary
Qur'anic schools in Morocco have incorporated more modern
methods into traditional features of Qur'anic schooling. Traditionally Qur'anic schools were for boys only; now they are mixed.
Since the mid-1960s the Moroccan government has made efforts
to harmonize the Qur'anic school system with the public school
system, in order to upgrade and standardize their instruction. The
classroom observations carried out in Morocco by the Morocco
Literacy Project led project workers to conclude that in the typical
present-day Qur'anic school traditional formats have been superseded by modernized pedagogy.

They noticed, for example, the use of 'bottom-up' teaching
strategies, starting with letter formation and recognition, combining letters into blends, then words, then sentences. Traditional materials of the wooden writing board and reed pens
have been superseded by pens and exercise books and chalk.
However, there is a prevalence of memorization of texts as a
learning strategy throughout the school system, and they conclude that learning by heart is an activity of central cultural
significance.

The other pre-school strand in Moroccan education is the public
system's modern pre-school. These are mostly taught by women
(whereas the Qur'anic school is male-taught), who have received
teacher training, in age-graded classes, with a wider range of
activities: oral expression, reading and writing practice in Arabic
and sometimes French; memorizing and reciting secular songs,
perhaps an hour a week of Qur'anic material, handicrafts, drawing, painting, role-playing, card-matching games and puzzles.
The project notes, however, a similarity between the methods
of the Qur'anic school and the modern pre-school in the use of
memorization and recitation in teaching reading.

In the London situation, voluntary, community-based Arabic

classes are trying to perform a number of functions: the transmission of Qur'anic literacy, the teaching of basic education in
standard Arabic, and articulating the concerns of parents that their
children should not grow up unable to read and write in Arabic.
To understand the background of these educational practices,
we need to know something about the linguistic situation in
Morocco.

THE LINGUISTIC SITUATION IN MOROCCO

The linguistic situation in Morocco is complex. On the one hand
there is a situation of diglossia (to use the technical linguistic
term), in which two varieties of the same language coexist: a
non-standard vernacular, which is the language of the home
and of informal, oral interaction, described in Arabic as the
lughat ad-darija; and a standard form of the language which is
the children's education, known as the *lughat al-fuṣha*. There is
also a large population of speakers of Berber and Berber Moroccan
Arabic bilinguals. The majority of the Moroccan settlement in
London are native speakers of Moroccan Arabic which has no
written form. So, in this discussion, when we talk about literacy,
we are talking about literacy in standard Arabic. There are very
strong social and political constraints against the adoption of
written forms of the *lughat ad-darija* in literacy development,
along the lines of the students' writing movement in the United
Kingdom, in which writing in non-standard dialect is valued and
seen to contribute to the literacy process.

THE LINGUISTIC SITUATION IN LONDON

The linguistic situation in London is complicated by the different
levels of oral competence in Moroccan Arabic of children who
were born here, or came here young. In Morocco, standard Arabic
literacy is taught on the basis of Moroccan Arabic oral fluency,
or fluency in Berber. In London, teachers sometimes complain
of having to explain things in English because the children do
not understand in Arabic. Oral language maintenance complicates
the process of acquiring literacy in a second, standard, dialect
of Arabic. Arabic classes for the children in London, as well as
attempting to perform some of the varied functions of the school
system in Morocco, are also coping with the needs produced by
the London situation. In the following story, a Moroccan mother
describes just such a communication problem with her daughter.

I = Interviewer; D = Drissia

I: And do you think you'll go back to Morocco?

D: I don't think so because my children now can't speak good Arabic.

I: Yeah?

D: Sometime I have trouble with them.

I: Yeah?

D: One day a man came to fix the roof and he asked me, 'Do you have a ladder?' I said, 'Sorry I don't.' So he went downstairs to get one and my daughter asked me, 'Mummy, what did that man say to you?' and I told her in Arabic, 'He asked me for a *sillem*' [*sillem* = ladder]. And she said, 'Mummy, what's a *sillem*?' So I told her it means 'ladder'. She couldn't understand.

I: Yeah?

D: Yeah, she forgets some words sometimes. She was a little bit over 3 when she came here.

I: Only 3.

D: Yeah, 3.

THE ARABIC CLASSES

Underfunding and the lack of organizational infrastructure, teaching carried out by dedicated volunteers also doing full-time jobs and some of the special problems mentioned above related to the linguistic situation, all create difficulties in London.

Si Mohammed, one of the teachers, complained of a number of organizational and practical problems in organizing his teaching. First, the lack of fluency in some children in Moroccan Arabic:

I = Interviewer; Si M = Si Mohammed

I: And how do you explain things to the children? Supposing you had to explain a particular word, how would you do it, in Arabic or in Moroccan Arabic?

Si M: I use both. If I use Arabic and they don't understand I use Moroccan language, if not I use English.

I: So sometimes you use English?

Si M: English, yeah.

I: Do some of the children not understand much Moroccan Arabic?

Si M: No.

I: Why is that?

Si M: Well, because you have some children born here in England.

Si Mohammed was teaching a mixed class of twenty, with an age range between 5 and 11 or 12. He aimed to teach 'reading and writing and some Qur'an', therefore not the traditional Qur'anic schooling, but something closer to the modernized Qur'anic schooling that Wagner *et al.* (1986) discuss. He is hampered by irregular attendance, a widely differing age range and levels of knowledge, and lack of suitable material. He notes in particular the difficulties of the older children.

In the following extract of an interview in which a 9-year-old boy (Driss) describes his experiences of the community-organized Arabic classes, we see a number of the issues we have referred to above highlighted.

I = Interviewer; D = Driss

I: So how have you been going to the Arabic classes?

D: Well, I used to go to an Arabic class, where was it now, in Lancaster Road, Ladbroke Girls' School.

I: Was S your teacher?

D: Yeah. It was about three years ago.

I: Yeah.

D: 1979. And she used to teach us. Then there wasn't any school any more and then there was Arabic school in Isaac Newton, and then last year in Bevington.

I: So what do you do there? How long do you stay? Is it an hour or two hours?

D: It depends what time the teacher gets there.

I: What, sometimes he gets there late?

D: He's supposed to get there at five, sometimes he gets there a bit late. No later than twenty to six, no earlier than five fifteen.

I: And is he strict?

D: He is strict, yeah.

I: Stricter than your teachers at . . .

D: Yeah, he carries his stick with him, a big chalk holder, like a stencil.

I: Yeah.

D: Like, oh gawd what do you call those things, pen holder, pencil holder to draw circles. I forgot.

I: I know, yeah, I know what you mean: a compass.

D: Yeah, a compass. He's got a big compass. He's got a metal one, a wooden one, and he hits you with it if you do something wrong. And the small children are still learning the alphabet, some of them, but now they're going on to other work, going on to words now.

I: So what did you do? What are you learning at the moment?

D: I'm learning, we're learning. Well, he writes something down, like about a tree, or about, last time he wrote about a dove or food or what you do in the morning, how do you get up. And he tells us questions and we have to say the answer. It's a bit difficult and he's strict.

D: And then after that we have to say Qur'an and I feared that. But then I just learnt. You have to learn Qur'an. And I didn't know any of it, just a bit of it. And then I kept it in my mind and learnt it. And the next day when we came he said we had to say it again at the end of time. And I said it that time. And then the day after that I didn't say it. 'Cos I'd said it to my mother's nephew and it was all right. And now I know it. I know, let me see, one, two, three, four, five, six, seven, I know seven verses.

A number of general issues emerge from Driss's rather frank account of the community-organized Arabic classes. First, we see evidence of the problems of organization and staffing, typical of unfunded or underfunded ventures relying on volunteer support. The volunteer teachers of these classes would more often than not be coming straight from work in a hotel or restaurant, hence the lateness that Driss speaks of. The fairly rapid opening and closure of classes in different venues, often with different organizations backing them, is disruptive of the continuity of educational processes.

In terms of teaching strategies, Driss describes a 'bottom-up' teaching method, such as we found in the literacy research project in Morocco. We notice a secular content in his description of the topics used by his Arabic school indicating that the model for instruction is not the traditional Qur'anic School, but the contemporary Qur'anic school, described by Wagner *et al.*, with its mix of the secular and the religious.

We notice also Driss's account of how he memorized the Qur'an. 'I kept it in my mind and learnt it' is a very literal translation of the Arabic *hafaẓa* (to learn by heart). We notice how this learning is supported within the family, when his mother's nephew tests him on his knowledge, before he is tested in class.

Driss's account of memorizing the Qur'an is told with a genuine feeling of triumph. It has frequently been noted that the learning in mainstream schooling diverges from the child's home experience (cf. for example, Shirley Brice Heath's *Ways with Words*, 1983). Here we have a case where a child's learning is being actively supported and validated by adult members of his family group, where learning is associated with membership, the feeling of achievement with belonging.

The education system in a complex and unequal society is bound to be a site of conflict and contradiction. We have in this short case study discovered a number of issues around which such conflicts and contradictions can adhere: in the polarity between traditional and modern, reactionary/progressive, rote-learning/reading for meaning, standard/non-standard forms of language, spoken and written. These conflicts and contradictions can be seen to adhere to 'the literacy issue', notably in the discussion of literacy practices in the community-organized classes in London, with their roots in the practices of Qur'anic schooling in Morocco. Comparing the research findings of the Morocco Literacy Project with the experience of the Moroccan community in London, however, has shown ways in which the practices of the Moroccan education system are reflected, adapted and reproduced in the activities of the community organizations in London. In all of these educational settings, there are different ideologies at work, different (or apparently different) conflicts and contradictions inherent in the literacy issue.

Activity

Earlier in the chapter, we saw how discourses are articulated, according to Kress, as a systematically organized set of propositions. How can we make explicit some of the ideological positions suggested in this case study? Take, for example, the ideological differences between

(a) the parents and the organizers of the Summer Scheme which had too much play and not enough hard work;
(b) the teacher who uses corporal punishment and a teacher who disapproves of corporal punishment;
(c) a proponent of 'reading for meaning' and a proponent of 'rote-learning and memorization'.

IMPLICATIONS FOR UNDERSTANDING LITERACY PRACTICES

What are the implications for understanding literacy practices if we adopt the shift of perspective from the *one language/one culture/one literacy* model and recognize that, within linguistic and ethnic diversity, there are a diversity of literacies, actual and potential?

First, we need to know more, and in greater depth, about the diversity of literacy practices in countries like the United Kingdom. The surveys carried out by the Linguistic Minorities Project have provided a baseline for such research, but the overview of survey research needs to be complemented by qualitative case-study research, which can illuminate literacy practices in multi-literate individuals and communities, and add to our knowledge about what it means to manage literacies rather than literacy. For examples of such studies, see Weinstein-Shr (1993) on the literacy practices of the Hmong community in Philadelphia, and a case study by Saxena (1994) on the literacy practices of Punjabis in Southall, United Kingdom.

Where there is the opportunity to trace connections between the literacy practices of individuals and communities settled in the United Kingdom and literacy practice 'back home', as there is because of the work in Morocco of the Morocco Literacy Project, research should make those connections. In this particular instance, the Morocco Literacy Project should be encouraged to consider further studies of the literacy practices of the migrant communities of Moroccans settled in a number of European countries (France, Holland, Germany and the United Kingdom).

We need to know more about the ways in which different participants in educational processes – parents, children, teachers 'in the community', teachers 'in the mainstream', administrators – manage or are defeated by the conflicts and contradictions which adhere to the literacy issue in multi-lingual societies. The work of Shirley Brice-Heath would provide a model for such research projects.

We need to pilot and evaluate programmes designed to bring the diversity of literacies onto the mainstream curriculum and support the initiatives of communities in providing out-of-school tuition.

Certain of the teaching/learning methods discussed in this case study – for example, rote-learning and memorization – appear to fly in the face of what is accepted as good educational practice in the 'new orthodoxy'. We need, perhaps, to examine whether the polarization

> traditional   modern
>
> reactionary   progressive
>
> rote-learning reading-for-meaning

which informs many discussions on good practice in literacy teaching, both with children and adults, is not an oversimplification.

There is a persistent and well-documented danger for those within the education system – teachers, administrators and researchers – to operate within a deficit model, by which users/learners are seen as educational have-nots, being topped up with learning by the educational haves. Freire's work exemplifies the critique of this deficit model of education, and its corresponding definition of users/students in terms of lack. Contextual studies of literacy practices outside the classroom, which demonstrate the richness and variety of literacies, may provide further evidence to counteract deficit-model thinking. The individual who struggles with reading and writing in English in a literacy group may be the same individual who teaches Qur'anic school, or organizes Saturday schooling for the children in his or her community. The child newly arrived in the English school may be a fluent reader/writer in one or more languages, one or more scripts.

RESEARCHING LITERACY PRACTICES IN CONTEXT

Academic researchers have developed their own responses to a demand for literacy research which challenges the one language/one culture/one literacy model, within the opportunities and constraints of their particular disciplines, as we shall see in Chapter 2. What about the practitioner researcher? How can students be involved in projects exploring literacy diversity? The material on which the case study above is based was derived from a mix of academic work and practical involvement in community education. The interviews quoted were carried out ten years ago. I am now struck with the similarity between the conversations that ensued in these interviews and the discussion that can arise in adult learning groups when both students and tutors are deeply involved in a topic.

Freire has suggested that we should routinely challenge the teaching/learning/research distinction. Every adult learning group, as well as every school classroom, is a potential site of linguistic/cultural/literacy diversity and therefore a potential site for research/exploration of some of the issues raised in this case study. Language awareness work, reflecting on our personal literacy histories and the institutional cultures that construct our experiences of literacy, can provide testimony of the complexity of literacy practices in multi-lingual societies and the opportunity for student/teacher/participants to deepen their understanding of the function of literacy in social processes.

CONCLUSION

Defining literacy involves making explicit a set of related ideological positions, not just on literacy itself, but on where literacy fits in social life as well as its role in constructing social life. One of these ideological positions is the contextual one: that language (and literacy) are meaningless out of context. Another is that it is not enough to look to the immediate context of situation: who is doing what with whom in particular instances. We need to investigate the ways in which relationships based on unequal power shape uses of literacy, both in terms of who is included and who is excluded, and in terms of how literacy is achieved in day-to-day life. The power of institutions and discourses impinge in countless ways on everyday communication, and the investigation of literacy practices, inside and outside classrooms, is a way of discovering this.

Chapter 2 will present a framework for investigating literacy practices outside the classroom. Chapter 3 will examine literacy practices in educational contexts. Both of these emphasize the social nature of literacy. Chapters 4, 5 and 6 are more language-based, although the emphasis again is on the social nature of language. We will return in Chapter 7 to the implications of researching literacy practices.

SUGGESTIONS FOR FURTHER READING

Gee, J. (1990) *Social Linguistics and Literacies: Ideologies in Discourses*, London: Falmer Press.

Graff, H. (1979) *The Literacy Myth: Literacy and Social Structure in the Nineteenth-Century City*, New York: Academic Press.

Graff, H. (1987) *The Legacies of Literacy*, Bloomington, Ind.: Indiana University Press.

Levine, K. (1986) *The Social Context of Literacy*, London: Routledge & Kegan Paul.

Street, B. (1984) *Literacy in Theory and Practice*, Cambridge: Cambridge University Press.

TWO

Investigating literacy practices in context

LITERACY AS SITUATED SOCIAL PRACTICE

What does it mean to talk about literacy as situated social practice? In this chapter we will introduce a range of the theoretical constructs that have been used to make sense of literacy in context, illustrated by case-study material. The literacy constructs that are significant in this chapter are as follows:

- *Literacy practices* Investigating literacy as practice is investigating literacy as 'concrete human activity', involving not just what people do with literacy, but also what they make of what they do, how they construct its value, the ideologies that surround it. The practice construct implies both doing and knowing.
- *Literacy events* Heath (1983: 386) quotes a definition of the literacy event from Anderson *et al.* (1980) as 'any action sequence, involving one or more persons, in which the production and/or comprehension of print plays a role'. Heath suggests that 'literacy events have social interactional rules which regulate the type and amount of *talk* about what is written, and define ways in which *oral language* reinforces, denies, extends or sets aside the written material'.
- *Mediators of literacy* A 'mediator of literacy' can be defined as a person who makes his or her literacy skills available to others, on a formal or informal basis, for them to accomplish specific literacy purposes.
- *Networks* Boissevain defines 'network' as follows: 'The social relations in which every individual is embedded may be viewed as a network. This social network may, at one level of abstraction, be looked upon as a scattering of points connected by lines. The

points, of course, are persons, and the lines are social relations. Each person can thus be viewed as a star from which lines radiate to points, some of which are connected to each other. These form his first order or primary network zone. But these persons are also in contact with others who our central person does not know, but with whom he could come into contact via members of his first order zone. These are the often important friends of friends. They form what might be called his second order zone.' (Boissevain 1978: 24)

Fingeret (1983), in a study of the social networks of illiterate adults, identifies two characteristic types of relationship between illiterate adults and others on their network, *interdependent* and *dependent*:

> Individuals create social networks that are characterized by reciprocal exchange: networks offer access to most of the resources individuals require, so that it is unnecessary to develop every skill personally. Therefore, many illiterate adults see themselves as interdependent; they contribute a range of skills and knowledge other than reading and writing to their networks. Some illiterate adults see themselves as having little or nothing to offer their networks. They are engaged in asymmetrical rather than reciprocal exchange relationships, and may be viewed as dependent. While their lack of literacy skills contributes to this condition, it is not the cause. (Fingeret 1983: 133–4)

- *Domains of literacy*   Domains of literacy map the main settings and contexts where people use literacy (home, workplace, school, shops, bureaucracies, the street). The term is borrowed from the literature on bilingualism; cf., for example, Fishman (1972), but also from the critique of the domain construct in bilingualism in LMP (1985).

The literacy research referred to throughout this chapter is empirical, based on interviews, observation, documentation and analysis of literacy practices in context.

Vignette

I am standing in the visa office of the French Consulate in London, waiting while my wife, who is an Australian citizen, queues to obtain a visa for a forthcoming visit to France. A Moroccan comes up to me, holding the application form, and asks me, in English, to help him complete it. This involves explaining what is required in each of the boxes in to which the form is divided.

The categories: SURNAME
FORENAMES
OTHER NAMES: maiden, professional, religious, pseudonym
DATE OF BIRTH
PLACE OF BIRTH: town, country
CIVIL STATUS: married, single, widow(er), divorced, separated are relatively unproblematic, as are
NATIONALITY and HOME ADDRESS. I explain to him what is required at each point and he fills it in. There are a number of questions relating to his travel document, a Moroccan passport, with information presented in both French and Arabic. I locate the information asked for:
KIND OF TRAVEL DOCUMENT
NUMBER
PLACE OF ISSUE: town, country
DATE OF ISSUE
DATE OF EXPIRY

I indicate what information should go where and again he fills it in. There are a number of questions relating to reasons for entering France, length of stay, dates of arrival and departure. In order to fill these in, we need to have quite a lengthy conversation. Once the form is completed, he thanks me for my help and moves off to join the queue.

Although the interaction was entirely in English, the texts we were working on were in English and French (the form) and French and Arabic (the passport). We find in this episode the typical mix of oral and literate activities characteristic of the literacy event, as well as the multi-lingual dimension of working with text in three languages. In addition we see how a stranger (myself) can be enlisted as a mediator to accomplish a literacy task.

The study of literacy in its social context has been advocated by anthropologists, sociolinguists and ethnographers of speaking over the last decade or so. In a programmatic paper, *The Ethnography of Writing*, Basso concludes with this statement:

Adequate ethnographies of writing do not yet exist because linguists and anthropologists alike have grown accustomed to investigating written codes with only passing reference to the social systems in which they are embedded. In this essay, I have suggested that the time has come for this strategy to be reversed. When all is said and done, we shall find that the activity of writing, like the activity of speaking, is a supremely social act. Simultaneously, I believe, we shall find that it is far more complex – and therefore more intriguing – than we have suspected heretofore.

(Basso 1974: 432)

This approach suggests that literacy practices are complexly patterned, like other communicative and social practices, and that the study of the social meaning of literacy can be enriched by a range of research methods, typically ethnographic fieldwork involving participant observation, gathering autobiographical accounts of literacy practices as well as analysis of texts.

Researching literacy in social context involves stepping back from the pedagogical issues involved in the teaching and learning of literacy and trying to find out how literacy is actually used in a range of contexts (in the home, at work, when dealing with bureaucracies, for study purposes). It is of course important not to set up a false polarity between 'social' contexts and 'educational' contexts, since the literacy classroom itself is another kind of social context, with its own typical literacy practices.

However, this approach to the study of literacy has greatly extended our understanding of the functions and uses of literacy across social groups and in different settings. It has helped to question the idea that there is one monolithic type of literacy, typically the literacy associated with schooling itself. Researchers have been led to the conclusion that instead of one literacy there are 'literacies' (cf. Gee 1990) because of the extreme diversity of literacy practices that they encountered

The Scollons (Scollon and Scollon 1981) looked at literacy in the context of inter-ethnic communication between Athabaskan Indians in Canada and the dominant Anglo culture, suggesting that for Athabaskan students to perform well in the literacy of the dominant Anglo culture they have to abandon preferred communicative patterns. They found that Athabaskan discourse patterns are in conflict with the discourse patterns of Anglo essayist prose and that, in order to write, the Athabaskan must adopt discourse patterns that are identified with a particular ethnic group, identified in Canada and Alaska as Anglo (Scollon and Scollon 1981).

They suggest that the demands of schooling, particularly of writing essayist prose, produce internal conflict in the Athabaskan writer, similar to the cross-cultural conflict that can be produced in oral communication when two speakers from different ethnic groups fail to identify the ground rules for mutual understanding.

Brice Heath's work shows how literacy can be studied in context, at the level of social groups and communities:

Ways with words: doing ethnographies of literacy in the Piedmont Carolinas

How is it that schooling and the institutions of the dominant, mainstream culture continue to reproduce themselves and legitimize the experience of middle-class professionals at the expense of working-class people, white and black? Shirley Brice Heath set out to explore this question by finding out 'from the inside' about the experience of two communities of working-class people, one black and one white, in the Piedmont Carolinas.

> The two communities – Roadville and Trackton – only a few miles apart in the Piedmont Carolinas. Roadville is a white working class community of families steeped for four generations in the life of the textile mills. Trackton is a black working-class community whose older generations grew up farming the land, but whose current members work in the mills. Both communities define their lives primarily in terms of their communities and their jobs, yet both are tied in countless ways to the commercial, political, and educational interests of the townspeople – mainstream blacks and whites of the region. The townspeople are school-oriented and they identify not so much with their immediate neighbourhoods as with the networks of voluntary associations and institutions whose activities link their common interests across the region.
>
> (Heath 1983: 1)

She focuses her attention on three groups, the people of Trackton, black working-class, the people of Roadville, white working-class, and, thirdly, the 'mainstream' townspeople.

Townspeople are tuned into the bureaucratic channels, the patterns of mainstream schooling. 'They choose their movies on the advice of the critics; they select their automobile tyres on the recommendations of consumers' guides; they seek out professional advice for marital problems, and for interior decorating and landscaping ideas.' Among other things, they are tuned into a mainstream, literate culture.

So what about Trackton and Roadville? What are the ways they have for using literacy? How do they use and value oral patterns of communications? Are the ways they bring up their children different from each other and from the mainstream culture? How do teachers and other representatives of mainstream culture deal with individuals who come to their institutions with different patterns of communication, different values, different priorities? Not surprisingly, she comes to the conclusion (Heath 1983: 235) that 'neither community's ways with the written word prepares it for the school's ways'.

How was Brice Heath able to find out about the 'ways with words' of these two communities, since she was not a member of either? She describes an extended phase of participant observation.

> In the years between 1969 and 1978 I lived, worked, and played with the children and their families and friends in Roadville and Trackton. My entry into these specific communities came through a naturally occurring chain of events. In each case, I knew an old-time resident of the community, and my relationship with that individual opened the community to me. I had grown up in a rural Piedmont area in a neighbouring state, so the customs of both communities were very familiar to me though many years had passed since I had been a daily part of such cultural ways.

This participant observation enabled her to observe and record the typical ways in which the different communities made use of literacy.

Instead of one monolithic way with literacy, typically defined as the school's way with literacy, close study of the ways in which people work with written texts in ordinary everyday settings shows up striking differences in ways of taking and making use of literacy, sometimes at odds with the mainstream definitions of what literacy should be about.

Conclusion

This brief example from an ethnography of literacy illustrates the kind of study that can throw light on the uses of literacy in groups and individuals. There is a danger that those who have come through the mainstream culture successfully (for example, those who have ended up as teachers) assume that how we learned to use literacy is the only way that literacy is used. Classroom-based research, designed to improve the work that goes on in literacy groups (or in other types of education for that matter) should be accompanied by attempts to study the uses of literacy in day-to-day contexts outside the classroom. Teachers should come to understand more about

class, cultural or ethnic bases for difference in communication, both
in spoken and literate modes.

Heath describes the uses of literacy at the level of social groups
and communities. Literacy in use can be studied in the different
domains of everyday life, for example in the workplace. (Keller-
Cohen (1987) for example, investigated the uses of literacy in a
credit union). What are the implications of a study like Heath's
for investigating literacy practices in the workplace?

INVESTIGATING LITERACY PRACTICES IN THE WORKPLACE

The workplace is a context where the connection between what
goes on in and out of classrooms is particularly striking. Literacy
courses in the workplace are generally designed to improve
the literacy abilities of sections of the workforce in job-related
literacy tasks in the hope of outcomes like increased productivity,
increased awareness of health and safety, increased ability to participate in new types of work practices and access to further training. This immediately raises the question of what the job-related
literacy tasks are and how can they be researched, documented
and analysed in order to provide material for job-related literacy
programmes.

One of the first issues in researching literacy practices in
the workplace, as in other contexts, is *negotiating access*. Heath
describes how she used a network chain of contacts to gain access
to the Trackton and Roadville communities (she was already a
member of the mainstream community). What are the issues in
negotiating access in a workplace? Negotiating access involves
identifying the key players in the organization (management,
unions) who must give consent to allow access to the workplace.
Literacy programmes in the workplace are generally the outcome
of extended negotiations between management, unions and the
training provider, but gaining access involves not just permission
to visit the worksite to gather data, but also permission to visit for
long enough to gain a useful insight into how literacy impacts on
work practices.

Gaining an understanding of the organizational culture of the
workplace involves not just the official or semi-official structures,
which are explicit and obvious, but also understanding the less

explicit network-type connections that can facilitate or frustrate action. Is the union perceived as effective by the workforce or by particular sections of the workforce? Are human resources in conflict with line management, because they are seen as pulling workers off the production lines for training? Does a particular section of the workforce feel under threat of redundancy and therefore unwilling to cooperate with a training initiative that may be preparing them for unemployment?

Once on the worksite, what kind of data need to be gathered? First, there is observational data, of the sort typically yielded by participant observation. What are the literacy tasks involved in accomplishing a given work process? But are observational data enough? The concept of literacy practice shows us that what can be observed is not enough. The observable needs to be complemented by the values and ideologies which participants use to interpret what they do. In order to get this information the researcher needs to talk to the different players, probably in the form of open-ended interviews which explore the meanings of the various uses of literacy observed.

A further source of data are examples of the different kinds of written texts in use, accident report forms, order forms, health and safety information and manuals outlining work procedures. So part of the data-gathering will involve sampling the range of texts in use.

One of the dangers of researching in contexts that are not familiar is that the researcher ends up taking the official explicit position as given, when there are other, hidden factors which crucially alter the situation. For example, the work procedures for a given manufacturing cycle may be laid out in a manual, and it is tempting to assume that this is a key text for this workplace. However, it may turn out on further investigation that the procedures in the manual are widely held to be inaccurate and that word of mouth is used to instruct new workers, while the manuals gather dust on a shelf.

Ethnographies of communication involve learning the ways with words and other cultural practices in cultures where the researcher is, to differing degrees, an outsider. Learning the culture of a workplace poses similar problems for the outsider coming in to investigate literacy practices, or any other workplace practices for that matter.

The arguments that have emerged from these approaches to the study of literacy in context have been synthesized by Street in his book *Literacy in Theory and Practice* (Street 1984). He argues that there is an 'autonomous model' of literacy. The autonomous model proposes that there are universalistic consequences of literacy, like the existence of fundamental differences of cognitive organization between literate and non-literate individuals and groups, and that literacy is a fundamental precondition for the development of logical thought and abstraction. Street argues that the proponents of the autonomous model, while claiming to read off large-scale consequences for literacy, are in fact naturalizing and universalizing the literacy practices of a particular dominant group, typically those who have successfully been through the school system, typically themselves. In opposition to this autonomous model of literacy, with its universalizing claims and tacit ethnocentric bias, Street develops an 'ideological model' of literacy.

The ideological model rejects over-ambitious generalizations about the consequences of literacy. Instead it proposes an attempt to understand literacy in terms of ideologies in which different literacies are embedded. Specifically he argues against a 'great divide' between orality and literacy (cf. Finnegan 1973, 1988). In contrast to a monolithic conception of literacy/illiteracy, the ideological model proposes that there are literacies, situated social practices which must be investigated in their own terms.

But first we will briefly review the approaches to the study of literacy which Street, Finnegan and others characterize as 'great divide' theories of literacy (cf. Finnegan 1973, 1988; Street 1984, 1988).

ORALITY AND LITERACY: THE GREAT DIVIDE

The cognitive and social consequences of the development of writing have provided a rich vein of research and speculation both historically and cross-culturally. Scribner and Cole (1981) provide a survey of some of the dominant themes.

The key tenet of the 'great divide' theory of literacy is that the development of literacy is somehow criterial in the great leaps forward of human history, that literacy is the key variable in distinguishing between 'primitive' and 'civilized', traditional and modern, that literacy is the key to personal and social development as it is conceived of in the liberal humanist tradition (cf., for example, Hoggart in the *Uses of Literacy* [Hoggart 1992]).

The consequence of literacy within this framework has been the development of logic, rationality and objectivity and the possibility of science. However, as Street (1987) points out, the corresponding implication is that those without literacy lack such qualities and are therefore, illogical, irrational, incapable of objectivity or scientific thinking.

We argued in Chapter 1 that the literate/illiterate dichotomy ('Can't you read!') was a powerful sorter of persons, as witnessed in the uses of terms connoting 'illiteracy' as abuse. Street's characterization of the implications of illiteracy, carrying traces of illogicality, primitiveness, childishness, begins to explain why this should be so and the kind of social power carried by the graffiti quoted at the beginning of Chapter 1. If literacy is tied to logic, development and progress, its opposite, 'illiteracy', is tied to illogical thinking, backwardness, underdevelopment, both at the individual and social levels.

We need to unstick the literacy variable from the progress and development variable. Literacy is necessary, but certainly not sufficient to explain key developments in the organization of knowledge and social transformations.

When we examine Scribner and Cole's research into the literacies of the Vai people in Liberia, exactly the same conclusions are reached in a fine-grained, empirical study: in order to pinpoint significant cognitive changes, we find that literacy interacts with other variables, such as the influence of schooling as an institution, the effect of moving from a rural to a city environment. In order to discover the social and cognitive consequences of literacy, we need a theory of literacy which engages in complex ways with social context. Literacy on its own (the decontextualized literacy of Street's 'autonomous' dimension) is not enough.

If theorists and researchers such as Finnegan, Street and Scribner and Cole have made us rightly suspicious of ambitious yet simplistic connections between the literacy variable and various kinds of social and cognitive re-orientation, does this mean that we must give up on any kind of connection between literacy and social/cognitive shifts? A new generation of literacy research, termed by Gee (1990) the 'new literacy studies', is attempting to re-theorize literacy in such a way that its interaction with social structure, its embedding in social practice and its status as social practice become central. Once this is achieved, it becomes possible to re-address the questions of social and cognitive reorientation and 'the literacy effect', based not on grandiose generalizations, which reify a great divide between literacy 'haves' and illiterate 'have nots', but on fine-grained studies of literacy in context, where the cognitive and social implications of literacy can be investigated empirically.

This approach to the study of literacy does not therefore deny the role of cognition in literacy acquisition and use, but it does emphasize the role of context in shaping cognitive processes. This is why it is important to emphasize that literacy is *situated* social practice.

In order to illustrate the shift inherent in the 'new literacy studies', we will review one type of cognitive re-orientation typically ascribed as an effect of literacy: increased ability in abstract reasoning skills.

ALPHABETIC LITERACY AND THE DEVELOPMENT OF LOGIC

Literacy among the Vai in Liberia

Scribner and Cole studied the literacy practices of the Vai people of Northwestern Liberia who have potential access to three literacies, an indigenous Vai script, Arabic and English, with the object of testing out dominant hypotheses on the effects of literacy: notably, that there is a great divide between the literate and the non-literate, that literacy is a necessary prerequisite for logical thinking, that becoming literate entails fundamental cognitive restructurings that control intellectual performance in all domains.

So, for Scribner and Cole, understanding literacy does not mean a focus on the technology of the writing system and its reputed consequences, such as: 'alphabetic literacy fosters abstraction'. They approached literacy 'as a set of socially organized practices which make use of a symbol system and a technology for producing and disseminating it. Literacy is not simply knowing how to read and write a particular script but applying this knowledge for specific purposes in specific contexts of use' (Scribner and Cole 1981: 236).

The example they give of a literacy practice is letter-writing among the Vai, the predominant use of Vai script literacy they discovered in their research. Letter-writing can be seen as practice, as it involves:

1 a socially evolved and patterned activity;
2 a technology – the Vai syllabic script, formerly leaves, now pencil and paper;

3 a means of communicating the message – formerly on foot or by
   canoe, currently by taxi;
4 shared cultural knowledge – the Vai writing system, left/right
   orientation on the page;
5 shared conventions of appropriate style for the letter;
6 ability to reconstruct pragmatically the letter recipient's current state
   of knowledge about the information to be contained in the letter;
7 ability to organize the information to be contained in the letter;
8 a complex set of skills (sensory-motor, linguistic, cognitive), which
   can be further broken down into component processes in order to
   implement the above.

(cf. Scribner and Cole 1981: 236–7)

In their review of studies which seek to establish links between
the development of literacy and cognitive restructuring, Scribner
and Cole examine the work of Havelock who, through analyzing
the oral, recitative mode of the poems of Homer and the written
mode of the dialogues of Plato, is able to characterize significant
linguistic differences between the two modes, in a manner remi-
niscent of Halliday's spoken/written modal distinction:

> Oral information is likely to be unfriendly to such statements as
> 'The angles of a triangle are equal to two right angles'. If, however,
> you said, 'The triangle stood firm in battle, astride and posed on
> its equal legs, fighting resolutely to protect its two right angles
> against the attack of the enemy', you would be casting Euclid
> backwards into Homeric dress, you would be giving him preliterate
> form . . . . Oral storage is hostile to the expression of laws and
> rules which are stated as such in terms which are connected by the
> timeless present. It is unfriendly to statements which place cause
> and effect in analytic relationship.
>
> (Havelock 1978: 42–3, cited in Scribner and Cole 1981)

Goody and Watt (1968) argue that the invention of written language in post-Homeric Greece made possible the development
of the disciplines of history and logic. History became possible
in that the permanency of writing made possible the maintenance of written records and archives, which could be checked
and re-checked. Logic, following the arguments presented by
Havelock, was facilitated by the written mode in that statements
which express cause and effect relations, most typically in the
Aristotelian syllogism, could be checked against each other when
written down.

Havelock and Goody and Watt make a strong claim about the

cognitive restructuring achieved through writing: a whole type of reasoning and logic becomes possible through its introduction, which, they argue, would be unavailable in the oral mode. It is an argument that leads from linguistic and social behaviour to generalizations about modes of thinking. What Scribner and Cole argue in response is that, while it may very well be that changing modes of linguistic and social behaviour bring with them corresponding cognitive changes, this is an empirical question which should be investigated within psychology; hence the title of their study, *The Psychology of Literacy*. Scribner and Cole draw on work carried out by Luria, investigating how non-literate, recently literate and literate peasants in the Soviet Union dealt with activities like classifying sets of objects, or reasoning through syllogisms.

Luria found significant differences between the groups he investigated, the non-literate group tending to classify objects not as logical sets (cooking utensils, kinds of food) but in terms of functional relationships (frying pan goes with egg because you fry an egg in the frying pan). The literate groups, in contrast, would deal with classification tasks by grouping objects into logical sets. In tasks which involved logical reasoning on the syllogism model –

> In the Far North, where there is snow, all bears are white.
> Novaya Zembla is in the Far North and there is always snow there.
> What colour are the bears?

the non-literate group would give responses like 'I don't know. I've seen a black bear. I've never seen any others . . . Each locality has its own animals' (Luria 1976: 108–9, cited in Ong 1982). A barely literate subject responds with 'to go by your words, they should all be white' (Luria 1976: 114, cited in Ong 1982).

The non-literate respondents respond to the syllogism, not in its own terms, but in terms of a situated logic, based on their own experience, while those becoming literate rapidly acquire the ability to respond to the syllogism in its own terms – that is, by reasoning internal to the syllogism itself.

Evidence of this sort might be taken as confirmation that becoming literate carries with it clear cognitive consequences, and this position is taken in a particularly strong form by Ong (1982), which is critiqued by Street (1988), 'A Critical look at Ong and the "Great Divide"' (see below). Scribner and Cole, however, caution against making the connection too simplistically because of the other variables that can interact with 'the literacy effect'.

The problem raised with this 'covariation of literacy with other major changes in life experience' of course implies that literacy is some sort of autonomous variable which could be extracted from context and isolated for study. As we are beginning to see, the other alternative is to re-theorize the literacy construct as situated social practice, contextually determined in many complex ways. This is indeed what Scribner and Cole attempted in their study and is the basis for Street's 'ideological' model of literacy: we re-theorize the separability of literacy from the troublesome overlapping effects of social context. These troublesome effects are in fact constitutive of literacy as situated social practice.

Scribner and Cole's research itself documents the shift from try-ing to investigate the general cognitive consequences of literacy, using a pre-set theoretical agenda, such as we have described above, in favour of an approach which emphasized literacy as situated social practice.

They shift towards investigating the cognitive consequences of literacy as they are mediated through the actual literacy practices the Vai engage in. For example, they examined the effect of memory in the context of the memorization involved in learning the Qur'an by rote. In studies aimed at investigating the commu-nicative demands of writing tasks, they based their investigation on the most common genre in Vai script literacy, the letter.

This shift is a shift away from ambitious cultural generalizations about the effects and consequences of literacy. For a number of significant theorists (Havelock, Goody & Watt, Ong) these generalizations can be seen as an attempt, *post hoc*, to explain how 'Western civilization' developed as it did and to universalize a specific set of circumstances surrounding the emergence of alphabetic literacy in Ancient Greece, using the implicit equation of the liberal humanist tradition:

LITERACY = PROGRESS = DEVELOPMENT = ENLIGHTENMENT

which, as we saw in Chapter 1, is implicit in many responses to 'the literacy debate'.

As Street argues, in the ideological model of literacy, literacy prac-tices are 'inextricably linked to cultural and power structures in a given society' (Street 1986: 59). Lévi-Strauss (1976: 385–99) argues, in fact, that the primary function of literacy historically has not been to facilitate great leaps forward in human development, but rather to facilitate slavery and social control. Given the generally benevolent, developmental or explicitly political tenor of the ideology of most literacy programmes currently, it might seem convenient to relegate Lévi-Strauss's argument to the functions of literacy in the ancient world. However, the current trend towards providing compulsory or semi-compulsory literacy programmes for the unemployed, which will be discussed in the next chapter, indicates that literacy may figure not just as a practice of freedom, but also in the context of state coercion.

LITERACY PRACTICES

Literacy as practice was defined in Chapter 1 as 'concrete human activity', involving not just the objective facts of what people do with literacy, but also what they make of what they do, how they construct its value, the ideologies that surround it.

Scribner and Cole adopted a practice-based approach to literacy research through a 'shift in strategy' as their theorizing became progressively more embedded in the uses of literacy among the Vai.

So the concept of practice requires us to theorize subjectivity, not simply to rely on the external evidence of behaviours. The concept of *values* developed by Barton and Padmore in the Literacy in the Community project at Lancaster University (Barton and Padmore 1991) focuses on the subjectivity dimension of practice – what people think about what they do:

> When people talked about writing, everything they said was imbued with values and attitudes. They evaluated themselves and others and talked about the power of writing, its pleasure or its difficulty . . . Neil, for example, was a section manager at a branch of a foodstore chain and had great difficulty writing. He was sent on courses where he trained with people who had passed all sorts of examinations. He didn't understand how he could talk and work so easily alongside these people who could produce pages and pages of writing effortlessly while he struggled to make a sentence. When discussing writing letters to the newspaper, two people, Pat and Bob, suggested it was laziness on their part that prevented them from writing such letters; Roger on the other hand said, 'It seems such a long, laborious task to write it out and then send it and then see if they're going to write it out', implying the

fault was in the process rather than himself. It is interesting that
Bob commented, 'I must be a lazy sort of person', because his
typical response to questions about writing was that he couldn't
write. Like Pat he was orally articulate and cared passionately about
local and national issues.

(Barton and Padmore 1991: 71)

We will return to the need to theorize subjectivity at the beginning
of the next chapter.

The importance of the idea of practice in understanding literacy
is that it provides a way of relating literacy in use not just to
the immediate context of situation, but also to the broader social
context and the role of ideologies, discourses and institutions:

in order to identify the consequences of literacy, we need to
consider the specific characteristics of specific practices. And, in
order to conduct such an analysis, we need to understand the
larger social system that generates certain kinds of practice (and
not others). From this perspective, inquiries into the cognitive
consequences of literacy are inquiries into the impact of socially
organized practices in other domains (trade, agriculture) on
practices involving writing (keeping lists of sales, exchanging goods
by letter).

(Scribner and Cole 1981: 237)

The concept of 'practice' is therefore quite an abstract one, on a
par with 'discourses', 'ideologies' and 'institutions'. Its value is
precisely that it forms a bridge between literacy as a linguistic
phenomenon and the social context in which it is embedded. How
are literacy practices routinely realized in everyday life? To understand that we will now turn to the idea of the literacy event.

LITERACY EVENTS

Literacy events can be defined as instances and occasions where
uses of literacy play a role. In terms of the Vai letter-writing
example above, a literacy event would be a specific occasion on
which a letter was composed in the Vai script, either by a Vai
literate on their own behalf or else by a Vai literate on behalf of
a non-literate other.

Under the heading 'Talk is the thing' Heath writes that 'in
almost every situation in Trackton in which a piece of writing
is integral to the nature of the participants' interactions and their

interpretation of meaning, talk is a necessary component' (Heath 1983: 196). To put it another way, as Street has pointed out there is no great divide between literate practices and oral practices, literate practices are typically a mix of the literate and the oral.

The question of mainstream or dominant literacy practices and their relationship to non-dominant literacy practices is one which we shall return to later. To conclude this discussion of the literacy event construct, I will briefly present the stages of a literacy event involving the reading of a letter and the drafting of a reply, taken from the fieldwork of a study into the communicative practices of the Moroccan community in London (Baynham 1988).

Case study: a literacy event

The scene is the sitting room of Touria's flat. I have arrived, armed with a cassette tape-recorder, to interview her. Touria's aunt, Menana, is also visiting. Menana has received a letter from the Department of Health and Social Security (DHSS) and asks me to tell her what it says.

I read the letter and tell her the gist of it. The DHSS claim that she has continued to cash her giro book after she started work, and demand repayment of £96.96. She angrily denies the DHSS claim. I am very careful to attribute each statement that I relay to her, making clear that the DHSS is making these claims, not me. No one wants to be the bearer of bad news and there is a thin line between bearing the accusations of others and making those accusations yourself. My care in attributing each claim in the DHSS letter reflects, I think, an awareness of the ambiguity, inherent in my position of mediator of literacy, bringer of bad news.

Menana's response to the gist of the letter is a vehement denial of the accusation which takes the form of a story, the story of what really happened ('the book I'm give him the book straight', 'yeah I'm give him the book back when me start work . . . straight . . .'). We can perhaps call the DHSS letter provocative: it provokes Menana's response, which is structured as an emergent narrative.

In response to Menana's denial, I propose a strategy to her for taking it further: go and see Souad, who is a Moroccan worker at the local CAB. Menana has the right of appeal. I try to explain the concept of appeal and then go on to paraphrase the contents of the letter more fully, producing what is, in effect, a simplified version of the text.

My paraphrase is, in effect, repeating the accusation and produces a repeated denial of the circumstances surrounding the cashing of the disputed giro cheque. Menana, assisted by Touria, continues to reconstruct the narrative of what actually happened, provoked by the challenge of the DHSS letter, mediated through my reading of it. The narrative serves to explain why she cashed the giro: she is paid a week in hand by the new job – for the first week she receives nothing – she has to pay the rent and buy food for herself and her daughter. How could she do that without cashing her giro cheque?

Menana then switches into Spanish, possibly as a way of regaining control of the conversation from her niece, who is beginning to speak for her. Menana again elaborates her narrative of what happened in Spanish and I again repeat my go-and-see-Souad (or rather my *tiene-que-ir-hablar-con-Souad*) strategy, supported by Touria, who although she cannot speak Spanish, presumably catches the gist of what is being said on hearing the name Souad, and re-enters the conversation with 'Yeah Souad she do it for you'.

I elaborate my advice, which up till now has been mainly focused on persuading Menana to go and see Souad (the professional), 'well what you should do you have to write a letter saying'.

At this point Menana challenges my advice in a very clear way, by drawing my attention to the fact that it is not necessary to write a letter at all; there is a space on the letter from the DHSS to register that you wish to appeal: 'what this write letter his letter (   ) fill this form small'. She points to the letter and asks, in both English and Spanish: 'what she tell him, que quiere decir?' At this point I give in, after a pause, and offer to write the letter.

Menana, Touria and I reconstruct the story of what actually happened, in this case working out which office Menana went to. This is for my benefit, as part of my work of composing the letter of appeal. After extensive discussion in English, Spanish and Moroccan Arabic, Menana points out the obvious: the address of the office will be on the letter she has received: 'yeah . . . look the letter where she come from.'

I finish off the letter. Menana herself wants to get off as she has to go to work. I am, however, keen that she should hear back what I have written, agree it and sign it. While I am reading it back, I get positive feedback from Menana ('Yeah . . . yeah . . . that's it'), who caps my final statement, 'I did not cash it after that' with her own 'nothing no eat one penny him' and provides her own evaluation of the whole incident in both English and Spanish: 'crazy *locos*'.

So what are we to make of this literacy event? First, we can say that the literate work that is done is grounded in talk: my silent reading produces a version of the letter which I convey to Menana.

The information thus conveyed provokes her response, in which she uses narrative strategies to deny the claim in the letter that she owes the DHSS money. The working out of the response involves interaction in English, Spanish and Moroccan Arabic. I read the reply I have composed and it is orally evaluated by Menana.

Secondly, we can see quite clearly the process by which Menana recruited me as mediator, first to tell her what the letter from the DHSS said and then, quite unwillingly on my part, to reply for her. Once she has recruited me to do the literacy work, that work is achieved jointly, with quite notable interventions from herself. We can perhaps distinguish these interventions as being (1) on the level of content, in that she contributes information which specifically contradicts the information contained in the DHSS letter, information structured as a narrative which is then transformed by me into a letter notifying the DHSS of Menana's wish to appeal, and the grounds for the appeal; and (2) on the level of *form* at those moments when she uses her knowledge of the forms of literacy to intervene in the shaping of the literacy event. It is intervention on the level of form which constitutes the powerful strategy by which she finally gets me to write the response for her.

Heath states that literacy events have social interactional rules that regulate the type and amount of talk about what is written. I am struck in reviewing the unfolding of this literacy event, in which I was participant, by the role that conflict plays in this unfolding. Candlin (1986) has spoken of 'explaining moments of conflict in discourse', citing examples from institutional settings. Fairclough (1985) refers to work on unequal encounters in institutional settings, and stresses the need for discourse analysis to explore the role of institutional power and status in overdetermining interactional patterns. Now I would argue that what is happening in this literacy event is that an institutional voice, the message of the letter that the DHSS sent to Menana, has intruded into a setting which would normally be regarded as marked for informality: her niece's front room. As mediator of literacy I am introducing this voice into the conversation. The message of this letter, with its demand that Menana repay £96.96, produces a response of anger and resentment and provokes her to tell her own version of events. This is the primary conflict in the situation, between the DHSS's demand for repayment and Menana's rejection of that demand. There is a conflict between my strategy for action and Menana's unwillingness to adopt it.

My strategy is typically professional: when in doubt, refer. I am in doubt as to the best thing to do, so I refer her on to Souad. Menana, who is not in good health, is not keen, understandably, to trail down to the CAB on her one day off in the week when she has someone on hand who is perfectly capable of fulfilling her purposes (namely, me). Menana is operating an informal network strategy of the type described by Wagner. She is able to use effective strategies to achieve the solution to her immediate problem in the face of quite spirited opposition from me, being doggedly committed to my professional strategy of referral.

Fairclough (1985) has criticized the notion that exchange of information between participants having equal discoursal and pragmatic rights and obligations is the unmarked case, focusing on Grice's cooperative principle. He regards the idealization underlying such theories of 'communication' or 'conversation' as being inadequate to deal with the discourse of unequal encounters. I would suggest, using this literacy event as prima facie evidence, that a useful pragmatic theory must be able to deal with the management of conflict in conversation, just as much as it must be able to handle the achievement of cooperation between participants. Menana's account of what actually happened is achieved in conflict with the accusation made in the letter from the DHSS. The development of this literacy event can be seen in terms of a struggle between participants to determine the way it should develop and its eventual outcome.

We will return to the text of this literacy event in Chapter 4, in order to look at how, from a discourse analysis perspective, we can characterize some of the social interactional rules, constitutive of the literacy event, that Heath refers to.

One of the results of empirical studies of literacy events is that the interaction of oral and written modes in the accomplishment of literacy become apparent. To understand the functions of literacy in context, however, we need to take this further and describe the interaction between literacy practices and other forms of social practice in contexts of situation.

Vignette

It is a bright sunny morning as Si Mohammed drives the office car into the brand new Afriquia petrol station in Berrechid, Morocco.

> When Allal, the petrol station attendant, has filled the petrol tank, Si Mohammed asks for a *facture* (receipt) for reimbursement. Allal rummages briefly through his leather money-bag and carefully extracts a pad of blank *factures* and a blackened stamp with the station's name and address. With a deep breath he exhales on the rubber stamp, moistening it slightly, and then presses it with deliberation into the *facture* paper. This small rubber stamp, like tens of thousands all over Morocco, serves as the guarantor of official literacy in Morocco. Allal, who cannot read or write, then hands the stamped paper to Si Mohammed, who fills in the date, amount of petrol and the price (data from Wagner *et al.* 1986).

The petrol pump attendant in this example is engaged in activities that are not just a mix of the oral and literate modes, but also a mix of linguistic and non-linguistic action. The literacy event in which Si Mohammed fills in the *facture* is part of the broader 'getting petrol' event. Here Steiner's proposition that communicative practices have to be integrated into a more general frame of social action (linguistic and non-linguistic) is relevant (1985). Halliday classifies contexts where language is central to the social purpose engaged in (for example, Heath's newspaper-reading example) and those where language has a support role (for instance, this transaction in the Moroccan garage or similar examples as in the literacy involved in waiting in a restaurant). This becomes relevant if we want to understand the situated inter-relationship of spoken and written language with other forms of social action, particularly when investigating literacy practices at work.

Activity

> To illustrate the difference between literacy events which are entirely language-based and those in which the spoken and written language use accompanies non-verbal activity, compare the different roles of spoken and written language in the following two situations:
>
> (a) taking a phone message in an office and leaving a written message for a colleague;
>
> (b) assembling a new computer, using an instruction manual.

MEDIATORS OF LITERACY

A 'mediator of literacy' can be defined as a person who makes his or her literacy skills available to others, on a formal or informal basis, for them to accomplish specific literacy purposes. Just as the literacy event construct was implied in the discussion of literacy practices, so the concept of 'mediators of literacy' arises out of the discussion of the literacy event.

Writing about the role of mediators of literacy in Morocco, Wagner *et al.* point out that 'historically to be illiterate was not considered a negative stigma, though it can be in contemporary Morocco' (Wagner *et al.* 1986). They note that 'literacy is now often perceived as a need and a right whereas it was once something that a person as a member of a group or neighbourhood might accomplish indirectly' (ibid.). They speak of traditional mediators of literacy, formal and informal. These include public writers, with differing degrees of specialized knowledge of legal literacies. The preparation of legal documents is the province of the notary or *'adil*. A second category of public writers, with a low level of self-taught expertise in legal matters, carry out day-to-day literacy work, often using typewriters to fill out forms for people or write personal letters. Wagner *et al.* assert that, despite the recent development of a 'modern' ideology of personal literacy, traditional mediators of literacy are by no means out of business. They estimate that considerably less than half the adult Moroccan population can read or write with fluency in any language. As well as these professional mediators of literacy, informal mediators are often found on family or neighbourhood networks. Parents may depend on their literate children to read to them. Wagner suggests that these 'joint literacy events' contrast with the modern ideology of individual literacy. They assert that 'literacy is not possessed and understood only by a small elite, even in countries where a majority can neither read nor write' (Wagner *et al.* 1986).

In the following extract from an interview, Z.T. describes how, after quitting school in Morocco she couldn't find a job and decides to migrate, illustrating the roles played by mediators of literacy in Morocco:

I = Interviewer; Z = Z.T.
I: what made you decide to come to England
Z: erm well really not eh to England but somewhere abroad
I: yeah
Y: and eh of course umm I quit my high school and I was looking for a job actually
I: yeah
Z: I couldn't find any so erm we had eh local whaddyoucallit eh the

man who does eh typewr- erm whaddyoucallit I forget now who
does writing by the machine you know for the public
I: ah hah
Z: and I think because he told me that someone in England came
to Meknes
Z: and he knew this man but he's very very very nice very educated
and he gave him the address of Grand Metropolitan Hotel
I: ah hah
Z: so friend of mine know him and she said I wanted to go to
see Mr n so and so and can you go with me says all right so we
we went
I: yeah
Z: and erm we were talking and he said do you want to go abroad
said oh yes I'd love to but how well I have got the address and you
can write to them yourself
I: uh huh
Z: and send them two picture of yours but you're going to get
reply in English so who's going to read it for me (Laughter) I
don't know English at all so erm we really did it is erm eh not a
seriously
I: yeah
Z: but just through our luck maybe yes or no
I: uh huh
Z: so I did and I wrote a letter for my friend as well
I: yeah because you could write in
Z: yes I wrote in eh in eh in French and we send two picture of each
and then in four weeks we get a reply
I: yeah
Z: in English but I and a friend of mine very old woman she's
French and she works at the co- uh French consulate so I took it
to her and she told me that you're going to get your work permit
within four to six weeks but didn't. . . I know I I wasn't lucky but
eh I didn't take it eh that much so I waited
I: yeah
Z: well that time three of us wrote letters already myself and Fatima
then another Fatima which I told her to do so and she did but
when we did get work permit the last one was the first my friend
was the second and I was three days behind them
I: yeah
Z: so I says well I know my luck is my sign is good go to work so
um so it did so I get my work permit

In her account of how she went about migrating to England, Z.T.
provides us with an interesting insight into the accomplishment of
literacy purposes in the Moroccan context, which is, in many ways,

similar to the practices described in the Morocco Literacy Project. Z struggles to find the right word in English for the *écrivain publique* (a semi-official mediator of literacy in terms of Wagner *et al.*)

> whaddyoucallit eh the man who does eh typewr-erm
> whaddyoucallit I forget now who does writing by the machine you
>   know for the public

It is through network contacts that Z gets to hear of the opportunity of contacting the Grand Metropolitan Hotel chain which, at that time, was recruiting hotel staff in Morocco.

Her contact tells her how to go about writing the letter, including the requirement of sending two photographs with the letter. A linguistic problem appears here, since the reply to her letter will be in English, a language she does not speak. Z, however, has been educated to secondary-school leaving level and is able to write a letter in French. She serves as a mediator for another friend, for whom she writes a letter. When the reply arrives, Z is again able to make use of a network contact to achieve her literacy purpose: getting the letters read. She takes the letter to her friend who provides her with the gist of the letter: 'You're going to get your work permit within four to six weeks'. The outcome is the arrival of another text: the work permit.

We see in this account how Z is involved in chains of network contacts to achieve her literacy purposes and is herself a mediator and facilitator for others. The account is informative, but also somehow tantalizing to the discourse analyst. How did Z go about writing the original letters? When her French friend told her the content of the reply in English, did she translate word for word, or summarize the gist of the letter? How, precisely, was the activity of aloud or silent reading, of relaying content, related to the other oral activities which constituted the literacy event (querying, commenting, asking for repetition or clarification)? These are the sort of questions that the discourse analyst wants to ask and which may indeed hold the key to the social interactional rules that constitute the literacy event, as Heath suggests. We shall return to this question in Chapter 4.

Activity

Can you think of any occasions when you have made use of someone else as a mediator to accomplish a literacy purpose? Conversely, have there been occasions when you have been enlisted by someone else to accomplish a literacy purpose for them? Here are two examples.

Example One: making use of someone else to accomplish a literacy purpose:

When I worked as an adult education worker in London in the 1970s and 1980s, I frequently needed to get publicity information about courses translated into different community languages. My friend, Mohammed F, who had been educated in Qur'anic school, had a beautiful Maghribi Arabic script and I would occasionally visit him to ask him to translate a publicity leaflet into Arabic. Conversely, I would often get a message at work asking me to drop round to see Mohammed. He would have a form that needed filling in in English. Both Mohammed and I were serving as mediators of literacy for each other in different languages and for different purposes.

Example Two: being made use of to accomplish a literacy purpose:

I am watching children's television with my eldest son (aged 4) in the early morning. We are tuned to a commercial channel and at regular intervals there are details of competitions with lavish prizes, which involve writing to a Post Office Box Address in Brisbane. My son becomes very excited about one particular competition and insists that I copy down the PO Box address so that we can do the competition. Here I am being enlisted to accomplish a literacy purpose by a 4-year-old, not yet able to copy the address down himself.

The concept of mediator of literacy is related to the concept of role discussed in Barton and Padmore:

> When people talked about the writing they did within the household and beyond it, it was often in terms of roles; they referred to themselves as parents, relatives, workers, neighbors, friends – each role making different literacy demands upon them. One clear role differentiation which was apparent within the household was that between men and women. Usually this followed the common division of women writing in the personal sphere while men dealt with the official world . . . We had many examples of this. If we take the example of dealing with household correspondence, everyone interviewed played some part in this but in most homes, other than wholly male set-ups, letter and card writing tended to be seen as the woman's responsibility, while dealing with forms and bills was the man's.
>
> (Barton and Padmore 1991: 66–7)

If the concept of mediator leads to the idea of the role relationship between the mediator and the person making use of their services, it also brings us to the concept of network.

NETWORKS

The ideas of the literacy event, the mediator of literacy and the impact of social role on the division of labour in literacy tasks all point in the same direction: to the social nature of literacy practices. Instead of the ideal writer/reader and the text in isolation, we come to regard literacy as socially constructed. Shuman (1986, 1993) writes of 'collaborative literacy', Wagner *et al.* of joint literacy events. Participating in literacy is not an either/or issue, individuals with relatively restricted access to personal literacy may routinely have access to literate others through whom they can achieve their literacy purposes.

Fingeret (1983), in a study of the social networks of illiterate adults, identifies two characteristic types of relationship between illiterate adults and others on their network – interdependent and dependent:

> Individuals create social networks that are characterized by reciprocal exchange: networks offer access to most of the resources individuals require, so that it is unnecessary to develop every skill personally. Therefore, many illiterate adults see themselves as interdependent; they contribute a range of skills and knowledge other than reading and writing to their networks. Some illiterate adults see themselves as having little or nothing to offer their networks. They are engaged in asymmetrical rather than reciprocal exchange relationships, and may be viewed as dependent. While their lack of literacy skills contributes to this condition, it is not the cause.
>
> (Fingeret 1983: 133–4)

In the literacy event described above, I am available on Menana's network to achieve a particular literacy purpose. Mohammed, the man who writes the publicity leaflets in Arabic for me, is another member of Menana's family network, married to her niece. The arrangement by which I help him with his forms in English, while he helps me with my publicity leaflets in Arabic, is an example of the reciprocal exchange relationship that Fingeret describes.

Barton and Padmore describe the role of network in the literacy practices of the people they interviewed in Lancaster in the United Kingdom:

> In our data we can see clearly that social networks of support exist for people. These networks are part of everyday life whether or not people have problems. Sometimes there was support for people

who identified problems. Often it was within the family. Neil, Paul and Bob all mentioned getting help from their partner. Mark took writing problems to his sister, while Duncan relied on his parents. Liz got help from her husband and her daughter, as well as from a friend who worked 40 miles away. Sometimes particular people were chosen for help; Julie's mother would approach an uncle 'because he worked in an office' – one of several examples where work skills extend into the home. When Sally got married she found that there were many everyday tasks she could not deal with, and she turned to her mother to help her learn the new writing tasks.

(Barton and Padmore 1991: 69)

Fingeret further distinguishes between individuals who have 'extensive contact with the institutions, norms and systems of the literate society' (1983: 137), who may be economically successful adults, working in public roles, passing as literate and functioning in networks which she terms 'cosmopolitan', and illiterate adults whose networks are 'local'.

There is a continuum of variation between the extreme poles of 'cosmopolitan' and 'local' networks. To exemplify this from the participants in the literacy event described above, Menana's network is almost entirely co-extensive with her family and family connections (although not exactly tied to one geographical location, in that she travels regularly back and forth between London and Morocco). I got to know her through my friendship with Mohammed whose network is 'cosmopolitan': he is head waiter at a West End hotel, for a period taught Arabic classes on a voluntary basis at the local primary school, and has a wide circle of friends both Moroccan and English. The difference between their networks is typical of the traditional social distribution of Moroccan society as described by anthropologists such as Geertz and Dwyer (Geertz et al. 1979; Dwyer 1978), in which women's social networks are co-extensive with the family and immediate neighbourhood, while men's networks typically extend out into 'school, coffee shops, workplaces, the market, the mosque and the street' (Geertz et al. 1979: 333).

It is important to realize that the significance of network in literacy practices is not simply a feature of adults with restricted access to literacy skills. We can see the importance of network in accomplishing specialized literacies as much more widespread, as the following vignette shows.

Getting a constitution (1)

I am sitting in a meeting called to set up a new organization to promote 'literacy in development'. A draft of proposed rules for the association has been prepared, and the next item on our agenda is to look at them. The person who prepared the draft explains how she rang round people she knew in similar professional organizations and 'modelled' the draft on similar rules and constitutions, adapting them to fit the needs of this particular organization.

We are invited to go through the rules, paragraph by paragraph, and suggest amendments. The discussion becomes quite lively at points, with people taking exception to certain forms of words and suggesting others. There is prolonged discussion, for example, on whether we should use the term 'literacy' or 'adult literacy'. Another contentious point is the 'exclusion clause', a commonplace feature of the constitution format, which allows the association to refuse or discontinue membership in certain circumstances. This is felt to be autocratic in its formulation, and there is considerable discussion about the form of words used and the idea of exclusion clauses in general. Finally, when all comments have been exhausted, the new committee of the association agrees to incorporate the amendments into a final draft. The discussion has been minuted all the while, and, presumably, the notes taken by the minute-taker will be used in the process of final drafting.

This fairly commonplace example of committee business involves a 'literacy event'. A written text was being jointly worked on by a large group of people. It had an oral and a literate dimension: discussion and argument round text, and reading or readings of it. Some members of the large group contributed quite vociferously, others remained silent. The written text appeared quite distinctive, both in format and discourse organization, lexis and syntax. Some members of the group – for example, the minute-taker and designated officers of the association – had roles which clearly differentiated them from other participants speaking 'from the floor'. This literacy event involved reading, talk, a jointly undertaken oral re-drafting of the written text, the note-taking of the minute-taker as well as the private note-taking of the more diligent or compulsive participants. It had a past (the way the first draft had been achieved) and a future (amendments would be incorporated into a final draft to be agreed at a future meeting).

In addition, it seemed to me that the person who drafted the rules had adopted a typically informal learning strategy. She was confronted with a new variety of literacy practice and responded by seeking out people 'on her network' who might be able to help, by providing model formats on which this new set of rules could be based. Having gone through this learning process she may then become someone who can be recommended to others about to go through the same process: 'Why don't you talk to so-and-so, she's been involved in drafting constitutions and rules of association.' And so it goes on. What we have here is an example of the use of informal networks for the transmission of a specialized literacy practice.

Getting a constitution (2)

This is how Saeed described the process of getting a constitution for his community organization:

> S: We were first a self-elected committee, because we had the idea to build this committee and we got together, we formed, because the organization in general, you know, you have to have management committee, such as chairman, honorary treasurer, secretary and so on. And we did, that. First thing we went to get some legal advice about how we can be formed and they say 'you have to form a constitution'. We receive tremendous help from the Law Centre.

> M: How did you know about the Law Centre?

> S: Well . . . first of all, before you start, when you're starting an organization, of that sort, you are all volunteers, there is no funds at all, so you have to shop around, you have to find the cheapest, the one that is free service first. If not, then you got to go to the cheapest. So we had to go to the Citizens Advice Bureau. We got some information about how we can get some legal advice freely, or rather cheaply. Then we been referred to the Law Centre. We spoke of our problem, then they help us. That's how we did it. So we got our constitution ready. Because once you have a constitution, that makes it easier, even if you want to go and rent a building to start a proposal, then you are identified, there are people with you. Because a constitution only can be composed at that stage if there are more people involved, say like chairman and so on.

In this extract, Saeed describes the transition from informal to formal types of organization that is implied in getting constituted. We see his network strategy of getting advice from available local organizations offering free legal advice: the Citizens Advice Bureau, the Law Centre. These organizations have access to the specialized forms of literacy required to draw up a constitution.

It might be argued that the role of network is simply a conservative mechanism, which anchors the low-literate into low literacy 'traps' (cf. Mikulecky 1987 and 1989). However, as the two vignettes above show, the role of network is pervasively a feature of literate as well as low-literate practices, and can be seen as a source of strength, not necessarily dependence.

Activity

> In what ways do the network strategies used to achieve the literacy purpose of 'getting a constitution' differ between Example One and Example Two above? Are their network strategies 'cosmopolitan' or 'local'? How do the protagonists become knowledgeable about where and who to go to for necessary information?
>
> If you became involved in an organization which required a constitution, what strategies could you make use of to gain the necessary information?

DOMAINS OF LITERACY

One of the strategies literacy researchers use is to map the main settings and contexts where their subjects use literacy and, borrowing from the literature on bilingualism (cf., for example, Fishman 1972, but also the critique in LMP 1985) they use the term 'domain'. The domain construct is a fairly rough and ready way of sorting the social space in which literacy practices are embedded. It is useful in that it provides an initial structuring of the 'social context' of literacy practices, while demonstrating, in the examples quoted, some aspects of the research design of studies of literacy in context.

Two literacy research projects using the domain construct

> 1 *Wagner* et al. *describe the domains identified in the Morocco Literacy Project.*

>> Our in-depth observations of eight households in Al-Ksour range from a divorced Berber woman (often joined by her daughter and a friend with a grandson) to a family of eleven; and primary breadwinners including a migrant factory worker in France, a taxi-driver, a woodcutter, a small-scale merchant, and a bathhouse

owner. Through these observations a set of literacy 'domains' has emerged, providing a heuristic model useful for describing the literacy landscape of the social strata represented in this study. Five such general domains, which are often overlapping in everyday Moroccan life, have suggested themselves: household, school, religion, entertainment, and work.

(Wagner *et al.* 1986)

2 *Klassen in his study of the uses of literacy among bilinguals in Toronto, Canada, uses the domain construct in a way that is modelled on Wagner* et al. *as a way of making sense of the variety of uses of literacy he encounters in his research*:

I started gathering data (in Spanish) by diagramming my informants' daily schedules and by mapping the 'domains' (a term I borrow from Wagner, Messick and Spratt 1986) that each person regularly entered in the course of their daily lives in order to capture the variety in their regular experience. With the schedules and maps as a basis, I then asked each informant to describe the kinds of print materials that she or he encounters, domain by domain. I then moved to questions about use (users, uses, and importance of the uses). I included questions about how the informants themselves interact with print, and the problems they have as a result of the print. The final topic of conversation in each round of interviews centred on feelings and opinions not only about the print that is encountered but also about the ways in which print is managed. . . . The domains that emerged over and over again in the data fall roughly into the categories of the home, streets and stores; bureaucracies; places of work; schools and church.

(Klassen 1991: 42–3)

Wagner *et al.* write about 'overlap' between domains, and Klassen points out in his data that 'all the domains tend to merge in the first category, the home, which is the center from which individuals venture out into other domains' (Klassen 1991).

Activity

1 In the literacy event described above (pages 55–6), what are the domains of literacy that are in play? Do the domains overlap in any way? How does this case study illustrate the point that Klassen makes about the home domain?

2 Try documenting your own uses of literacy over a period of time – up to a week, for example. You could do this by keeping a journal and recording the use of literacy, the purpose, the setting, other participants involved and any other information that seems relevant.

> When you have collected these data, you might review them to see what domains of literacy use emerge.

LITERACY PRACTICES, IDEOLOGIES AND SOCIAL CONTEXT

Constructs such as network, mediators of literacy, role and domain are clearly significant in determining the structure and contextual embedding of literacy events. However, Street is keen to emphasize the limitations of theorizing social context solely in terms of face-to-face interaction.

The limits of such contextualizations are elegantly expressed by Bourdieu when he argues that

> 'interpersonal' relations are never, except in appearance, individual-to-individual relationships and that the truth of the interaction is never entirely contained in the interaction. . . . In fact it is their present and past positions in the social structure that biological individuals carry with them, at all times and in all places, in the form of dispositions which are so many marks of social position and hence of the social distance between objective positions.
>
> (Bourdieu 1979: 81–2)

Street argues for this broader conception of context in literacy research, emphasizing social structure and systems as well as the categories derived from the study of face-to-face interaction:

> I would like to argue that the analysis of the relationship between orality and literacy requires attention to the 'wider parameters' of context largely under-emphasized in Anglo-American linguistics. Within social anthropology, for instance, these would be taken to include the study of kinship organization, conceptual systems, political structures, habitat and economy etc., which are seen as 'systems', and analyzed in terms of function and structure rather than simply of 'network' or 'interaction'.
>
> (Street 1988: 62–3)

We have already above had two instances, where the close-grained social interactional constructs of network and role reveal the workings of a broader sociological and ideological category: that of gender – firstly, when Barton and Padmore described the distribution of family correspondence on a gender basis; secondly, in the glimpse of Menana and Mohammed's social networks, revealing gender-based differences in their network structure.

The research studies quoted in this chapter in different ways argue for the contextualization of literacy in broader socio-economic and ideological structures. For Scribner and Cole, in order to identify the consequences of literacy it is necessary to consider specific social practices.

> And in order to conduct such an analysis, we need to understand the larger social system that generates certain kinds of practices (and not others) and poses particular tasks for these practices (and not others). From this perspective, inquiries into the cognitive consequences of literacy are inquiries into the impact of socially organized practices in other domains (trade, agriculture) on practices involving writing (keeping lists of sales, exchanging goods by letter).
>
> (Scribner and Cole 1981: 237)

This is why the emphasis is placed in this book on literacy as practice. It is important to study literacy from a linguistic base, as the analysis of texts, but we also need the further dimension of literacy as strategic, purposeful activity in social interactions. Beyond this we need to understand literacy as social practice, the way it interacts with ideologies and institutions to shape and define the possibilities and life paths of individuals. The literacy/illiteracy polarity is in itself a major means of sorting and categorizing individuals. The uses of literacy which we examine in the close focus of the literacy event need to be understood in terms of the social power relations that are operating, and the values and ideologies which they express implicitly or explicitly.

It follows that critical literacy draws on the dimension of literacy as social practice, because it is here that it becomes possible to understand the relationship between literacy and social power.

There is a danger of ahistorical descriptive literacy studies, which simply emphasize and document the infinite variety of 'literacies', re-inventing notions of cultural pluralism and mask-ing power relations, such as the fact that, at particular times, particular modes and practices of literacy may be dominant. As we shall see in the next chapter, adults' experience of literacy is strongly shaped by the dominant institution of schooling (turning inside out, as it were, the problem noted by Scribner and Cole inherent in separating the 'literacy effect' from schooling and other types of social organization, like city living, a complex, highly bureaucratized culture, technological change, shifts in work practices). If we re-theorize literacy as situated social practice, then it becomes obvious that literacy practices will shape and be shaped by social factors.

It should be clear from the above that an autonomous model of literacy (like an autonomous model of language) will not be adequate to specify the ways in which literacy practices shape and are shaped by social contexts. In Chapter 4 we will take up these issues further when we try to specify the theory of spoken and written language required to underpin a theory of literacy as situated social practice.

SUGGESTIONS FOR FURTHER READING

Barton, D. and Ivanič, R. (1991) *Writing in the Community*, London: Sage.

Hamilton, M., Barton, D. and Ivanič, R. (eds) (1994) *Worlds of Literacy*, Clevedon: Multilingual Matters.

Heath, S.B. (1983) *Ways with Words: Language, Life and Work in Communities and Classrooms*, Cambridge: Cambridge University Press.

Scribner, S. and Cole, M. (1981) *The Psychology of Literacy*, Cambridge, Mass.: Harvard University Press.

Street, B.V. (ed.) (1993) *Cross-cultural Approaches to Literacy*, Cambridge: Cambridge University Press.

THREE

Educational contexts for literacy development

> Learning to read and write has often been described as a journey, with stops and starts. It has also been described as a race, where you run around the running track and the hurdles are seen as obstacles which have to be overcome. Sometimes you trip over these hurdles, but pick yourself up again and carry on or you may drop out for a while and carry on again later.
>
> I look at my literacy in a slightly different way. I think of literacy as entering a large maze. When you first enter the maze, the way to the centre seems nearly impossible, with all the blind alleys and dead ends, but gradually you manage to work your way further into the maze. You may have to go over the same ground two or three times, but with persistence you eventually make it to the centre.
>
> I think that the whole journey, from the outside to the centre, is extremely difficult and full of many setbacks, which can be the cause of much dropping out. You can never be completely sure whether you can make it to the centre or not. It has taken me over ten years to make this journey. I think that the journey from the outside to the centre was when my literacy was a major problem to me and this was when I had so much difficulty working in groups. Fortunately, I have at last overcome this problem with groups, largely because I now have much more confidence in my abilities. I think that this was when I reached the centre of my maze.
>
> (Johnson, undated: 44–5)

The metaphor of the maze is the organizing metaphor for John Johnson's experience of becoming literate. It contrasts with the linear metaphors of the journey with stops and starts, the race with hurdles, which correspond to a more conventional way of theorizing education as 'development'. Entering the maze can be read as entering the complexities of a system, on one level the complexities of education as an institution, on another the complexities of the system of written language itself. John Johnson's text provides a way into this chapter, which will examine, first, the ways in which experiences of schooling shape and construct the subjectivities of adults who have been educationally disenfranchised, as John was, and, secondly, the range of educational settings where adults can work to improve their literacy. These settings will include:

- literacy in community adult education;
- literacy in vocational education;
- literacy in preparation for further study;
- literacy in the workplace.

Like all institutions, the education system looks more logical if you are on the inside. For the potential user, particularly the educationally disenfranchised, going back into education is indeed like entering a maze as John Johnson points out. It is a maze sown, like all good mazes, with ordeal and challenges: negotiating public spaces, like college offices and initial interviews, forms to fill in, discretionary fees for certain categories of students, re-entering classrooms, often after many years' absence, re-visiting experiences of schooling. Educational institutions are sites of both procedural and linguistic complexity, demanding of potential users that they should present themselves in public contexts and in public modes of discourse. Naturally, the best efforts of adult literacy practitioners have been aimed towards short-circuiting the damaging effects of educational institutions on the potential of adults to learn. Much adult literacy in countries like the United Kingdom and Australia developed initially within community education contexts, where buildings and programmes could be designed, interview procedures set up, methods of teaching developed, which would maximally contrast with the experience of schooling.

There will be twin themes in the chapter: adult literacy education for *empowerment*, and adult literacy education for *access*. I will argue that these two dimensions of empowerment and access are central to the problematic of adult literacy education in complex, unequal societies, like the United Kingdom and Australia. I will be drawing on examples from both the Australian and British contexts.

Experiences of schooling shape the subjectivities of adults returning to learning, especially those who either have not had the chance of schooling, or those whose experience of schooling has constructed them as failures. Adult literacy education aims to re-orientate learners towards a new range of possibilities: from a sense of failure to success, from disempowerment to empowerment. One aspect of this is to work on the experience of schooling, to unpack the subjectivity constructed over an adult life by previous experiences of education.

THE EXPERIENCE OF SCHOOLING

If the concept of critical literacy is to be developed in conjunction with the theoretical notions of narrative and agency, then it is important that the knowledge, values and social practices that constitute the story/narrative of schooling be understood as embodying particular interests and relations of power regarding how one should think, live and act with regard to the past, present and future. At its best a theory of critical literacy needs to develop pedagogical practices in which the battle to make sense of one's life reaffirms and furthers the need for teachers and students to recover their own voices so they can retell their own histories and in so doing 'check and criticize the history they are told against the one they have lived' (Inglis 1985: 108).

(Giroux 1988: 201)

In the *Prison Notebooks* Gramsci says: 'The starting-point of critical elaboration is the consciousness of what one really is, and is "knowing thyself" as a product of the historical process to date, which has deposited in you an infinity of traces, without leaving an inventory.' The only available English translation inexplicably leaves Gramsci's comment at that, whereas in fact Gramsci's Italian text concludes by adding, 'therefore it is imperative at the outset to compile such an inventory.'

(Said 1978: 25)

A critical literacy education must start with an awareness of the powerful effect of these traces and develop strategies for bringing them into play.

Adults talking about their childhood and school experience or lack of it represent, in autobiographical discourse, shaping experiences, both at school and in the family, which in significant ways have made them what they are as adults. Their accounts constitute a documentation or inventory of traces, such as that which Gramsci proposes. The very notion of 'trace' carries with it interesting connotations of writing: adult learners are marked with traces of their previous experiences as learners. These traces construct them as successes or failures, 'literates' or 'illiterates', within the pervasive and dominant social discourses, which were found to accumulate around the concept of 'literacy' in Chapter 1. In some sense, social roles and potentials are inscribed on (and ascribed to) learners, through these early learning experiences, now documented in first-hand accounts of what it was like to learn in specific social and cultural contexts.

Extract one

This text was recorded off air from a radio phone-in on literacy. The caller, who identifies herself as having literacy problems, briefly describes her school experience to the phone-in host:

(C = Caller, H = Host)

C: I couldn't read or write and with those forms you know . . . worse than a piece of blank paper but I put the blame on the school where I started when I was a little girl at school I was um I was taught by how clever you was you know if you was backward or clever or . . . you know

H: yeah

C: they taught you by how clever you was and when I was seven I had to go to another school and when I went to that one they taught you by your age you know how old you was

H: mm

C: and umm from that day even now I still blame the second school what I started at because instead of teaching by what you knew they didn't they taught you by your age if you know what I mean

H: yeah . . . do you still have the problem of finding it difficult to read or write

C: oh yes I still do and I feel ashamed of it

H: how bad is it I mean can you write anything or read anything

C: well I can read me name and address and things like that but when it comes to reading forms you know or filling a form in

H: mm

C: I'm you know it's just a sort of blank you know what I mean just like I just sort of can't do it

The caller here makes an explicit connection between her own experience of failure in school, in particular her transfer from one school to another, and the transfer from the system of allocating children to classes on the basis of what they knew 'if you was backward or clever', to one based on age-grading, 'instead of teaching you by what you knew they didn't they taught you by your age if you know what I mean'.

Word choices ('blank', 'blame', 'ashamed') project a sense of helplessness, blame and guilt. The host also seems to be buying into this stereotype with lexical choices like 'problem', 'bad', with overtones of the field of medical discourse. ('Illiteracy', as we saw in Chapter 1, can be powerfully constructed as a medical condition.)

The introductory section of the extract, and its conclusion, significantly echo each other in their modal choice ('I couldn't read or write . . . I just sort of can't do it') as well as in the repetition of 'blank' ('worse than a piece of blank paper . . . it's just sort of like blank you know'), 'blank', perhaps, referring both to a mental blankness and and the blankness of a sheet of unreadable text.

Sandwiched in between the introduction and conclusion is a section in which she powerfully lays blame on the school system, and describes the ways in which she feels it failed her. Again there is a structural parallelism in the way that she organizes the text ('but I put the blame on the school where I started . . . and um from that day even now I still blame the second school what I started at').

There is a contrast in the way she gives her reasons for blaming the school: first, through a narrative report in which she summarizes her early schooling:

> when I was a little girl at school I was um I was taught at Blackfriars and um they taught you by how clever you was you know if you was backward or clever or . . . you know they taught you by how clever you was and when I was seven I had to go to another school and when I went to that one they taught you by your age you know how old you was

The speaker is using a situated generalizing strategy (cf. Baynham 1988): she generalizes about the teaching strategies employed in the two schools, using the pronouns 'they' (the teachers) and 'you' (the children). The extract follows the temporal sequencing of narrative ('when . . . and when . . . and when'). The emphasis is on 'them' doing things to 'you', and the whole extract has the stringing of coordinate clauses typical of spoken narrative.

What immediately follows the repetition of the structural parallelism is organized in an interestingly different way:

> I still blame the second school what I started at because instead
> of teaching by what you knew they didn't they taught you by
> your age

in which the narrative like sequence above is summarized in a way that sets up an atemporal contrast between the two teaching approaches:

> Instead of doing X they did Y.

The effect is to summarize and contrast the main point of difference between the first and second school, as perceived by the caller.

I have dwelt on the richness and complexity of the way that the caller's spoken language is organized in order to make the point that her adult abilities to organize her ideas in spoken discourse contrast quite dramatically with her sense of blankness, when faced with the written language.

The other point worth making relates to the caller's interpretation of why she had problems at school. In a sense, it is not significant here whether she is objectively right or wrong about the types of school organization (ability versus age-grading) which she contrasts. What is significant is that she is taking up her own critical perspective on her own schooling and education. By taking up a perspective on her own 'failure' in school, which makes it the school's failure, she unsticks her own subjectivity from the concept of failure, thus opening up a new range of possibilities, including of course, success.

Extract two

Trying to read to Mum
by Mary Smith

> I was about 10 years old and I know I had a big problem. I was
> dyslexic. I could hardly read apart from small words like 'is' and 'on'
> and so on. My mum really wanted to do her best for me and wanted

to help. We had a set of Walt Disney books, so we tried them. It was: 'Once a something time', and my mum would say, 'Once upon a time.' So I would say that and try again with a few more words I could not read. Then she would say, 'Try from the beginning again'. And it would be 'Once a something time', and she would tell me off and say, 'You know that word. I told you what it was, so try again.' I would say 'Once a . . .' and I would stop. 'I don't know, Mum,' and she would start shouting at me and I would shout back and say, 'I don't care, I hate you!' and we would be like this for about fifteen minutes and we would shout one word and my dad would say, 'Right, that's it. You shut up and get upstairs the pair of you. Calm down.' Nowadays I can read the newspapers. Sometimes I get stuck but it's the really big words. Now her eyesight is getting very bad.

(in Billington 1985)

This written account, in which Mary Smith's narrative graphically illustrates a reading lesson within the family, shows how bound up the process of learning to read as a child can be with the emotional interplay between learner and teacher, both within the family and at school. Mary dramatically replays her mother's attempts to help her with her reading. She emphasizes repeated attempts to do so with the iterativity of 'My mum would say so I would say then she would say'.

Mary's ability to replay this childhood incident dramatically as an adult is an indication that this is a key event in the formation of her own sense of herself as a learner and a reader. The caller in Extract One goes blank when confronted with text. Mary rejects the text and the intervention of her mother. 'I don't care, I hate you!' she says in response to her mother's frustration.

Mary's is an account 'from the inside' (cf. Horsman 1990) of the experiences of a learner reader in difficulty. As I argued in Chapter One, 'illiteracy' is socially constructed 'from the outside', as part of the literate/illiterate dichotomy, which is a powerful sorter and categorizer of persons.

A feature of Mary's text is the interplay of different voices (cf. Silverman and Torode 1980; Bakhtin 1981). The orientation and coda of the narrative are indexed to present time and Mary's adult self. (The orientation is the scene-setting part of the narrative's schematic structure, while the coda comes at the conclusion of the narrative and provides a bridge between narrative time and the time of telling – cf. Labov 1972).

Orientation

I was about 10 years old and I know I had a problem. I was dyslexic. I could hardly read apart from small words like 'is' and 'on' and so on. My mum really wanted to do her best for me and wanted to help.

Coda

Nowadays I can read the newspapers. Sometimes I get stuck but it's the really big words. Now her eyesight is getting very bad.

The adult voice evaluates the reading lessons from Mary's current perspective.

In the action sequence of the narrative, Mary dramatically replays the exchange with her mother, culminating in the furious argument between them. It is possible to reconstruct the power relations operating in the replayed interaction, or at least Mary's perception of them:

1   Mary attempts the beginning of the text, 'Once a something time'

2   Her mother corrects her, 'Once upon a time'

3   Mary attempts 'a few more words I could not read'

4   Her mother directs her back to the beginning again.

5   Mary tries again, with the same result: 'Once a something time'

6   Her mother starts to lost patience, 'You know that word. I told you what it was, so try again.'

   (Claiming first-hand knowledge of other people's experience is a very powerful strategy, typical of the therapeutic interview, as Labov and Fanshel [1977] point out.)

7   Mary tries again, but stops before the problem area, 'Once a . . I don't know mum.'

8   They start to argue, and Mary withdraws with 'I don't care, I hate you!'

The interaction, as replayed by Mary, has a kind of entropy, in that each time Mary is attempting less and ends up by withdrawing.

As I suggested above, it is an indication of the intensity of the experience that Mary replays the incident in sufficient detail for this partial reconstruction of the interaction around text with her mother.

The narrative Coda, quoted above, returns to a kind of equilibrium between Mary and her mother, textually carried in the structural parallelism of 'Nowadays . . . Now'. Mary's achievements as an adult and her mother's failing eyesight have somewhat closed the gap between them. Maybe Mary will end up reading the paper to her mum.

Activity

Mary Smith's account of her reading lessons with her mother would make an interesting thematic prompt for a discussion on experiences of learning to read and being taught reading. This could be done either as part of teaching, either in a literacy group or with students training to teach literacy, or as part of a research project investigating experiences of being taught to read.

Design a series of questions for discussion, to explore issues raised in Mary Smith's account.

Extract three

In the previous extract, we saw how bound up the process of learning to read was in the interaction between a mother and daughter, and began to analyse the power relationships in play. In the following extract, we will look at an extract from an interview in which the protagonist, P, describes an incident from her schooldays.

JM: Does that go back to anything that happened to you as a child, or at school or anything like that, that you felt shown up in front of everybody else?

P: Yes I was shown up in front of people. Yes, a couple of times, at school. One teacher, my sister was very clever actually, she passed her exams and everything, you know, she was a couple of years older than me. And I went in her class after, you know, when we was in this school, and I know I put something down in

the book that I hadn't got a clue how to spell it, because I'm
terrible, absolutely shocking still at spelling. I mean I was more
concentrating on the getting to the reading first, and I thought if I
got over that, perhaps I could get on with the spelling. And I wrote
down, I didn't realize I wrote down something to do with – so she
comes up to me and says, 'Who's Dutch in your family?' you know,
like that. I can remember, it sticks there, you know. But I had –

JM: Who's Dutch?

P: Dutch, yes. Because, 'That's double Dutch. You don't take after
your sister' you know. And she said,' 'Who's Dutch in your family?'
Well we have got Dutch in our family, so naturally I turned round
and said, 'My grandfather', you know. And all the class laughed.
And I didn't mean to be rude. I was, you know, kind of knocked
out, and 'Get out the class!', you know.
                    (Interview conducted by Jane Mace; from Baynham and Mace
                                                                1986: 51–2)

I suggested above that adults returning to learning had to confront the public spaces and public modes of discourse of educational institutions. P's account of a humiliating moment in her
schooldays exemplifies one of Gramsci's traces: an experience she
carries with her, formative of other, later experiences.

In the domains of a child's social world (family, playground,
classroom, street), the classroom is a public space, in which she is
expected to learn the norms, routines and communicative practices
of schooling. A significant component of children's language
acquisition is learning the ability to interpret meanings in context,
particularly interpreting types of indirection (cf., for example,
Cazden *et al.* 1972). What P characterizes here is a typical instance
of communication breakdown, where P fails to understand the
communicative intent of her teacher's question, 'Who's Dutch in
your family?' The teacher's question was linked to P's 'shocking
spelling', and could be unpacked only if the expression 'Double
Dutch' with its connotations of incomprehensible nonsense was
shared knowledge between participants.

Looking back on the incident as an adult, P reads a further
reference into the teacher's question, in that for her 'in your
family' implicitly sets up a contrast between herself and her
clever sister. In contrast, instead of interpreting the utterance
as it was presumably intended, P activates the frame of literal
meaning, interpreting the utterance literally as a question about
her family. As luck, or ill luck, would have it, her inference is

supported, in the real world, by the fact that there was Dutch in her family. Her response, 'My grandfather', is perfectly coherent, within the interpretative frame she is operating, but within the teacher's interpretative frame counts as a *non sequitur*.

We might surmise that the teacher's question did not expect a response other than embarrassed silence, and was simply a demonstration of the abuse of interactive and institutional power, so the fact that P replied at all can be interpreted as cheek.

The classroom is a public space in the child's social world. Its inhabitants are the teacher and the child's peers. Getting it wrong, in public, is a major source of humiliation, and P's account shows how she gets it wrong both with the teacher and her peers. P's misunderstanding leads her to mix the domain of the family with that of the classroom: the teacher is commenting on her work in the current context of situation; P in effect starts talking about her family. It is hard to gauge from this account whether the children are laughing with P, since she is cheeking the teacher, or against her, seeing her as demonstrating naïvety in misunderstanding the teacher's question.

The public space of the classroom has sharply defined power relations (adult/child, teacher/pupil), and participants in classroom interaction are playing on a public stage. We see in this account the potential for interactive and institutional power to be abused, particularly when some participants are still only developing their abilities to interpret indirection.

If the response of the caller in Extract One to written text is 'blanking' and Mary's response to the interaction with her mother around text in Extract Two was 'I don't care if I can't read it, I hate you', P's response in Extract Three demonstrates what happens when you don't know the interpretative rules and betray that ignorance in public settings.

Extract four

In the preceding extracts, the focus of attention has been the protagonists' experiences of schooling. In this extract, taken from an interview with Rhimu, a Moroccan settled in London, she talks about the reasons why she didn't go to school, due to her mother's bereavement and the ensuing hardships for her family, which include her working as a domestic servant as a child.

(I = Interviewer; R = Rhimu; A = Rhimu's son Anwar)

I: And did you go to school?

R: I'm tell you about this problem. My father dead, died, because I have eight years, me. Just my mother. My mother all, because she can't work (she couldn't because she never work you know). All take it all furniture, no clothes, nice clothes, you know 'spensive, all selling this time, this time ( ) have Spanish Spana Spain aš kayaqulu l-guerra? (How do you say 'war'?)

A: War

R: War

I: A war

R: Yes. All my mother can't work. She don't know you know because is never work in her life you know. All the furniture, all, everything just the floor, n the, n the, as ka . . .

I: The carpets?

R: The carpet (just) the carpet, n aš kayaqulu mantat (how do you say 'blankets'? . . . Blanket, just blanket for sleep on the floor. (that's) everything gone. I remember. I'm been school. This time I remember my mother. I can't remember because, you know, I don't like remember this time. My mother e take me the mm the doctor, you know, the doctor, Spanish doctor you know. Because my, my family, this eh T wife T sister, is work eh nurse in hospital, you know, for the doctor.

I: Where, where? In Tangier?

R: The doctor Spanish. No, in Larache.

I: In Larache.

R: Yes, I'm little girl, me eight years. Well, nine years like this this time. You know I'm, I'm, I'm go work for the doctor you know. I'm look after the baby. I'm nanny.

I: Nanny

R: I'm nanny too. Look after me. You know this time e give me five pound. Eh no, no no five pound, no erm twenty five penny a month.

I: Blimey.

R: Twenty five penny. I remember. Twenty five penny month.

I: How many hours did you have to work?

R: I'm keep here. Because my mother e can't keep it al the children e can't keep it the children because my father died my mother can't work. You know, my my my he go for auntie auntie's sister de my father you know 'nother country. Arcila, you know . . .

I: Arcila.

R: Arcila, you know. Is eh he going army. Small, small, fifteen years, my brother. Ten and five.

I: You went to live with your . . .

R: With my, with her auntie, brother de my, sister de my father, sister.

I: Auntie.

R: Auntie, auntie, yes. Well just my brother small one you know, Abdelkader is in army now. Nn my sister Aisha stay with mother, with my mother you know, because we can't keep it all. That's it, I'm no, I can't read, I can't do nothing you know.

The interviewer's question provokes a lengthy response in which Rhimu explains why her schooling was interrupted at a very early age, why her family was separated and why:

I'm no, I can't read, I can't do nothing you know

Whether an individual has been through schooling and failed, or been failed by it, or has never had the opportunity to go to school, not being able to read and write is socially constructed as an absence or lack, as illustrated in the literacy/illiteracy dichotomy.

What significance is placed on that lack or absence will vary from social group to social group and from context to context. The variability in literacy practices and the ways these are constructed by participants in given social contexts was a major theme of Chapter 2. We saw, based on the research of Wagner *et al.*, how literacy/illiteracy was rather differently constructed in the traditional Moroccan society in which Rhimu grew up, how not being able to read and write was not especially stigmatized and how there were well-established social mechanisms for individuals to achieve literacy purposes by drawing on mediators of literacy.

In contrast, I argued in Chapter 1, that the literate/illiterate dichotomy was a major means of sorting and grading individuals in societies like those of the United Kingdom and Australia, and that access to literacy was an essential prerequisite to participation as an adult in dominant communicative practices. In a complex multi-lingual society, like the United Kingdom or Australia, there are a necessary variety and diversity of literacy practices, corresponding to the variety and diversity of other cultural practices. It is important, however, not to underestimate the significance of the dominant culture in defining and setting the parameters for a whole range of cultural practices, including literacy (cf. Kalantzis *et al*. 1989).

The individuals whose life experiences of literacy have been discussed in the previous illustrative case studies express a range of responses to written text and interactions round written text: blankness, anger, disempowerment, humiliation in public domains, rejection. This does not of course exhaust the whole range of possible responses to the dominance of the written mode (for example, accommodation, or opposition and resistance to dominant or normative discourses which are discussed in Ivanič and Roach 1990). This presentation has tended to emphasize those who have been disempowered by their experiences of schooling.

Literacy work within community-based literacy programmes aims at turning around the expectations of disempowerment in the face of dominant modes of discourse and changing the inventory of possibilities from the expectation of failure to the possibility of success.

To understand the role of literacy programmes in community education settings, it is important, however, to be able to 'place' community-based literacy provision in the context of other educational and social institutions (further education, the workplace). It is important to 'place' the experience of adults returning to study in the context of their previous experience of schooling. Placing community-based literacy education in the context of mainstream institutions opens up the possibility of progression on to further study or vocational training, into the workplace, but it also puts into question the ideologies of community-based literacy education, with its emphasis on empowerment and access. In this context, does access mean simply a process of acculturation into the norms, values and communicative practices of the dominant culture, or does it imply the possibility of challenge or transformation of these practices? How can literacy education foster and maintain a critical stance?

IDEOLOGIES OF ACCESS AND EMPOWERMENT IN COMMUNITY LITERACY EDUCATION

Vignette

I remember a few years ago, with some time to spare in Liverpool, spending a few hours in the public gallery of the law courts. The case I sat in on was one of 'sus', and the white working-class youth who was the defendant was being cross-questioned by a lawyer. Why had he been walking down that particular street at that particular time of night in such a way that the watching police might think he was trying garage doors? Well, he didn't really know and he mumbled away implausibly, contradicting himself, tripping himself up, inexorably drawn into the appearances of guilt in the face of the studied eloquence of the lawyer. The appearances of guilt were being manufactured in a way that seemed to me quite independent of actual guilt or innocence. The defendant was being projected as incoherent, inept, suspicious; the lawyer as coherent, capable, trustworthy.

In this vignette, the defendant and the lawyer were participants in a particular kind of highly formalized and public discourse: court-room interaction. There is a notable disparity of power relations between lawyer/defendant, lawyer/witness, and we can perhaps draw out some general similarities with teacher/pupil interaction in terms of concepts like who has the right to speak, to open up and close exchanges, to nominate topics and to expect other co-participants to respond to nominated topics. The defendant is caught in a public discourse, in a situation of unequal power. His situation provides a kind of metaphor for the situation of many educationally disenfranchised adults.

It is worth pointing out here a distinctive feature of adult literacy in community education settings (as opposed to school-based literacy), which is that the 'curriculum' of community-based literacy education is potentially the whole range of written communication that an adult is expected or wishes to engage in as part of their daily life. It follows that the potential input into a community-based adult literacy programme is a selection from the whole range of communicative demands which are daily made on adults. This includes not just written modes, but also participation in formal, public, spoken modes of discourse (participation in meetings is an obvious example of this).

Given this bewildering potential variety of literacy demands on adults and the potential diversity of students in any given literacy group, particularly in multi-lingual inner-city contexts, how does the literacy tutor select and organize material to develop a teaching/learning programme? A critical language awareness approach can provide a unifying framework for literacy education.

CRITICAL LANGUAGE AWARENESS AND LITERACY EDUCATION

The model of language presented in Chapter 1 involves a number of layers. The innermost layer is language as text, the middle layer is language as social process (getting things done through language) and the outer layer is language as social practice (how ideologies and institutions operate through language). Literacy education has to enable learners to deal with text. It has to enable learners to get things done with text. But it also has to enable the learner to 'read' the dominant discourses, to understand what they have to offer, but also to have the possibility of taking up an oppositional stance, to say, in effect, 'I recognize what this discourse is doing and I'm not going to buy into it.'

Literacy education for community uses can therefore engage with the whole range of ways in which power is exercised through language in the institutions of everyday life: banks, social security offices, college offices, law courts, the public spaces that are associated with public discourses. Joining a literacy class is in itself a way of 'going public' and, in fact, one of the gains that literacy students often report is simply that of increased confidence in public participation through joining in the activities of the literacy group.

Discussion

Associated with this range of uses of literacy are the range of text types or genres (spoken and written) that come into play in each domain. What are the kinds of writing and spoken language use typically associated with using a bank? To answer this question it is useful to 'walk through' a series of transactions (opening an account, ordering a new cheque book, paying in or taking out money) and try and work out what the language and literacy demands might be.

It is worth remembering that literacy practices shift and alter as other social practices and technologies shift and alter. An example of a shifting literacy practice might be the increasing use of cash points for withdrawing money and doing other transactions. What are the language and literacy demands of interacting with a machine?

The experiences of schooling presented above in Extracts Two and Three are encodings of the dynamics of unequal power (parent/child, teacher/pupil). It is possible to imagine a range of ways of using them in educational settings: as prompts for sharing experience, or as leads into the discourses of social and political analysis. The following case study takes an everyday public setting, where power is distributed unequally as its focus, although with a rather unexpected outcome.

My bank account: speaking up in official contexts

This activity was carried out with a group of bilingual literacy learners with post-elementary spoken language skills. It was based on a simplified version of a Stephen Leacock story, 'My bank account'. The aim was to explore, through reading the text, situations where members of the group had felt humiliated or embarrassed in a public, and official settings and to look at ways of increasing confidence in objecting or answering back when the power relations of the situation put you at a disadvantage.

The story presents in a humorous way an encounter between a timid prospective bank customer with the snooty staff of a bank where he is trying to open an account. He is humiliated and embarrassed because he has an insignificant amount of money to do it with. The story starts:

> When I go into a bank I am frightened. The clerks frighten me; the desks frighten me; the sight of the money frightens me; everything frightens me.

The discussion following the story can be used to evaluate the feelings of the hero in the bank. Has anyone ever been in a situation like that? If so, what happened? Each story told to illustrate the point enriches the discussion, gives it depth and meaning, creates a grounding in which the 'language as social process' point can emerge later: how to confront rudeness and unhelpfulness from a position of relatively less power. The story and the discussion that comes after provide a critical contextualization for the communicative work that follows after. In addition to evaluating the subjective

feelings of the hero/victim, the discussion can go on to judge the
behaviour of the bank employees. What are the rules for treating
people well when you have knowledge or power and they don't,
when you are an insider and they are outsiders? How should the
bank manager have behaved? How could the protagonist have
challenged the bank staff? These issues can be worked on in a
number of ways: through evaluative response to the initial story
prompt, through autobiographical writing, through working on
strategies for challenging when in a situation of unequal power using
role play, through exploring ways of responding through writing,
letters of complaint, for example.

In this teaching/learning sequence, therefore, the critical dimension of language as social practice precedes and contextualizes
the work on language as social process. We start from the ways
in which institutions and discourses operate, through a kind of
critical reading of the social world and from that lead into the
practical ways in which, through spoken and written language,
it is possible to intervene, to get things done through language.

It is worth remembering that any group of learners/teachers
will be operating within specific sets of discourse/cultural conventions, expectations about what is and should be in social
practice. The expectation of the teacher here was that the lesson
would follow the sequence of *fictional stimulus* leading to *autobiographical response* leading to *language-based strategies for action*. As
it happens, one of the students altered the expected course of the
lesson by telling a Mullah Nasreddin story, which exemplified in
a folk-story genre the point of the lesson:

Version one

This was the first draft, written by the student.

One day Molla-Nasraddin was invited to a party, he went to the party
without changing his ordinary clothes, but the receptionist stoped
him to go there, and told him he couldn't go while he is wearing
ragged clothes, but he rushed backed home and changed his clothes
to the best clothes ever he had.

He came backed to the party everyone bowed to him, and offered
him nice place to sit down.

It was time for dinner, they served best food, but Molla instead of
eating the food he was putting the food in his sleeves.

> Everyone was astonished, what was he doing, probably they
> though he was mad. Somebody asked him why is feeding his
> clothes.
> He said I am hear because of my clothes.

Through a process of group editing and with suggestions from the
teacher, a second version was arrived at.

Version two

MULLAH NASREDDIN AND THE PARTY

> One day Mullah Nasreddin was invited to a party. He went to the
> party without changing out of his ordinary clothes. When he arrived
> at the party, the doorman stopped him from going in.
> 'You can't come in here wearing ragged clothes like that', he said.
> So Mullah Nasreddin rushed back home and changed his clothes.
> He put on the smartest clothes he had. Then he hurried back to the
> party. Everyone bowed at him when he arrived and offered him a
> nice place to sit down.
> It was time for dinner. They served the best food. But Mullah,
> instead of eating the food, started putting the food in his sleeves.
> Everyone was astonished. What was he doing? They thought he
> was mad.
> Then somebody asked him: 'Why are you putting food in your
> sleeves?'
> And Mullah said: 'My clothes have been invited to the party, not me.
> So I'm feeding them.'

We will look at the drafting and redrafting involved in these two
versions in more detail in Chapter 6.

The teacher's expectations as to what constituted topic continuity were operating within a specific set of discourse and cultural
conventions, while the student's contribution operates within a
different set, through which the topic of judging people by outward appearances does not trigger an autobiographical, 'reality'
frame, but a folk-story frame, which maintains topic continuity,
although via a very different genre.

The moral of this story is not to assume that all members of a
culturally diverse group will share the same set of discourse and
cultural conventions. The teacher here treats as natural the move
from thematic prompt to autobiographical accounts to strategies

for practical action through language, but this expectation is not shared by at least one student.

LITERACY ACROSS CURRICULUM AREAS

Clearly, literacy is an issue across a wide range of curriculum areas and not just within classes, narrowly designated as literacy. It follows from this that teachers of other content areas need to have a basic awareness of how literacy impacts on their curriculum. In adult numeracy classes for example, written texts containing material drawing on maths concepts are part of the critical numeracy curriculum. Critical reading involves being able to read the ways in which statistics, for example, convey information or indeed disinformation. The following extract from the *Sydney Morning Herald* (Figure 3.1, page 93) was used in a maths workshop as a critical reading (Cassar Patty 1991).

Discussion

In what different ways could this text be read critically? For example, how is AIDS constructed as a 'problem' for life insurance companies? Are there any other perspectives on the AIDS/insurance issue except that of the life insurance companies? What perspectives would AIDS organizations have on this issue? How are the statistics used in the article? What do you make of expressions like 'downward revised death estimates'?

What kind of moves would be possible from the critical reading stage (language as social practice) to the active doing-things-with-words stage of 'language as social process'? For example, how could a group of students become involved in documenting the current state of affairs on life insurance and those who are HIV-positive? What uses of language spoken and written would arise out of making contact with the insurance companies by letter, asking what their policies are, gathering documentation of health insurance application forms, reading these forms for information as to clauses which might restrict the access of HIV-positive people to health insurance, contacting AIDS organizations by phone or by letter asking for their response/perspective on the issue, inviting a speaker from an AIDS organization to come and speak to a group?

It is clear that the connection between the critical dimension of language as social practice and the social process dimension of

Insurers overstated AIDS by 100pc

By ANNE LAMPE

AIDS is still a problem for the Australian life insurance industry, but not as major as first thought.

The industry has acknowledged that projections of deaths from the disease made two years ago overstated the position by more than 100 per cent. These earlier projections gave rise to some alarmist predictions that unless some way was found to curb AIDS-related claims, life insurance premiums for the entire population would soar.

According to a periodical news-letter on AIDS and insurance published by the Life Insurance Federation of Australia, the industry now estimates that AIDS-related deaths in Australia by mid-1995 will be between 6,000 and 12,000 compared with projections made two years ago of 13,000 to 26,000.

The downward revised death estimates mean earlier forecasts of rocketing life insurance premiums may now be avoided.

At the end of the March quarter 1989 LIFA member companies, which include many of Australia's largest life insurers, had paid out almost $20 million on AIDS-related death and disability claims on 443 lives. Of 315 individual claims, 76 per cent were under-written on a non-medical basis. An analysis of 109 group claims showed that the majority were granted on an automatic basis and without a medical. Only 12 of the 443 claims were from women.

At the end of 1989, LIFA member companies recorded a cumulative total of 112 group claims totalling £8.2 million. In the three months to the end of the March quarter this year, there were another 16 group claims which added $1.4 million to the group total.

LIFA's executive director, Mr David Purchase, said yesterday that of continuing concern to the industry was that 35 per cent of the claims were made on policies that had existed for less than three years and two-thirds of group claims were made in the first five years of fund membership.

Some life insurers ask detailed questions about sexual preference in their proposal forms, some ask if the potential policy holder has had a blood test in the past which has shown up HIV positive, while others require individuals to undergo medicals.

Figure 3.1

getting things done through language is a close one. It is not a stage-by-stage process of first become communicatively fluent, then begin to question. Both dimensions of language in use are intertwined and presuppose each other. In fact, as we have seen, the critical dimension can be seen to precede the language as social process dimension, contextualizing the communicative work of developing literacy for real purposes in contexts of use.

Access and empowerment are key issues in community-based literacy education. However, the focus so far has been on personal empowerment and individual access back into the education system. What are the implications of literacy for access and empowerment not in terms of individuals achieving their personal own ends, but also in terms of whole groups and communities?

LITERACIES AND COMMUNITY ORGANIZATION: THE LITERACY INVOLVED IN 'GETTING FUNDED'

The acquisition and use of specialized literacy knowledge in the formation and setting up of community organizations, and the role of informal networks and chains of transmission in getting to this knowledge raise important issues of access to knowledge, resources and power. In British or Australian society a degree of formalization of organizational structure, clearly defined aims and goals, a committee structure with roles such as secretary, chairperson and treasurer, are basic prerequisites for getting funding to carry on the activities of the organization. How do individuals come to be experienced in these matters? How do the organizational formats required get transmitted to those with little or no previous knowledge of them? How do these individuals acquire formats and accompanying literacy practices which involve an acculturation into the norms and values of dominant social groupings?

Having achieved an organizational format that is, in principle, acceptable to funders, one that has structures, procedures, identifiable roles, explicit goals, accountability, what next? After 'getting organized' comes 'getting funded'. Although it is possible to organize without getting funded (voluntary organizations and pressure groups are examples of this), it is not possible to get funded without getting organized (at least on paper). Various forms of organization are open to a group who wish to further their objectives through obtaining funding: becoming a company limited by guarantee, becoming a charity, forming a cooperative. All of these forms of social organization have legal status and open up possibilities of obtaining funding from government and private sources. A constitution is a basic prerequisite for setting in motion the processes involved in attaining, for example, charitable status. 'Getting a constitution' and 'getting funded' involve the acquisition of complex bodies of social knowledge and specialized forms of literacy. Informal learning and networking play an important role in the transmission and acquisition of such knowledge.

In the next section, still within the community education context, I will examine the access to dominant literacy practices
needed in order for a community organization to obtain funding
to pursue its goals.

This case study is based on the introductory session of a community education course entitled 'Running a community group'.
The object of this course was to provide for participants, who were
drawn in the main from local voluntary organizations, an introduction to the organizational and communication skills necessary
for the setting up and management of an effective organization.
The course tutor was an experienced community worker and the
course had been jointly organized and set up by myself (a language
and literacy worker) and by the community education worker in
the centre where the course was held, an adult education centre
in an area of considerable ethnic diversity and with a history of
community organization, successful and unsuccessful.

The object of the introductory session was to outline the scope
of the course, to enable participants to describe what they wanted
to get out of the course, and to provide a case study of some of
the issues involved in setting up a community organization. Saeed,
the worker on a Moroccan community project, had been invited to
describe how his organization was set up.

Getting a constitution

S: We were first self-elected committee, because we had the idea to
build this committee and we got together, we formed, because the
organization in general, you know, you have to have management
committee, such as chairman, honorary treasurer, secretary and so
on. And we did that. First thing we went to get some legal advice
about how we can be formed and they say 'you have to form a
constitution'. We receive tremendous help from the Law Centre.

M: How did you know about the Law Centre?

S: Well . . . first of all, before you start, when you're starting an
organization, of that sort, you are all volunteers, there is no funds
at all, so you have to shop around, you have to find the cheapest,
the one that is free service first. If not, then you got to go to the
cheapest. So we had to go to the Citizens Advice Bureau. We got
some information about how we can get some legal advice freely,
or rather cheaply. Then we been referred to the Law Centre. We
spoke of our problem, then they help us. That's how we did it. So

we got our constitution ready. Because once you have a constitution, that makes it easier, even if you want to go and rent a building to start a proposal, then you are identified, there are people with you. Because a constitution only can be composed at that stage if there are more people involved, say like chairman and so on.

We saw on page 67 how getting constituted involves a transition from informal to formal types of organization, and considered the role of networking. Saeed also points out the *function* of the constitution in the fund-raising context: it signals an organization as having a formalized, reliable structure, with explicit goals and procedures, an organization that can be trusted with money. A constitution is a signal of a particular kind of organization. The kind of organization implied by a constitution has explicitly defined roles and responsibilities, a calendar of events round which the organization functions (committee meetings, annual general meetings), procedures for calling meetings and recording them. All this involves formalizing what up till now may have been fluid and not explicit, finding forms of words (aims and objectives) for a range of activities and objectives not up till now defined.

The textual organization of the constitution implies, or, more strongly, requires, a corresponding kind of social organization and the adoption of certain strategies for organizing time, recording decisions and providing financial accountability. All of these serve to mesh in with the purposes of funding bodies which are similarly organized and structured. For groups and individuals who have up till now not had access to the institutions of the dominant cultures, the process of getting constituted can be seen as a process of acculturation into the communicative and social practices of the dominant group. The carrot for this is the possibility of funding for your group. There is a particularly tight mesh between access to this particular kind of literacy, particular types of organization and access to resources.

Getting funded

Saeed's organization had been singularly successful in obtaining funding from a number of organizations, which suggests considerable access to institutional knowledge, and the ability to draft funding applications which fall within the guidelines laid down by the funding bodies. There may also be the need to enlist support for a project by lobbying influential individuals on the neighbourhood network. Oral skills and literacy skills, formal institutional knowledge and informal network knowledge are all brought into play in the activity of getting funded. In the following extract, Saeed describes how his organization went about fund-raising:

> When you do really make your application form, you got to get advice about the application itself. Before sending them you got to contact people like the Community Relations Advisers and so on and those people they give tremendous help, because they can correct you. Because just little things can make a big difference in an application form. When we made our application form for Urban Aid we (somebody else did it, I was away) and just by typing just typing mistake, which is we applied for a Centre and the person who typed it, she put Cultural Centre and that makes the application form fail, because it's large difference between Community Centre and Cultural Centre.

Part of learning the specialized type of literacy involved in making funding applications is to be able to interpret the funding guidelines of a potential funding agency correctly and to mesh the application with its categories. Here we see how a fairly subtle lexical choice can rule an application out, because it does not fit the required funding categories.

The whole process of applying for funding is a process involving complex uses of literacy, interpretative readings of funding guidelines and access to kinds of social knowledge about the organizations offering funding. The literacy processes at work are embedded in similarly complex oral processes of consultation, correction and redrafting. Saeed, as we have seen, treats it as an informal learning process: by making a mistake they learned the importance of staying within the funding guidelines.

Saeed draws on individuals available on the neighbourhood network to help achieve his literacy purpose: making a funding application that stands a chance of being successful. The community relations advisers and the like are in a position to point out the little details that can make an application succeed or fail. In addition to being available on the neighbourhood network for this kind of consultation by community groups, a community relations adviser may well be one of the individuals consulted during the stage when applications are being considered, so enlisting the support of such a person has multiple functions: as a source of information and informal learning, but also as a valuable ally when applications come to be considered. Once again we have an exemplification of how literacy processes are embedded orally.

Passing on 'the knowledge'

Participants in the course are invited in turn to identify what they hope to get out of attending the course. Three musicians from Brixton have come along, who do not at first appear to fit the aims of the course, since they are not involved in community organization. They do, however, have 'a project': the idea of setting up low-cost rehearsal rooms and recording studios in Brixton. When their turn comes round, they express uncertainty as to whether their project can be seen as a 'community project', since they stand to benefit from it themselves:

> The idea started off as a private thing, because we were all involved in playing activities, we thought that instead of paying out money every week to rent rehearsal rooms and at a later stage recording studios, what we thought we would do was do it ourselves and then in turn, because of our interest in it, so that we don't have to make a profit on it, so when someone else comes along and uses it, then they can use it at a cost, but not so as we make a profit on it.

What the speaker is here identifying is uncertainty about the categorization of his project: is it 'private' or 'community', 'profit-making' or 'non profit-making'? Does it fit within the community frame? (A frame consists of the sum total of background knowledge and rules of interpretation needed to participate in a discourse or activity type, whether going shopping, ordering food in a restaurant, participating in meetings or, as here, fund-raising for a community project.) In a sense the musicians are uncertain whether they are in the right frame. As the interaction develops, we find that the larger group adopts a basically helpful strategy to the problem of frame or categorization presented by the musicians. Different participants try to tease out the senses in which the studio project might be of benefit to different sections of 'the community', what kinds of information the musicians might need in order to go further. What develops, as we shall see, is a search for overlapping frames, by which the aims and goals of the musicians can be made to mesh with available funding possibilities.

Saeed points out that, for the funding of arts projects, both charitable (that is, non-profit-making) and profit-making activities can attract funding, and he identifies a number of possible funders for the musicians' project. He provides an important piece of background information: the funding cycle of the relevant committee requires that the application be submitted by the 31 March. The musicians here are being introduced to some basic components of the funding process: the submission of applications and the funding cycle, with its accompanying notion of 'the deadline'. Successful achievement of this literacy activity is reliant on all sorts of external, social contextual factors, including timing.

Another preparatory activity to the application itself is getting hold of the form. Saeed describes how you phone the relevant organization, ask to be put through to the relevant committee, who will send you the form. Another component of the funding process is being able to gain access to the right section of the right bureau-cracy at the right time. Again this is an example of the embedding of literacy practices in complex oral and social processes.

Saeed then goes on to sketch the format of the application form: Section A for applicants who are charitable and non-profit-making; Section B for those who are profit-making, or individual artists. Members of the group, with Saeed taking a conspicuously vocal role, continue to elaborate, for the benefit of the musicians, on the requirements for obtaining funding under either of the two categories: financial accountability being one, getting support from local individuals and key organizations being another.

We begin to see that the process of getting funding is a complex of processes, oral and literate, interacting with relevant back-ground knowledge, such as knowledge of funding cycles, how to gain access to organizations, the formats of funding applications and the need to make your project fit into them. In addition to this relatively 'overt' knowledge is a perhaps less accessible 'network' knowledge as to who are the key individuals and organizations to lobby and get on your side and also, what potential advice-givers and mediators of literacy are available.

In the following extract, one of the musicians tries to clarify his understanding of the requirements of an application form:

D (the musician): When you apply for these things and they have to be in by the 31st of March, is that like submitting a complete finished application, all the details there, and asking for a set amount of money and they say yes or no, or is it more flexible?
G (course coordinator): I don't know how much scope there is for flexibility: I would imagine that some people don't fill in all the details and do it in outline, but does anybody know the answer to that question?

M (the writer): I would say that, off the top of my head, that people, the sort of thing that people, when they're on committees looking at it, they'll say, 'These guys can't do their figures', so I think they probably will be quite tight on

D (a musician): like set

M: sort of set format for doing it

D: You're asking for an amount and they could say yes or not, it's not like you could keep.

G: Can you negotiate, beat you down.

D: It's not like, 'oh you have to go and fill another form then redo it all again'.

G: Probably what you need to do is to talk to the people who are organizing this at County Hall, whoever's dealing with it, sending out the application forms, could advise you on who could give you this kind of guidance.

What D is doing here is trying to learn something about the funding applications genre: do you have to present the application in final form or can you leave aspects of it open for negotiation? The text of the application form requires a specific, detailed budget, broken down into expenditure headings. The final form of the application requires at least the appearance of a complete, rounded project, thought through and costed; while at a later stage, when the written application form is considered (orally) by the funding committee, there may indeed be room for negotiation, with possibly some aspects of the project receiving funding and not others. The funding application genre requires complete specification of the scope of the project (or, as we suggested above, at least the appearance thereof).

Conclusion

Literacy is often constructed as an individual and individualized activity. In this case study, we have been looking at the development and use of specialized literacies in a community organization, in which achievement through literacy furthers the purposes of a group rather than an individual.

Question

Where do you see the role of *informal learning* in the account that Saeed gives of how he became knowledgeable about fund-raising and setting up a community group?

What kind of informal learning is going on in the section where the musicians from Brixton are getting advice on fund-raising for their project?

What would be involved in *formalizing* the informal learning portrayed here into a course on 'How to Apply for Funding'? Consider the role of:

- spoken language
- written language
- socio-cultural knowledge

in making a successful funding application.

In this section we have looked at literacy education in community education contexts. We emphasized the importance of participants situating themselves within their own experiences as learners, documenting the traces, as Gramsci puts it, developing a critical literacy, with the aims of empowering students in their uses of language, both spoken and written.

The typical scope of the community-based literacy class is a selection from the whole range of possible uses of literacy (community literacies, as Barton *et al.* (1991) put it).

It is important to go beyond the individual learner and recognize the need for forms of literacy education that can empower communities and groups of people to achieve their purposes, as illustrated in the example of fund-raising applications.

INTO THE MAINSTREAM: ACCESS TO FURTHER EDUCATION AND TRAINING

Literacy is also a means of access to further education and training, both for continuing study and vocational training.

The further education context has been documented in a number of studies and curriculum development projects, focusing on both spoken and written language needs. Work done at Shipley College, Yorkshire, United Kingdom by Jean McAllister and M. Robson (McAllister and Robson 1984) has been influential in setting the agenda for approaches to language and literacy education involving language support and language across the curriculum. The Inner London Education Authority's Afro-Caribbean Language and Literacy Project (reviewed by Roz Ivanič in RaPAL No 2, Winter 1986) was influential in engaging with the language requirements of students of Afro-Caribbean background, through a programme of curriculum and staff development activities.

The British Further Education Unit has produced reports of a series of curriculum development projects, under the umbrella of 'Curriculum development for a multicultural society' (cf., for example, Robson 1987; Roberts 1989).

The primary emphasis of literacy provision in the further education sector is on access into further education and training. Pre-vocational work will concentrate on developing the skills of students to participate in and achieve in accredited courses, leading to qualifications and opportunities for work, further training and study. Continuing literacy support for students on courses may be organized on a team-teaching basis. Tutorial support may be provided in addition to regular teaching in subject/vocational areas. As Scheeres points out (1991), awareness of the language and literacy dimension of education and training courses should not be limited to 'literacy specialists':

> There is an increasing demand on all educators to be aware of
> and respond to the language needs of both non-English-speaking
> background and native-speaker students. The learning environment
> may be a university, a Technical and Further Education College, a
> workplace or other context, and the course could be Civil Engineering,
> Hairdressing or Care of the Horse. No matter what the content area,
> the teaching and learning will usually involve reading and some
> writing . . . People teaching and training in the huge variety of
> courses and workplace skills areas will undoubtedly be appropriately
> qualified and experienced. But do they know how people read
> and write, what processes are involved, what skills and strategies
> are used? I think that some knowledge, and how to translate this
> knowledge and understanding into relevant and sound practice
> – whatever the content area – will enhance both teaching and
> learning.
>
> (Scheeres 1991: 8)

So the emphasis in language and literacy development for further education and training is on language support across the curriculum and the integration of language and literacy instruction into content area teaching, whether through team-teaching situations, in which a language specialist works alongside a content specialist, through extending the teaching repertoire of the content specialist or else through providing tutorial support. Literacy in further education contexts involves a move into mainstream areas: the education and training systems, preparation for entry into the labour market.

If community-based literacy provision can have as goals the building of confidence, self-esteem and empowerment in the domains of everyday life and can be set against the disempowering nature of given experiences of schooling, in the traces they leave long after schooldays are over, entry into further education can be seen as a return into the mainstream of qualification-driven courses, offering access into further study, training and work.

Earlier in this chapter I wrote that schooling and education in general involves the negotiation of public spaces and public discourses. In the next section I would like to look at language and literacy education in an area that aims to assist students in making the transition between community-based education and further education: so-called 'second-chance education', aiming to provide adults with the opportunity to develop the confidence, language skills and study skills to go on to succeed in formal courses, often for people after a long period out of education, or else for people with significant gaps in their education. These courses have been documented by practitioner-researchers like Gardener (1985, 1988) and Edwards (1986, 1988).

LITERACY EDUCATION AS TRANSITION

The concept of 'transition' is a helpful one in characterizing the ways in which individuals move through the education systems available; for example, going from a literacy group into a second-chance course in a community education context and thence gaining a place on a course which provides a vocational training and qualification at the end, or going on to study in higher education. Movement within and between educational institutions will involve different kinds of transitions. In the next chapter we will relate this to the 'theory of transitions' that Stubbs proposes (1987) to describe the ways in which learners move through education systems and their corresponding linguistic demands. To move from a community education setting to a further education setting is a transition that makes many demands on the individual making the transition, both in terms of social organization and participation and the linguistic demands of the new environment.

In her research on the development of written language in second-chance education Gardener (1985, 1988) writes as follows about issues of development and transition in student writing:

One form that the issue of development presented itself in was a pair of terms which we could neither accept nor escape: anecdote and analysis. It is a caricature of what goes on to suggest that all adults embarking on writing from a position of difficulty with literacy, or embarking on it again after a long gap, find the storytelling mode and the first person narrative in particular easier and more congenial, and abstract and generalizing discourse both unfamiliar and difficult, and at the same time a goal for writing in education. But even if the polarity is not that simple, something like it haunts both us as tutors and the apprentice writers we work with. We don't want to describe it like that but we haven't an alternative description.

This issue links in our minds to what we understand about transitions from speech to writing, and how we think students see these transitions. We work in part with a popular consciousness that 'I write like I speak'; though most inexperienced writers don't, in important ways, not the least of which is that few of them can transfer the fluency and unconsciousness of speech to writing. We worry that students understand this to mean, 'I write in bad English, which is how I speak.' But we also know about their pride in their speech forms. We know that they both fancy and are anxious about learning and using the long words that are the easiest marker of educated language: problematic in terms of group loyalty, but not to be withheld, especially by those who have 'Swallowed the dictionary'. What we began to discuss as the study progressed was how openly we share these different perceptions with our student groups, how clearly we put the language of learning on the agenda of a return to study course.

(Gardener 1988: 106–7)

An interesting issue in the passage quoted above is the focus on identity and group affiliation, on areas of conflict for teachers of writing, on an emerging awareness of the need for a 'meta-dimension' to writing instruction, through which learner-writers reflect on such issues as the transitions involved in learning certain ways of writing and the accompanying issues of identity and choice, taking up their own position and 'stance' in relation to their discourse. (These questions are addressed in Ivanič and Roach 1990.)

Immediately following the section quoted above, Gardener concludes: 'what we also faced is that we are untrained, or self-trained, as teachers of writing. We want more opportunities to confront these issues and to learn what there is to learn from other research' (1988: 107).

Within the research/practice dialectic, practice can often throw up problems and issues, intuitively grasped, which require explicit development and elaboration. In the next chapter we will explore the extent to which an understanding of language and its embedding in social context can throw light on some of these issues raised for adult literacy practice by Gardener.

In the next chapter, our starting point will be the idea that institutions can be construed as discourses and, correspondingly, discourses can be construed as institutions. If the further education setting presupposes the discourses of academic disciplines, content areas, vocational areas, then the language and literacy preparation for students entering further education must include an ability to come to terms with these discourses.

An essential part of preparation for going into further education is study skills: skills for organizing time; gaining access to information; preparing and carrying out study tasks; engaging in complex uses of spoken and written language, like participating in classroom discussion; writing assignments, projects and essays. All of these involve complex uses of literacy which can be seen as prerequisites for successful study. The following activity is intended to 'walk the reader through' the literacy demands of a particular study skill area, using a library, to consolidate awareness of the language and literacy demands of the further education context, but also to prepare the way for material to be presented in Chapter 4.

Activity: gaining access to print material

Suppose you decide you want to follow up a particular writer. How do you get access to their work? What kinds of knowledge about literacy, literacy practices or other kinds of social knowledge are involved in getting hold of a book you want to read?

Choose a book to follow up from the references cited in this book, or any other you are using for study purposes. Keep a log of the stages you go through in getting hold of it, the kinds of knowledge about literacy and uses of literacy involved.

Use as a checklist the framework for the book developed in Chapter 1. In other words, what kinds of

social contexts
learning/acquisition processes
interactions as reader/writer/participating others
text production & interpretation
texts
media

discursive practices
ideologies

are involved in using a library to follow up a reference?

Some hints for this activity:

- What kind of *social* and *institutional context* is a library?
- What are the *learning/acquisition processes* involved in getting the hang of the Dewey system or an on-line book search facility?
- What kind of *interactions* might a potential library user have with a librarian when joining a library? What kinds of literacy work, oral interaction might be involved?
- What kinds of *text production & interpretation* (filling in form to join the library, filling in a form to reserve a book, reading information on a computer screen, scanning shelves, noting down the Dewey classification number) might be involved?
- What kinds of *texts* might be involved?
- What kinds of *discourses* would you be engaged in? Does it make sense to think of the divisions between subject areas in a library as divisions between discourses?
- What kinds of *ideology* might be involved – for example, beliefs about how knowledge should be organized and located, who should have access to it?

In the above activity, you have been documenting the literacy practices involved in using a library, thus making explicit your implicit knowledge as a library user. How could this explicit knowledge be organized as part of a study skills course for new users of libraries for study purposes?

LITERACY IN THE WORKPLACE

Kostadin

Kostadin is from Macedonia and has been in Australia for 20 years. He has been working in a steel works for those 20 years and is now aged 53 years old. He had four years of schooling, with frequent gaps even during those four years, as he was often sent out of class to look after the teacher's sheep!

Kostadin is an Operator I, which is the highest grade before becoming a Leading Hand or Foreman. As part of the award restructuring process, Kostadin, among others, is being required to broaden his skills and become certified by the Department of Industrial Relations in areas like Fork Lift Driving, Crane Driving and Crane Chasing. He is practically skilled in these areas, but lacks basic reading and writing skills to participate in the training courses. Other areas where he needs literacy are in form-filling, report-writing and computer literacy.

Kostadin is a skilled and experienced worker, but he is convinced that he is too old to learn. He is attending a Basic Literacy course in the workplace, but wants to supplement this by attending classes in his spare time. Since he is on shifts, he can attend a class every fortnight.

The workplace context differs from the two previous contexts for literacy education that we have examined – the community context and the further education context – in one significant way: whereas the first two settings are marked as 'educational' settings, the workplace isn't. Its goals and purposes are some form of production, whether of raw materials or value-added products, or the delivery of a service. The literacy educator in the workplace, even if located within the organization (in an in-house training department, for example) is something of an outsider, and we will see how, in the researching and planning phases of workplace literacy programmes, ethnographic models of investigation tend to suggest themselves. In the workplace, the educator is not on home ground, so the need to negotiate that ground becomes a central issue in planning and implementing literacy education in the workplace.

If the need to create educational contexts in non-educational settings is one of the 'problems' of workplace literacy education, the ready availability of context is one of its challenges and strengths. In the conventional classroom, students and teachers are at some remove from the contexts of literacy use, and through dialogue, in the sense that Freire and Shor use the word, can reconstruct and problematize these contexts. The availability of context in the workplace provides a rich source of information about literacy in its contexts of use, which can inform course planning and design.

Factors for course planning and design in the workplace

Literacy educators working in the workplace need to take into account a range of factors:

- the macro socio-economic factors affecting the industry;
- projected changes in work practices;
- the educational profile of the workforce;

- the perspectives of the 'key players' in the workplace (management, unions, workforce);
- the literacy and communication demands of work processes in different sectors of the workplace;
- strategies for designing programmes to close the 'skills gap' between literacy and communication demands of the workplace and the educational profiles of the workforce;
- strategies for evaluating programmes and accounting to the 'key players': management, unions, workers for the success or otherwise of a programme.

Language and literacy issues in the Australian textile, clothing and footwear industry

Writing about the textile, clothing and footwear industry in Australia, Durie (1991) outlines the macro socio-economic factors affecting the industry and the profile of its workforce:

> A thumbnail sketch of the TCF workforce is that the 'average' worker is a woman over 35 years of age from a non-English speaking background. Across the industry there are variations with clothing having the highest proportion of women and migrant workers – around 90% and 70% respectively – and textiles the lowest at around 50% for both women and migrant workers. For the TCF industry as a whole the proportion of workers from overseas countries, mainly from countries where languages other than English are spoken, is higher than for the manufacturing sector and the economy as a whole.
>
> Within factories the mix of English-speaking and non-English speaking workers varies enormously. In country factories most workers are Australian born of anglo-celtic background. In the cities the story is very different. Some factories might be all or mainly English-speaking and others might be comprised of workers from a number of different backgrounds, very few with English language proficiency. Yet other factories might have workers who all speak the same language, for example Chinese or Vietnamese. . . .
>
> As a general rule then, we are looking at workers with low levels of English proficiency. This applies to both workers from overseas and native English speakers. Most workers have low levels of formal education, no formal qualifications and little or no training for the job. English speakers often have very low literacy and numeracy skills and many workers from other countries do not have literacy in their first language let alone in English.
>
> (Durie 1991)

Sonnenburg and Nussbaum (1991) carried out a project in the textile, clothing and footwear industries in Sydney, Australia. They found that:

the two main themes coming out of the workplace observations affecting operators' language and literacy skills are:

- new technology;
- changes in workplace organization viz. moving from line product system to teamwork production.

All new technology involves 'paper work'. The 'paper work' is used to track production, productivity and quality. An operator has to be able to deal with it accurately and efficiently.

In operating as a member of a team, an operator must not only be technically proficient i.e. be able to perform a number of operations on a number of machines, but must also be able to work as a fully participative team member –

- work cooperatively;
- attend meetings
- do budgeting
- do interpretative analysis of charts, statistics, scales, etc.

(Sonnenburg and Nussbaum 1991).

The themes which Sonnenburg and Nussbaum identify through their investigation in the textile, clothing and footwear industry can be read as generative themes in the Freirean sense, perhaps organized round 'impact of new technologies' and 'participation'.

Case study

Lite and Lo (Low Alcohol) Brewery (SA) is moving to a new total quality control work process in its Adelaide brewery. Staff will be required to participate in quality circle meetings and to learn to operate new equipment as well as computerized record-keeping. In order to bring in these new work processes a new award structure has been negotiated, which requires a substantial component of training. There will be no redundancies, but staff will be expected to take more responsibilities for higher wages.

You have been asked to organize a workshop for fifteen process workers to explain the relationship between increased responsibility and pay rises in the new award, and to explain how the new procedures will demand increased communication skills, in both spoken and written language and increased flexibility skills.

All the members of this group have been employed for the company for more than fifteen years. They were familiar with the work processes that are being replaced and are extremely worried that the new training demands will point out their lack of basic skills, and that, despite the no-redundancy agreement reached, they will end up out of a job.

Shifting communication demands, brought about by changes in work organization and technology can have an impact on the literacy demands of roles throughout the organization. Supervisors may have an increased volume of written record-keeping and report-writing. Managers, trainers and those designing new work systems need to have high-level communication skills to communicate complex information in effective ways.

Case study

The State Water Authority (Training Division) has carried out a large-scale survey of its workforce of 5,000 staff: 1,500 are semi-skilled workers; 1,500 are supervisors or inspectors; 2,000 are management.

The survey has shown very low levels of literacy and numeracy in the semi-skilled group, and there is a proposal included in the industry restructuring negotiations for workplace basic skills training. However, the survey also showed a worryingly high level of literacy and numeracy problems in the supervisory grades, along with an extreme reluctance to admit to the problem.

Under the new restructured awards, supervisory grades will have an increased responsibility in report-writing, organizing and recording meetings and on-the-job training.

You have been asked to run a workshop for fifteen supervisors, explaining the importance of literacy and numeracy for the new award structure in the SWA. You plan to focus on the identified needs of the semi-skilled workforce. However, you know that at least some of the supervisors' group themselves will be experiencing literacy and numeracy difficulties in the new set-up and you want to provide a tactful opportunity to raise those issues. How would you do it?

PLANNING A WORKPLACE LITERACY PROGRAMME

Drew and Mikulecky (1988) provide guidelines for the research and investigation phase of planning a workplace literacy programme, including methods such as:

- site tours;
- observation of communication demands of meetings, quality circles, etc.;
- observation of performance of literacy tasks;
- interviews with operators, supervisors;
- analysis of literacy tasks identified;
- collection and analysis of workplace written texts.

The following case study of a company in the process of restructuring and introducing new work practices encapsulates some of the literacy issues that arise in workplace contexts:

The company

Emcol Plastics Pty Ltd is a medium-sized manufacturing company, based in an inner suburb of an eastern state capital city. Its range of products are plastic components for aerosol sprays which are sold in Australia and to a small but expanding market overseas. Management is currently updating the plant, renewing equipment and work processes. It is also introducing innovative quality-control procedures, which involve increased decision-making on the part of all staff. In addition to this, a new award is being negotiated which will involve a simplified career-path structure. All of the above will require a comprehensive training programme, and the newly expanded Human Resources Division is working on this.

The Human Resources Division has begun implementing the training programme, but has encountered problems in a number of areas. A substantial number of process workers, both Australian and overseas-born, have limited literacy and numeracy skills and are having difficulty with the training required to implement the new processes, as well as participating in the quality-control process. Staff working in the warehouses are having to switch to a computerized system for processing orders and seem unable to adapt to it. There is an apparent loss of productivity, instead of the hoped-for increase. Superiors feel that certain older staff lack the education skills to deal with the new system.

The management

Some members of the management team feel that a training budget spent on topping up the literacy and numeracy skills of their workforce is money wasted. They regard basic skills training as the responsibility of the school, and believe that, in the face of increased sophistication of work processes, a better-educated workforce should be recruited, and those older workers who are unable to make the transition should be encouraged to take voluntary redundancy. This is not the view of Human Resource Division or the unions who believe that upgrading basic skills will be an effective way of enabling the workforce to adapt to the changes in their workplace.

The union

The union has been aware of the lack of basic skills of a section of their members but until recently it hasn't been a high-priority issue. For many of the shop stewards it still is not, although they recognize the language problems of some of the NESB (Non-English Speaking Background) workers can cause health and safety problems. However, during the award negotiations, training in general, and literacy and numeracy training in particular, have come to assume increased importance in ensuring a good deal for their members in the new agreement.

The workforce

One of the fears of the workers at Emcol Plastics is that the new work processes and procedures will mean redundancies. They have already experienced a 'slimming down' of the workforce in the early 1970s. Many older workers remember with bitterness job losses then. In particular, workers with little education feel threatened by the proposed changes, the training programmes and the demands of increased participation. There have been basic education courses in the workplace previously. A number of English in the Workplace courses for NESB workers were given to some men in the mid 1980s. These caused considerable resentment in the ESB section of the workforce. 'Why were these blokes being given time off to study, while we have to cover their work?'

The literacy issues

At Emcol Plastics a literacy and numeracy skills gap has been informally identified among process workers required to adapt to new work processes, equipment and procedures. In addition, some 40 per cent of process workers come from an NESB. Of these, a number have limited education in their first language, which uses a different script from English. None of the NESB workers has difficulty in oral communication for day-to-day purposes, but a significant number have problems with reading and writing.

Take, for example, George, whose first language is Macedonian, which has a different script from English. Age 47 years. Lived in Australia for 25 years. Can communicate well in English but never studied English. Can't read and write in English except name and address and basic form-filling. Left school at age 10 to work on his uncle's farm.

Some supervisors are also feeling unconfident in the literacy demands that will be placed on them, when the new work processes come into operation. They will also have to run meetings for their section on a regular basis.

An increasing number of staff will have to take on training roles as part of new responsibilities. Many of these, although quite confident in their literacy abilities at work and for day-to-day purposes, do not have the skills to present information in training clearly and effectively.

Task

What kind of arguments could you present to

- the management,
- the union, or
- a group of process workers at Emcol Plastics

on the benefits of literacy and numeracy training in their workplace?

Workplace literacy education raises a number of issues for the literacy educator. First, literacy theory and practice has developed, as we saw earlier in this chapter, within a social justice paradigm. In the workplace, economic rationalism may seem to be the dominating consideration.

Secondly, a concern with measurement and outcomes of literacy programmes may lead to an emphasis on a narrow, skills-based conception of literacy. What arguments and what allies are there, within the industrial context for broader critical conceptions of literacy?

CONCLUSION

This chapter has presented a range of contexts for literacy education (community-based, further education, workplace) while emphasizing differences between these contexts and the different range of constraints and opportunities working on and for a critical literacy education in these different contexts.

There are other contexts for literacy education that have not been included here, such as literacy work with the unemployed or with workers being made redundant, literacy work in prisons, in the probationary service, as part of youth work.

While recognizing discontinuities and differences, as well as the difficulties of transitions between educational sectors, it is also worth emphasizing, however, the continuities within and between educational sectors. These continuities are often characterized as 'pathways of progression' as users of education move between sectors. In the following extracts, workers on a literacy course in their workplace talk about their previous experiences with English classes and their current situation:

Previous experiences in work and learning English

'No school, go for the ship, go for the factory.'

'I'm coming sixteen and a half years, my sister take me. Who give me food? My brother-in-law? No! . . . find a job . . . pay rent . . . seven dollars all week . . . bus . . . food . . . no time go to school.'

'I'm coming my husband together, bring five kids, seven together.'

'Old days, pick up shovel and work.'

Q: What made you decide to do the course?

'Very hard to locate another job . . . cut back . . . must understand write and read for other job, can't understand, kick me out.'

'When I start steel work, nobody give me chance. This year special for the writing and reading.'

'I'm Australian twenty years, steel works seventeen, now this first time. "I'm too old." Teacher say "Please come!"'

This group were getting their first chance at education after nearly twenty years in Australia. On arriving in Australia they went straight to work and did not have the chance to take up 'community-based' learning opportunities. The prospect of re-deployment at least, if not redundancy, hangs over them, and the need to improve their language and literacy skills.

The reader will notice many ways in which these comments pick up on themes introduced earlier in the chapter, in the focus on learners' previous educational and life experiences. The differences between educational settings lie in the domains of literacy that are typically their scope, the discourses that are presupposed within them, their ideologies and institutional practices. The continuities lie in the pathways and possibilities for movement between these educational settings, which are a key goal for equal opportunity in education.

SUGGESTIONS FOR FURTHER READING

Horsman, J. (1990) *'Something in my Mind Besides the Everyday':* *Women and Literacy,* Toronto: Women's Press.

Mace, J. (1979) *Working with Words,* London: Chameleon.

Shor, I (1992) *Empowering Education: Critical Teaching for Social Change,* Chicago: University of Chicago Press.

FOUR

Spoken and written language

This chapter will focus on language, and I will argue that the approach to literacy as social practice presented in previous chapters needs to be complemented by a linguistically based analysis of literacy as text and textual practice, that what is needed to complement the social contextual analysis of previous chapters is what Stubbs calls an 'educational theory of (spoken and written) language' (Stubbs 1987). In Chapters 1, 2 and 3 I argued that literacy is a socio-political and educational construct, not a linguistic one, and in this chapter I attempt to characterize what an educational theory of (spoken and written) language ought to look like and how it should underpin and complement our understandings of literacy as social practice.

If literacy as social practice suggests research alliances with fields like sociology and anthropology as well as social history, and literacy as educational practice suggests research alliances with educational theorists, then the educational theory of (spoken and written) language suggests that linguistics and applied linguistics are the disciplines to turn to.

Educational linguistics is an emerging field (cf., for example, Halliday 1985b; Stubbs 1986,1987; Christie (ed.) 1990 Hammond 1990), and we are beginning to see the kinds of theories of language that can adequately underpin our understanding of literacy as social practice, providing a complementary perspective to the ethnographic approach. Halliday (1985a) points out that traditional approaches to language typically focused on written language. As the title of this chapter suggests, a theory of language that can adequately underpin literacy as social practice must be able to characterize both the spoken and written modes of language, in their similarities and differences. It needs to be highly responsive to context, both in the ways that context constrains and shapes language in use and in the ways that language in use shapes and constrains context: it needs to be a contextual theory of language. It needs to be a theory of language which can deal with the organization of whole texts, but it also needs to be a theory of language that is a theory of practice as well as of text.

This theory of language needs to be sensitive to ideological constructions (implicit in the 'pedagogical and everyday stereotypes' that Stubbs writes of), and capable of deconstructing them (cf. Kress 1985; Martin 1986; Fairclough 1989): a theory of language that can deal with the politics of unequal communication and the ways in which inequality is institutionally and socially embedded.

A theory of language underpinning literacy as social practice must also characterize the linguistic aspects of what Stubbs (1987) calls 'a whole theory of transitions' involved in becoming literate. These transitions include:

- from spoken to written;
- from casual to formal;
- from spontaneous to planned;
- from private to public;
- from non-standard to standard;
and in the case of bilinguals
- from L1 to L2

(cf. Stubbs 1987: 23)

To sum up, then, a theory of language relevant to the understanding of literacy as social practice will have to be able to:

1 account for the linguistic organization of whole texts;
2 account for the ways in which language (both spoken and written) is embedded in and constitutive of social context;
3 account for the ways in which power relations are linguistically encoded in both spoken and written language;
4 characterize the similarities and differences between spoken and written language;
5 present a framework to describe how those differences might be realized in a range of communicative contexts;
6 characterize in linguistic terms the interaction between spoken and written language in context (as typified in the 'literacy event' construct introduced in Chapter 2);
7 account in linguistic terms for significant cross-cultural and

inter-group variation in the functions and uses of spoken and written language (cf. Gumperz 1982; Cook-Gumperz 1986; Scollon and Scollon 1981).

It goes without saying that such a theory of language will be critical and context-sensitive, but it is also worth saying here that it ought to be comprehensive. Stubbs (1986) has argued that linguistic theories underpinning educational practice should provide a comprehensive account of the characteristics of language and not limit themselves to the seductive areas of discourse and ideology, in a form of cultural criticism without a descriptive base. The relevant model of language needs to include the different *levels* of linguistic organization, which, for the purposes of this book we will treat as:

- text
- lexico-grammar
- phonology

These levels correspond in the model of language presented in Chapter 1 to the innermost section of *language as text*. Between each level there is a relationship of *realization*, with the units of a lower level (sounds and their combination into syllables in the case of phonology) being realized at the next level (words and strings of words at the level of lexico-grammar), which are in turn realized in text (spoken and written).

Seen from another perspective, each successive level of language provides the *context* within which units of the previous level make sense: out of context a string of sounds (typed at random)

abacaradag

while having a recognizable syllabic structure, mean nothing (although of course any string of random sounds will trail kinds of associated meanings, since it is difficult to drain language of meaning even for demonstration purposes). A rather similar string of sounds

abracadabra

can be made to yield meaning as a lexical item. But the lexical item 'abracadabra' on its own needs to be recontextualized in a grammatical utterance to 'mean' effectively:

'Abracadabra,' said the conjuror, waving his wand.

Outside the discourse of linguistic texts, in which this might serve as an example, say, of the grammatical feature of direct speech reporting, this string is again incomplete, suggesting, for example, a story-book discourse in which it can again be recontextualized as a narrative event at the level of text.

The above examples have taken us on a 'bottom-up' trail, in which sounds combine to make syllables, which combine to form words and groups of words, which again combine to form texts. We could equally well take a 'top-down' trail, attempting to take to pieces or deconstruct a whole text, spoken or written, to find out how it is constructed, what makes it tick.

The text which we have so far imagined, a story book about a conjuror, needs to be further recontextualized into its contexts of use: as a story read to a group of pre-school children; as a story read to herself by an older child; in the context of its visual presentation on the page with the images associated with it. We can further imagine the reading child asking an available adult how to read 'abracadabra' or possibly what a 'wand' is, creating a metalinguistic frame for the text.

A tape-recording of the literacy event involved in an adult reading the story to a child might well involve a whole series of glosses and asides to the text, in which the spoken mode interacts with the 'aloud reading' mode through which the words on the page are shared with the listening child.

It is important to emphasize at this stage the interaction between text and context and between a given written text and the social context and literacy practices in which it is produced and read. The work of Heath (1983) provides evidence of how literacy practices are differently constructed in sub-groups of a given society.

Beyond the focus of face-to-face interaction, we also have to recognize the ways in which ideologies, values and institutions impinge on text, its construction and reconstruction in literacy events. If, as Heath suggests, middle-class parents systematically introduce their children to ways of meaning congruent with the ways of schooling, is this a reason for class-based differences in educational achievement? If, as Michaels (1986) suggests, teachers can systematically misunderstand and undervalue the ways of making meaning in spoken discourse of black children in an ethnically diverse classroom, this provides concrete evidence of the loaded nature of situated discourse and the ideological filters at work in its interpretation.

The procedure of this chapter will be to start from context, picking up issues raised in previous chapters, and work inwards towards text. In the following sections we will:

1   examine how spoken and written discourse is embedded in social structures, but also creates and reproduces them;
2   examine the similarities and differences between spoken and written language;
3   examine the role of spoken language in literacy development;
4   examine the interrelationship of spoken and written language in the literacy event, via the concepts of 'code-switching', 'mode-switching' and 'register-switching'.

LANGUAGE AND INSTITUTION

In this section we will examine the interrelationship of language and institution through an extract from the novel *Kes: a Kestrel for a Knave*, by Barry Hines.

Billy, a working-class teenager, hero of the book, has become fascinated with kestrel hawks. He arrives at the city library, determined to borrow a book on hawking.

Episode one: in the library

'Got any books on hawks, missis?'
   The girl behind the counter looked up from sorting coloured tickets in a tray.
   'Hawks?'
   'I want a book on falconry.'   5
   'I'm not sure, you'd better try ornithology.'
   'What's that?'
   'Under zoology.'
   She leaned over the desk and pointed down a corridor of shelves, then stopped and looked Billy over.   10
   'Are you a member?'
   'What do you mean, a member?'
   'A member of the library.'
   Billy pressed a finger into the ink pad on the desk and inspected the purple graining on the tip.   15
   'I don't know owt about that. I just want to lend a book on falconry, that's all.'
   'You can't borrow books unless you're a member.'
   'I only want one.'
   'Have you filled one of these forms in?'   20

She licked a forefinger and flicked a blue form up on her thumb.
Billy shook his head.
      'Well you're not a member then. Do you live in the Borough?'
      'What do you mean?'
      'The Borough, the City.'   25
      'No, I live out on Valley Estate.'
      'Well that's in the Borough, isn't it?'
      A man approached and plonked two books on the counter.
The girl attended to him immediately. Open. Stamp. Open.
Stamp. She slotted the cards into his tickets and filed them in   30
a tray. The man pulled his books to the edge of the counter,
caught them as they overbalanced, then shouldered his way
through the swinging doors.
      'Can I get a book now, then?'
      'You'll have to take one of these forms home first for your
father to sign.'   35
      She handed Billy a form across the counter. He took it and looked
down at the dotted lines and blank boxes.
      'My dad's away.'
      'You'll have to wait until he comes home then.'
      'I don't mean away like that. I mean he's left home.'   40
      'Oh, I see . . . Well in that case, your mother'll have to sign it.'
      'She's at work.'
      'She can sign it when she comes home, can't she?'
      'I know, but she'll not be home 'til tea time, and it's Sunday
tomorrow.'   45
      'There's no rush, is there?'
      'I don't want to wait that long. I want a book today.'
      'You'll just have to want, won't you?'
      'Look, just let me go an' see'f you've got one, an' if you have I'll
sit down at one o'them tables an' read it.'   50
      'You can't, you're not a member.'
      'Nobody'll know.'
      'It's against the rules.'
      'Go on. I'll bring you this paper back on Monday then.'
      'No! Now go on home and get that form signed.'   55
      She turned round and entered a little glass office.
      'I say.'
      Billy beckoned her out.
      'Now what?'
      'Where's there a bookshop?'   60
      'Well, there's Priors up the Arcade. That's the best one.'
      'O ye! I know.'
The library as one of the paradigmatic institutions or sites of
literacy (along with the school or college, the workplace). Billy

attempts access into this institution/site through spoken language (although the adept user, as we see in lines 28–32, may be able to gain access and accomplish his business non-verbally and new technologies can give access by electronic means).

In discourse terms, we can characterize conversational interaction as a series of *moves* (cf. Burton 1980; and Toolan 1989). In this interaction Billy makes the first move, which opens up and initiates the interaction, just as a chess player might:

'Got any books on hawks, missis?'

Grammatically it is a *question*, but it also functions as a *request*. As the initial move in the interaction we have already described it as an *opening*. (It is worth remembering that utterances are typically plurifunctional, they will fulfil a number of communicative purposes.)

In response to Billy's initiating request, the librarian first shifts her gaze from the task of sorting cards. (The interaction of verbal and non-verbal features in discourse, and the embedding of discourse in context are important aspects for analysis. The counter positions participants in relation to each other. Billy is standing, the librarian sitting. Billy is drawing her attention away from the task in hand. The novelist filters this information for us, as part of his contextualization of the scene. The discourse analyst working on naturally occurring data would have to rely on video-recording or participant-observation in order to capture the richness of contextual embedding of the dialogue so far.)

The librarian's non-verbal reaction to Billy's request is followed closely by her verbal response:

'Hawks?'

(A video-recording of a similar interaction, occurring naturally, would give the analyst information about the synchronicity of the librarian's response: would her shift of gaze count as a separate move in the interaction, or would it be more or less synchronous with her response? The information on conversational interaction yielded by the novel, contextually rich in some respects, is impoverished in others.)

Two moves, the second in response to the first, make up the minimal unit of interaction, the *exchange* (cf. Burton 1980; Toolan 1989; Coulthard 1992). The organization of exchanges in conversation is its *exchange structure*.

Between lines 1 and 8 we can discern a bounded sequence, since the librarian subsequently shifts the topic away from locating the book Billy wants, and starts to query Billy's right to be in the library at all, by questioning his institutional membership. We will examine this chunk of discourse in more detail below.

The librarian's response to Billy's request is to query the request, drawing from Billy a *reformulation*:

'I want a book on falconry'

which has interesting properties. The plurifunctional nature of language is confirmed here in that Billy uses another grammatical form, the *statement*, to specify his request.

An interesting shift in this reformulation is from the casual 'books on hawks' to the more formal register of 'a book on falconry', which we can call register-switching or shifting, on the analogy of code-switching (cf. Gumperz 1982). We will discuss register-switching, code-switching and a further variable, 'mode-switching', in a later section of this chapter.

In response to Billy's reformulated request, made more definite and authoritative by the shift in register, the librarian responds with a move that falls into two parts:

'I'm not sure'

This refers back to Billy's initial request, since 'I'm not sure' is not a coherent response to 'I want a book on falconry' (although an utterance like 'I'm not sure that we have one' would do in that context). We can therefore interpret the exchange in lines 4–5 as a *side-sequence*, which is nested within the ongoing exchange structure. The side-sequence works to clarify misunderstanding and allow the interaction to proceed.

The first part of the librarian's move denies the expertise to answer Billy's question herself and serves as a preface to the second part of her response:

'you'd better try ornithology'

in which she suggests a course of action for Billy to follow on his own (the organization of the library is predicated on the basis of autonomous users, like the borrower in lines 25–32).

Her advice raises the stakes in register by drawing on an item from the lexical taxonomy that serves to organize the library collection ('ornithology'). This moves the interaction out of the range of Billy's repertoire and his countering move:

'What's that?'

is a request for clarification, rather similar to the librarian's in line 4, though operating in a different direction, in that the librarian queries an everyday lexical item and is offered a more technical one (hawks – falconry). Here the librarian offers a technical term 'ornithology' and, instead of a clarification, she offers back a term on the same level of technicality, the hyponym 'zoology'.

Billy has come bang up against the library as discourse: the organization of knowledge and information into taxonomies is represented by the organization of the library. His initial request for information draws him into the discourse of the library and, successful at first, he soon betrays himself as someone who does not have access to the kinds of knowledge implied in library use. Initiation into the library as discourse is an initiation into ways of organizing knowledge and information, procedures for gaining access to it.

If the first interactional chunk brings him up against the library as discourse, the next brings him up against the library as institution, the key concept here being *membership*. Something about Billy's demeanour and behaviour leads her to query Billy's basic right to be participating in the interaction at all:

'Are you a member?'

Again we note the plurifunctional nature of the utterance: on one level a request for information: on another it counts as a challenge to a participant's rights to be participating. The librarian's move opens up a further exchange in which Billy queries an aspect of her utterance:

'What do you mean, a member?'

Cooperative conversation (cf. Grice 1975) is based on the abilities of participants to gauge what is shared and not shared information and background knowledge. In the event of one participant assuming wrongly in an utterance that a particular item is shared knowledge, a conversational partner may query that aspect of the utterance. The librarian assumes knowledge of the membership structure of the library as a given in the conversation, Billy queries the term and the librarian attempts to repair the misunderstanding by being more explicit (rather as Billy did in line 5).

The exchange structure of the interaction analysed so far shows certain recurrent patterns, most notably the frequent requests for clarification (lines 4, 7, 12) themselves a sign of conversational difficulty. While on one level conversation is being conducted cooperatively, on another the conversation betrays consistent cycles of struggle and difficulty. So far the interaction has been accomplished by verbal and non-verbal means. The question of membership brings in the written mode, in that a pre-condition for membership is having filled in a form.

The question of membership arises through another pre-condition for library membership: residence in the area served by the library. Again we find another three-part exchange in which a request for information move is followed by a query move, followed by a move that attempts a clarification:

'Do you live in the Borough?'

'What do you mean?'

'The Borough, the City.'

We find again that the basis for misunderstanding lies in one participant's assumption of knowledge as given, when in fact it is not shared. 'The Borough' is a bureaucratic and geographic entity, clearly part of the librarian's mental landscape, yet not part of Billy's. His request for clarification produces an attempt at clarification using the register-shift strategy noted above: instead of the bureaucratic term 'the Borough', she substitutes the more everyday term 'the City'. Billy again fails to interpret this as a bureaucratic/geographic entity, giving rise to the misunderstanding in the following exchange:

'No, I live out on Valley Estate.'

'Well that's in the Borough, isn't it?'

Within his mental landscape, the City (centre) contrasts with Valley Estate (periphery), while the bureaucratic entity includes both centre and periphery.

Billy runs into difficulty both on the level of discourse (the organization of the library as the organization of discourses, exemplified in the taxonomy within which he is expected to locate the book on falconry) and on the level of institution (the organization of the library as institution, with procedures for membership, range of possible members and so on). He shows considerable *personal power* in his persistence in asking for a book, but the librarian is working within a framework of *institutional power*, which is informed by her position, her knowledge base, as well as her understanding of the library both as discourse and institution. The librarian acts as a *gatekeeper* (cf. Erickson and Schultz 1982) in the interaction.

Episode two: in the bookshop

He went out into the sunlight. People crowded the pavements and gutters, and on the road the traffic was jammed honking in two straight lines. Billy screwed the form up and dropped it onto a grate. It bounced on the bars, then fell between them. He squeezed between a car and a bus and jogged down the centre line of the road. Car drivers with their arms resting on window ledges looked up at him as he passed. The vehicles at the head of one line began to move. Billy slipped back on to the pavement before the reaction in the chain could reach him.

He looked in at the window display, then walked through the open doorway and crossed to a rack of paperbacks. Walking round the rack, and revolving it in the opposite direction, he examined the room as it flickered by between the books and the wire struts. All four walls were lined with books. Disposed around the room were racks and stands of paperbacks, and in the centre was a table with a till and piles of books on it. There were three assistants, two girls and a man. Several people were browsing, and one young man was buying. The shop was as quiet as the library.

He started in one corner, and, working from the top shelf, down, up, down, moved along the sections, scanning the categories, which were printed on white cards and stuck on the edges of the shelves: CRAFTS . . . DICTIONARIES . . . DEVOTIONAL . . . FICTION . . . GARDENING . . . HISTORY . . . MOTORING . . . NATURE–ANIMALS, one shelf, two shelves. BIRDS, birds, birds. A *Falconer's Handbook*. Billy reached up. The book was clamped tight in the middle of the shelf. He pressed the top of the spine and titled it towards him, catching it as it fell. He opened it and flicked through it back to front, pausing at the pictures and diagrams. A sparrowhawk stared up from the glossy paper of the dust jacket. Billy glanced round. The man and one of the girls were serving. The other girl was shelving books with her back to him. Everyone else had their heads down. Billy turned his back on them and slipped the book inside his jacket. The man and the girl continued to serve.

The other girl continued to shelve. Billy continued round the walls, to the door out into the arcade.

Activity

Like the library, the bookshop is a 'literacy site'; a place constructed with and around written text. We saw how the library was organized round the Dewey classification system. How are the books organized in the bookshop? How does Billy go about finding the book he wants? How is space organized in the bookshop? What similarities and differences do you find between the library as a literacy site and the bookshop?

SPOKEN AND WRITTEN LANGUAGE

In the previous section, we looked at the organization of conversation, using examples from the constructed text of a novelist, rather than the naturally occurring conversation we might obtain, if we were able to leave a tape-recorder running at the library counter, or observe such an encounter as 'participant-observers'. In this section we will try to characterize in linguistic terms some salient similarities and differences between spoken and written language, drawing on the work of Halliday (1985a, 1985b), Kress (1988, 1989) and others like Hammond (1990), who have addressed the issue.

Some myths about spoken and written language

As we saw in Chapter 1, the whole area of literacy, both in education and in everyday social practice, is highly ideologized, with the construction of powerful literate/illiterate cleavages and feelings running high about what the 'solution' to the 'problem' might be. When we turn to the relationship between speech and writing, we find similarly powerful ideas, not necessarily fully articulated, but nevertheless underpinning our everyday understandings of spoken and written language.

Myth one: writing is talk written down

Solomon asked an afreet about the spoken word. 'It is like the passing wind,' replied the afreet. 'And how do you capture it?' asked Solomon. 'With writing.'

(traditional Arab saying)

In this anecdote, we find a very clear example of the myth that writing is talk written down. In fact, the organization of spoken and written language, in linguistic terms, is different in significant ways, as we shall see in this section, while drawing from the same underlying grammatical system.

Myth two: writing is organized and grammatical; speaking is disorganized and ungrammatical

According to this myth, spoken language is disjointed, full of half-completed, reformulated utterances, fillers like 'umm' and 'ah', and 'you know', while written language is organized into complete grammatical sentences, expressing complete ideas.

Underlying this myth is a misconception, or rather a cluster of misconceptions, about the organization of language. Halliday (1985b) points out that the emergence of written language is a necessary pre-condition for the development of linguistics, in that it enables language to be focused on as an object, thus making possible the objective study of language. This of course should not be taken to mean that non-literate cultures do not have metalanguages available to them. The objectifications of language available to non-literate cultures are more likely to focus on genres, performances and contexts for performances, of the type revealed in ethnographies of communication (cf. Bauman and Sherzer 1974), than on the features that organize text, and again are more likely to focus on genres and contexts for performance which are in some way culturally salient, like rituals or ceremonies, rather than the everyday, more invisible uses of language. The emergence of writing makes possible the comprehensive analysis of language.

In fact, as we began to see in the previous section, spoken language is organized, but it is organized differently from written language. Halliday (1985b: 81) argues that the modal tendency of written language is to represent phenomena as products, while the modal tendency of spoken language is process-orientated, and that this is reflected in the grammar in significant ways.

Halliday argues that, typically, written language is *lexically dense* (meanings are packed into nominal groups, rather than carried in verbal processes). In contrast, spoken language is lexically sparse, but *grammatically intricate*, in that its complexity is carried not by meanings packed into nominal groups, but by complex orchestrations of clauses, each made up of a verbal process. In a striking metaphor, he describes the organization of written language as *crystalline*, to capture the objectification that is its modal tendency, and the organization of spoken language as *choreographic*, to capture its process orientation.

A correlate of these modal tendencies of spoken and written language, is that spoken language tends to be *lexically sparse*, in that the work of encoding meanings is being done by verbal processes in clause complexes, while written language is lexically dense, but *grammatically simple*.

If follows therefore that, in written language, the nominal group carries a heavy functional load, and in fact one of the significant processes in written English is that of *nominalization*, the turning of verbal processes into nouns.

The previous sentence can itself be used as an illustration of what is meant by nominalization. If we look in more detail at a segment of it –

in fact one of the significant processes in written English is that of nominalization, the turning of verbal processes into nouns

– we can see initially that the grammar of this clause is, as predicted by the analysis of the spoken/written mode, rather simple, consisting of one relational process –

X is Y

– while on the other hand the nominal groups, as predicted, are rather complex:

1   one of the significant processes in written English
2   that of nominalization, the turning of verbal processes into nouns.

We find a number of nominalizations embedded in the nominal groups:

the significant processes
written English
nominalization
the turning of verbal processes into nouns

Nominalizations can be 'unpacked' (cf. Hammond 1990), to recapture the centrality of the verbal process:

the processes are significant
English is written

people write English
verbal processes are turned into nouns
the grammar turns verbal processes into nouns
people turn verbal processes into nouns

A progressive unpacking of the lexical item 'nominalization' would look like this:

1   nominalization
2   the turning of verbal processes into nouns
3   verbal processes are turned into nouns
4   the grammar turns verbal processes into nouns
5   people turn verbal processes into nouns

In which the basic functional relationships of

X does Y to Z

are progressively restored.

1 and 2 , both in themselves nominalizations, are formed in interestingly different ways: the first as a descendant of the Latin word-stock '-atio', the second more in the pattern of the Germanic word-stock. The work of Corson (for example, Corson 1985) points to the significance of Latin- and Greek-derived lexical stock in written English.

If we look at the way in which the unfolding of meaning is organized in the text (namely, its information structure) at this point, the following is interesting:

nominalization, the turning of verbal processes into nouns

Here 'the turning of verbal processes into nouns' functions in the grammar as an elaborating expansion of the lexical item 'nominalization'. The function of the expansion can be interpreted as 'glossing' or 'giving the word meaning', and the expansion can be seen as a shift in register, from the technical term 'lexically realized', in the direction of a partial unpacking of the underlying process. In a later section of this chapter, I will argue that such subtle shifts of code, mode and register are organizing principles in the 'literacy event'.

The progressive unpacking of the lexical item 'nominalization' corresponds to the direction of rewriting into 'plain English'. Halliday (1985a) points out that simplification in one part of the language system is at the expense of complexifying in another part of the system and this is illustrated here: the 'plainer' gloss of the original single lexical item 'nominalization' is made up of seven lexical items and brevity is sacrificed.

The grammar of writing in a railway station announcement

The following is an announcement heard on the platform of a London station. It was repeated in exactly the same form of words a number of times, so may have been an example of a written text read aloud:

> good morning ladies and gentlemen following the London
> Underground having to investigate a reported emergency between
> Regent's Park and Oxford Circus . . . the Bakerloo line has now
> resumed normal service

The grammar of the clause 'following . . . Oxford Circus' is quite complex and can be unpacked to reveal an underlying minimal narrative sequence:

> an emergency was reported between Regent's Park and Oxford
> Circus
> London Underground had to investigate
> the Bakerloo line has now resumed normal service

However the grammar works to subordinate the information contained in this clause, to the 'main' information that service has been resumed. The way the grammar is organized serves to background the emergency and the investigation and foreground the resumption of normal service, which is after all what commuters waiting on a chilly platform want to hear. In another circumstance – say, for example, a railway worker involved in the incident – the whole thing might be replayed as a performed oral narrative and the information organized in a completely different way, as a sequence of events, with vivid dramatization of the reactions of participants. The ability to build up complex clauses and organize them in order to foreground certain kinds of information and background others is part of the resources of English.

The following extract from Kress (1985) presents the modal distinction between spoken and written language in a particularly lucid way, while making clear the ideological underpinnings that make written language dominant:

Writing has a structuring logic which differs fundamentally from
that of speech. It is a logic of the nominal rather than of the verbal;
of objects rather than processes; of abstraction rather than
specificness/concreteness; a logic of hierarchy and integration
rather than a logic of sequence and addition. Western technological
societies value the forms and logic of writing over the forms and
logic of speaking. They represent a kind of technology which is
homologous with other technologies in our society. Writing also
represents permanence and control rather than the impermanence
and flux of speech. For these and other reasons writing is the
medium of the domain of public social and political life while
speaking is the medium of the domain of private life. The 'public'
person has to adopt the modes of writing in speaking. For the
powerful therefore, there is effectively only the one mode, that of
writing; both in writing and in speech.

(Kress 1985: 46)

While arguing for the distinctive modal tendency of written
language, the above text also embodies it, as an analysis of
its verbal process types, largely of the relational 'X is Y' type,
characteristic of expository writing, and the lexical density of its
nominal groups demonstrates.

If the modal tendency of writing is best expressed in expository
prose, that of speech is casual conversation:

If we want to bring out the essential differences between spoken
and written language, we can best do this by the strategy of
selecting a kind of paradigm case and treating it as representative
of the category. For spoken language, then, we shall take natural
spontaneous conversation as the paradigm form.

(Halliday 1985b: 46)

Another way of looking at this modal opposition between speech
and writing is to say that casual conversation best realizes the
potential of the spoken mode, while expository prose best realizes
the potential of the written mode, using 'potential' in the sense
of meaning potential. Halliday is careful to point out that the
differentiation of spoken and written modes does not mean that
each is associated with invariant types of language. He writes
of 'a whole cluster of different varieties – a scatter of types
of variation – that share the written medium' (Halliday 1985b:
46). Mixes and blends are also envisaged in the theory, which is
exactly what is predicted by the ethnographic accounts of literacy
in practice.

Case study

The following spoken and written texts (from Kress 1988) are both on the same topic: the proposed building of a dam at Tillegra, NSW, with consequent loss of farming land.

Spoken text

and ah/. . . we're down like/further/. . . but they said at the time/
it'd be seven acres/they thought that they'd be taking of ours/down
there like/you know/that was a good while ago/. . . well/. . . whether
whether they came here/oh/. . . look/I forget/. . . and ah Perce went
round with them/or whether they came here/and . . . judged for
themselves/I don't know/but they never looked in the house/. . . if/. . .
if they did come here/they didn't come to the/. . . come in the house/
or anything/. . . and ah/. . . well/whether they will come/or whether
they won't come/or when they're ready to come/I don't know/. . .
'spose they'll notify us/but oh we've had/. . . oh/. . . had letters from
them/. . . but oh gosh/eh/. . . they/. . . well the letters they write
are way over your head/. . . you know/er/. . . about this/and about
something else/. . . well I said to Perce/well look let the/. . . let the
tail go with the hide/I said if they want the place/they'll take it/and
if they don't want it/well we'll still live here/. . . we're not going to
worry about it/

In the above spoken example, we see the typical constructs of spoken language. The discourse type is narrative, but narrative is being used not just to recount what happened (the visit of the outside experts, 'they') but to present a perspective or point of view on the threatened developments ('if they want the place they'll take it'). Notice the role of repetition in the organization of the discourse:

if they want the place they'll take it and if they don't want it well
we'll still live here

whether they will come or whether they won't come or when they're
ready to come I don't know

Another typical spoken feature is the dramatization of speaker's perspectives using direct quotes:

well I said to Perce well look let the ...let the tail go with the hide

Another typical feature is reference to people and places that can only be interpreted within the discourse context:

> down like

can only be interpreted if you know that the speaker means down stream on the Williams River.

> down there

only makes sense if you imagine the speaker pointing out the direction of the seven acres that are threatened.

This is an 'us'/'them' text, which is constructed from the 'us' point of view, with 'them' impinging on our space. The only example of a word using a bureaucratic register is a reference to something that 'they' will do to 'us':

> 'spose they'll *notify* us

Notifying is something that they do to us, bureaucracies do to ordinary people, as this choice of words signifies.

The speaker here specifically points out that the language of the written bureaucratic notification goes over her head:

> we've had . . . oh . . . had letters from them . . . but oh gosh eh . . .
> they . . . well the letters they write are way over your head . . . you
> know er . . . about this and about something else

The following written text, a letter from the bureaucracy concerning the proposed dam, is an example of just this:

Written text

Dear Ms Sylvia,
I am writing to acknowledge your further letter in regard to the proposed Tillegra Dam.

I share your concern for losses to the local dairy and beef industries which will arise from future dam construction at Tillegra. You must appreciate however that the Government is obliged to take into account all the likely effects of each alternate proposal when making any decision with such far-reaching consequences. Economic, social and environmental impacts must be examined not only on a local base but regionally and, if applicable, at a State-wide level. Not the least of these considerations is the need for an economical and reliable source of water to the people and industry of the Lower Hunter. The decision favouring Tillegra was based on the widest considerations. The Government has accepted that Tillegra is the right choice. You may of course be assured that every effort will be made to minimise negative impacts of the scheme. In comparing the Johnson's Creek/Karuah option with Tillegra, the results of

broad-based consideration indicated that the overall impact on the
environment was similar if not somewhat greater for the Johnson's
Creek/Karuah case than for Tillegra. On a simple economic comparison
the result was quite clear, with costs favouring Tillegra by 38%
on a discounted cash-flow basis and by 18% on the unit cost of
production of water.

The alternative which you mention, construction of a large dam
at Chichester, has been examined in detail. The existence of an
ancient landslide area above the left abutment of the present dam
has posed serious problems about the safety of any structure with
a significantly higher water level. Even if an engineering solution
could be found, the costs involved would be prohibitive. Part of
the overall scheme for the Tillegra project does include the priority
enlargement of the existing Grahamstown Reservoir. Raising the full
supply level at Grahamstown by about 1.5 metres will add some
36,000 megalitres or twice the capacity of the Chichester Dam. This
additional water will be drawn from the existing flow of the Williams
River, which will later be supplemented by water stored at Tillegra.

One of the interesting features of this letter is its *intertextuality*,
or reference to preceding texts. (The concept of intertextuality
has been widely used in literary theory and originates in the
work of Kristeva [cf. Kristeva 1986], referring to the idea that no
text occurs in isolation but must be interpreted in the context of
a web or network of preceding texts.) The letter starts with an
acknowledgement of the recipient's letter, implying it is not the
first, but a 'further letter'.

So important is the intertextual reference to preceding texts here
that one could almost reconstruct the content of Ms Sylvia's letter
from the content of this one:

I share your concern for losses to the local dairy and beef industries
which will arise from future dam construction at Tillegra

suggests that Ms Sylvia argued against the construction of a dam at
Tillegra on the basis of losses to local dairy and beef industries.

The alternative which you mention, construction of a large dam at
Chichester, has been examined in detail

suggests that the letter started by an argument against the proposed dam at Tillegra, followed by a suggestion of an alternative.
Using knowledge as to how such letters from bureaucratic sources
might be organized, it is possible to reconstruct the letter that Ms
Sylvia might have written.

Although the letter starts in an I/you mode, acknowledging Ms Sylvia's letter and purporting to share its sentiments, it very quickly shifts the 'doer' role to 'the Government', and rebuts Ms Sylvia's arguments with a number of appeals to wider factors than the points of view of the inhabitants of the area threatened by the Tillegra dam construction.

The letter also contains a number of typical features of the bureaucratic written mode, such as nominalizations:

The existence of an ancient landslide area above the left abutment of the present dam

The decision favouring Tillegra

the results of broad-based consideration

and passive constructions:

construction of a large dam at Chichester, *has been examined* in detail

in which it is not made clear who did the examining. The reader is left to conclude that it has been done by a bureaucratic 'they' such as intrudes into the spoken text quoted above.

These and many other features combine to make up the typical written texture of this letter.

It is, of course, important to bear in mind that the above texts exemplify typical aspects of spoken and written language and that the features described can be found distributed across genres and texts in both the spoken and written modes. For example, repetition and the dramatization of speech exchanges is a feature of fictional narrative. In fact researchers such as Polanyi (1985) and Tannen (1989) have made direct comparisons between aspects of the rhetorical organization of spoken language and literary language. Similarly, public, spoken discourse regularly displays features typical of written language, as the following case study based on Masing's study of literacy practices in a ni-Vanuatu village (Masing 1992) shows.

Case study: a ministerial speech

Masing describes how a minister came to give a speech in the village where she was doing her fieldwork on the need to develop land for agricultural purposes. Feeling that the language used in the speech was going over the heads of the village audience, she carried out a small naturalistic experiment by taping the speech and playing it back to members of the village community, pausing the tape at intervals to ask them how much they understood and what they thought that portions of it meant.

The speech was delivered in Bislama, and here are some examples of utterances that were not understood:

1   *Yufala i gat potential blong developmen ples ia* (Bislama)
You have the potential to develop this area (English translation)

The meaning was not clear, although one person said that 'to develop' means something you do to make it go up.

2   *Polici olsem i adresem situation bilong yumi tedei* (Bislama)
This type of policy addresses our present situation (English translation)

This sentence, similar to the bureaucratic discourse of the Tillegra letter quoted above, places the policy in the 'doer' position. Those questioned said they did not understand what it meant.

3   *Niu direcsen we yumi wantem tekem* (Bislama)
The new direction we want to take up (English translation)

Apart from its derivation from the learned Latin-based lexicon of English, 'direcsen' is used here in a metaphorical sense: it is not direction in geographical space, but rather in the conceptual space of policy formation and implementation (compare the use of 'broad' and 'wide' in the letter to Ms Sylvia).

The above example shows how some 'written-like' language features can occur in spoken language. The government minister was using a language register that drew heavily on abstract terms ('potential', 'developmen', 'policy', 'adresem', 'situation', 'direcsen') and conceptualized the abstract space of policy formation.

Discussion point

Look back at the two Tillegra texts. In what ways do they refer to space? In order to read the letter, you need a map of New South Wales in your head (geographical space) as well as the ability to conceptualize a three-tiered organizational structure – local/regional/state (bureaucratic space). What is the space referred to in the oral text?

To put it another way. Suppose you were asked to draw visual representations to accompany the two texts, what might suggest themselves? For the oral text, it might be perhaps a map of the farm, or even a sketch of the land in its relationship to the house. In the case of the letter, the visual representation might be a map of the state, with administrative entities indicated visually. Some of the facts and figures quoted could be represented in diagrams and charts.

Consider now the misunderstanding between Billy and the Librarian as to the meaning of 'the Borough'. Billy and the Librarian live in different conceptual spaces.

SOME OTHER DIMENSIONS OF LANGUAGE USE

Changing technologies can dramatically alter the shape of communicative practices, both spoken and written, simply by altering particular variables in the communicative context. Take, for example, the face-to-face meeting in a workplace or elsewhere, with its typical roles of chairperson, secretary, its distribution of communicative roles, in both spoken and written modes, the mechanisms by which participants bid for space to contribute, the different distribution of rights to talk.

Now shift the frame somewhat and imagine a group linked up in a teleconference. What will be the differences? One of the most salient differences will be that participants can no longer rely on the visual channel and a whole range of paralinguistic features for organizing the conduct of the meeting. One mechanism for establishing a turn to speak in a face-to-face meeting is to catch the chairperson's eye, or through a gesture, like raising a finger to indicate a desire to speak. Such a mechanism is not available once the mode of communication shifts from face-to-face, with a consequent loss of visual communication. The whole mechanism for ensuring turn-taking in the meeting will have to be radically different.

In this section we will look at the effect of some of these variables on the organization of spoken and written discourse.

Stubbs's 'theory of transitions' involved in becoming literate include a number of other dimensions of language use, which we can consider in this context. He presents the following dimensions:

casual/formal
spontaneous/planned
private/public

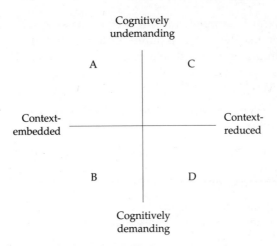

Figure 4.1   Range of contextual support and degree of cognitive involvement in communicative activities (Cummins and Swain 1986)

Two other relevant dimensions are contained in the Cummins
BICS/CALP (Basic Interpersonal Communication Skills/Cognitively
Advanced Language Proficiency) framework for determining language proficiency (Cummins and Swain 1986). Hood (1990) dis-
cusses its application to the understanding of literacy. These
dimensions are:

cognitively undemanding/cognitively demanding
context embedded/ context reduced

If we superimpose the spoken/written dimension in the form
of a grid, we can begin to develop limit cases, illustrating the
functional variability of spoken and written language.

An example of a casual, spontaneous, private, cognitively undemanding, context-embedded use of spoken language might be a
request at the breakfast table:

Pass the butter

A casual, spontaneous, private, cognitively undemanding, context
embedded use of written language might be a message left on
the fridge:

Don't forget to buy butter.

or even:

Butter!

which would be enough for a reader possessing relevant shared knowledge to interpret as a reminder to buy butter.

An example of a formal, planned, public, cognitively demanding, context reduced use of written language might be the minutes of a meeting:

> It was noted that figures on butter sales would be available at the next meeting.

An example of a formal, planned, public, cognitively demanding, context-reduced use of spoken language might be a lecture or seminar presentation:

> One thing I'd like to say at this point is that our research shows that consumption of butter in this population is well above the national average.

A given communicative event may well be a mix or blend of some of these variables. For example, a public lecture (entitled perhaps 'Some additional reflections on the butter question') might involve out-loud reading of a prepared text, extemporized sections in which the lecturer improvises on the theme, prepared overhead transparencies, off-the-cuff use of a white or blackboard, or asides referring to aspects of the immediate context of situation. While the dimension 'public' holds constant, virtually every other one can be varied.

Characterizing task difficulty

As Hood (1990) suggests, the BICS/CALP dimensions can be used as a way of characterizing task difficulty. The left-hand variable will, all other things being equal, represent that which is relatively easier. In other words, cognitively undemanding, context-embedded language uses (spoken and written) will tend to be simpler in relationship to cognitively demanding, context-reduced uses of language.

It is, of course, possible to imagine circumstances when this will not be the case. An obvious and not uncommon one is when a learner has learned another language primarily in its written form and finds extreme difficulty in communicating orally in everyday casual contexts, while being at home in written, public mode. Language which is highly context-embedded poses its own problems, as anyone starting a new job in a new place of work, and discovering many context-specific work practices and uses of language, will be aware. This may be a typical situation for particular types of second-language learner, in which case their communicative repertoire needs extension in the casual, unplanned, informal areas (cf. Slade and Norris (1985) on casual conversation). We can therefore treat the relative easiness of the left-hand variable as the unmarked case, while acknowledging that in certain circumstances and for certain types of learner the ordering of difficulty may be quite different.

Activity

> Work through some combinations of the variables presented above, trying to find examples of how they might be realized: e.g., what might be an informal, planned, private, cognitively demanding, context-reduced use of spoken or written language? Are there any combinations which are unlikely or impossible?

THE ROLE OF SPOKEN LANGUAGE IN LITERACY DEVELOPMENT

When we looked at literacy as social practice in Chapter 2, we found that in many contexts literacy practices were typically orally embedded: reading and writing were not individual, solitary activities, but occurred in contexts where meanings were actively negotiated by groups of people using spoken language. Nowhere is this more true than in the classroom, where reading and writing is typically preceded and accompanied by a whole range of oral contextualizations.

If we leave a tape-recorder running in a literacy classroom, we find first of all that the classroom is a place created through talk: in the ways that the teacher opens and closes activities, the ways that students intervene and participate, the ways that the different roles of teacher and student constrain and shape the ways in which classroom interaction develops. Although the literacy classroom is focused on written language, spoken language constantly impinges on its activities.

TEACHER TALK

If the focus is on the participation of the teacher, we need to examine teacher talk: the ways in which the teacher uses

spoken language to set up activities, to move from one phase
of an activity to another, to organize the work of a group into
purposeful learning. In the following extract, following a lengthy
discussion in a literacy classroom on the topic of child abuse , the
teacher tries to move from the oral mode of discussion towards
the written mode:

> T: we've said quite a lot actually i don't know whether it's ten to
> eight em not that that matters very much em whether we want to
> try and write something down about because we've said quite a lot
> about child abuse really em
>
> (unpublished data from Wendy Moss)

What the teacher is trying to do here (in a very hedged and
tentative way, in which the use of the pronoun 'we' appears to
neutralize the student/teacher role differentiation) is move the
activity on from a fairly free-flowing, open discussion within
the group, in which she was by no means the most dominant
participant, into doing a piece of writing on the topic. Strategies
for introducing activities, moving them on from stage to stage and
concluding them are normally the responsibility of the teacher.
Expectations placed on the students will vary from stage to
stage. Here is a description of the writing classroom, based on
a participant observation study (Gardener 1988) which captures
the relationship between talk and writing development:

> I heard more talk than I saw writing, and the talk was about new
> subject matter as well as about learning processes and processes for
> reproducing what is learned. The vexed question of the transition
> from anecdote to analysis raised itself through the styles of classroom
> talk as much as through writing. These are classrooms that use and
> value discussion, and where students and tutors make contributions
> that approach equal and reciprocal status at times. (They are not
> wholly equal, whatever the rhetoric of adult education tells us: I
> think there are no tapes which would present a new listener with
> difficulty in assigning tutor and student roles, and I witnessed one
> occasion when a student took on functions more usually exercised
> by the teacher, like questioning time use and asking why certain
> data were being presented, which produced an interestingly high
> level of stress.)
>
> (Gardener 1988)

It is interesting in the light of what Gardener says about teacher/
student roles to imagine the utterance quoted from the literacy

teacher above if it was spoken by a student. Coming from a student the suggestion of moving from talk to writing might, in that case, read like a not so subtle criticism: 'we've done all this talking, what about some writing?'

However subtly achieved, the social differentiation of teacher/ student roles is a significant variable in classroom organization. It should be part of a teacher's critical equipment to be able to monitor the ways in which they organize the literacy classroom as an interactive environment. Gardener concludes that observation and monitoring of classroom practice is a valuable way of gaining this critical awareness:

> My last comment on the classroom observations is simply to underline the value of observation and taping as a way of finding out what we all do in classrooms, and the variety of ways in which language issues in particular are present. It takes time and willingness to expose yourself to surprise, but it is a method of working that is available to tutors for development of their awareness and skills.
>
> (Gardener 1988)

Activity

In the following extract, the teacher (Jane) is jointly constructing a Nasreddin Hoca folk story with two Turkish students (Figen and Shoray). Shoray is telling the story to Figen in Turkish, Figen is telling it to Jane. The whole communicative event is a prelude to writing the story:

FIGEN: Nasreddin Hoca is really a man.
JANE: He's a . . .?
FIGEN: Really . . . and he died Aksehir . . .
JANE: Ah . . . he was a real man.
FIGEN: Yes.
JANE: When?
FIGEN: Long time ago (SHORAY: Yes.) Yes.
JANE: And where did he live?
FIGEN: Turkey . . . Aksehir.
SHORAY: Aksehir.
JANE: Do you know more about him, Shoray?
SHORAY: I know . . .
JANE: Can't you . . . all right, tell it, tell it to Figen.
SHORAY: (speaks Turkish)
JANE: Can you tell it, Figen?

FIGEN: W¹ at do you call water . . .?
SHORAY Floor.
JANE: W ter?
SHORA : Garden, garden, no house.
JANE: A pond, when you have water in the garden?
SHORAY: Yes.
FIGEN: Like a pond, but, you know . . .
SHORAY: Inside.
JANE: In the house?
FIGEN: No, garden.
SHORAY: Garden, yes.
FIGEN: Like a pond, and you get water . . .
JANE: Oh, you mean . . . for . . . to drink? A hole, the well, a well.
When you put a bucket in (SHORAY: Yes!) and you bring the,
yes . . . It's called a well.
SHORAY: *(speaks Turkish)*
FIGEN: It was a night time, Nasreddin went to the . . .
JANE: To the well *(writes on board)*.
SHORAY: Yes! Well.
FIGEN: To get some water (JANE: Yes.) And he saw the moon.
SHORAY: Water, you know, moon, night.
JANE: Yes. In the water.
FIGEN: He thought he pulls (SHORAY: Out.) the moon (JANE:
Yes.) and he pulls, and the rope . . .
SHORAY: *(speaks Turkish)*
FIGEN: He said very heavy (JANE: Yes.) and . . . he thought he
pulls the moon . . .
JANE: He thought he'd pulled the moon . . . out of the water.
FIGEN: And pulled, and pulls, pulls and he . . .
SHORAY: *(speaks Turkish)* Broken.
FIGEN: The rope.
SHORAY: *(speaks Turkish)*r
JANE: The rope broke.
FIGEN and SHORAY: Yes.
FIGEN: He lays down.
SHORAY: . . . up and after see . . . *(speaks Turkish)*
JANE: So he fell over.
FIGEN: Yes, he fell over; when he fells over, he lay down, and he
saw the moon . . .
SHORAY: On the sky.
FIGEN: In the sky . . . and he thought he pulled the moon out.
(Laughter from class)

(Data from McLaughlin 1986)

Questions

1 In what ways are Jane, Figen and Shoray collaborating to get this story told?
2 Look at Jane's moves. What 'teacher-work' is she doing?

The example above is drawn from literacy work with bilingual students, with relatively restricted command of English. The classroom focus on spoken language is unproblematic here. The situation is somewhat different in a class drawn mainly or entirely from monolingual students, in which the spoken language is somehow assumed, taken as given, however much it informs, as we have seen, every aspect of the ongoing work of the literacy classroom. Yet Gardener writes:

> I am increasingly convinced that it will help if we recognize that the adult classroom is itself a new social situation of the kind that extends people's language use and their capacity to generalize, sequence and pursue cause and effect, to identify only a few of the skills that systematic study demands. We may need to teach discussion itself more deliberately.

> (Gardener 1988: 108)

So how do students participate in oral interaction in the literacy classroom?

STUDENT TALK

In the 'traditional' classroom (cf. Cope 1986, and Cope and Kalantzis 1990), the teacher retains a very rigid control over the content of teaching and the way in which it is organized. In terms of its interactional structure, the typical pattern is a series of moves involving

Teacher initiation (I)
Student response (R)
Teacher feedback (F)

for example:

T: How do you spell Australia?
S: umm A-U-S-T-R-A-L-I-A.
T: That's right, well done!

(cf. Sinclair and Brazil 1982; Sinclair and Coulthard 1975; Coulthard 1992)

As will be clear from what Gardener has to say about the

organization of the literacy classroom, there has been a conscious attempt in the practice of adult literacy teaching to shift the balance of power in the classroom away from the traditional teacher-control mode, towards a situation in which the rights to speak and participate are more equally distributed.

Crude quantitative measures of this interactional shift would simply be an increase in the amount of time that students held the floor. Nunan (1989) points out that classroom observation tends to confirm that teachers do most of the talking, and certainly the most powerful kinds of talking, to do with framing activities, nominating topics, nominating others to speak, and so on.

An emphasis on participation, on the contextualization of educational work, makes oral discussion central to the literacy process.

A discussion on child abuse in a literacy group

In the following extract, from a discussion on child abuse, prior to writing on that topic, the teacher (T) is playing an ambiguous role, both as participant in the discussion and as shaper of its outcomes:

T: and there's this thing about not interfering isn't there that
neighbours don't like to
C: well not like they used to do they used to do they used to do
didn't they
T: do you think so   5
C: the neighbours used to be more friendly than they used to be
nowadays
K: mmm
C: they used to come and have a cup of tea with you and sit
on the doorstep and sit and have a natter and sit and watch   10
television till 12 o'clock in the house with you know your neighbours
K: like coronation street (laughs)
C: but now its very very rare you see your neighbour
K: yeah
C: you know you'll be lucky if you see your neighbour one   15
day t' next only she's going to the shop
T: mmm
K: and a lot of people think if you sort of say and are you all right
and you go around and say do you want any help they think
you're being   20
C: being nosey now
K: or funny but you know you know

T: whereas before people were lived in each other's pockets that
K: that's it that's right
C: yeah yeah   25
T: yes I suppose that gave the children a bit more protection cos
you couldn't hide behind closed doors as much
                              (unpublished data from Wendy Moss)

Activity

> Summarize in your own words (in writing) the points made in the
> above discussion about changes in relationship between neighbours
> in recent years and the ways that might impinge on the safety of
> children from abuse.
>   When you have done this, compare what you have written to the
> discussion. What spoken/written mode differences do you find in the
> two texts?

In this extract, as I have suggested, the teacher manages a double role, both as conversational participant and shaper of the
interaction, in the direction of written work. In the early part
of the interaction, C clearly has the floor, in that she takes up
T's topic nomination (neighbours who don't like to interfere),
but also expands it into a contrast between before and now. K
collaborates with C's contribution to the discussion, contributing
the odd comment that does not interfere with the flow of C's turn
(for example, line 12), until line 18, when K takes a substantial
turn, which itself flows on quite smoothly from C's previous
contributions, while C takes the role of contributing additional
comments. T's final contribution is in the direction of bringing the
transaction back onto topic (not just 'neighbours', but 'neighbours
in the context of a discussion on child abuse').

The whole of the extract quoted is in a mode of 'situated
generalization' (cf. Baynham 1988), common in informal conversation. Participants are talking sociologically, about generals not
particulars, but are using the particular as a means of generalizing
their experience. In the following section –

> the neighbours used to be more friendly than they used to be
> nowadays they used to come and have a cup of tea with you and sit
> on the doorstep and sit and have a natter and sit and watch television
> till 12 o'clock in the house with you you know your neighbours

– the organization has some narrative-like features on the generic
level, with an *abstract*:

> the neighbours used to be more friendly than they used to be
> nowadays

an *event structure*, or *complicating action*:

> they used to come and have a cup of tea with you and sit on the
> doorstep and sit and have a natter and sit and watch television till 12
> o'clock in the house with

a *coda*:

> you know your neighbours

Yet other features of the canonical narrative are not present. The subject is not person-specific (my neighbour/s) but generalized (neighbours in general). The aspect selection of 'used to' is iterative, representing a sequence of events as recurring typically, another generalizing strategy. These speakers are using aspects of narrativity to situate generalization in oral discourse.

K's interjected comment –

> like coronation street

– itself completely topic-coherent, is also very interesting. In making an explicit reference to a well-known soap opera, whose organizing theme is precisely to portray a society of neighbours, living in one another's pockets, in one another's houses till 12 o'clock, K is adding a dimension of intertextuality to the discussion, the locus of which is in a kind of proto-literary discourse.

What is significant at this point is that the discussion is itself tending towards different kinds of abstraction, trailing the possibility of a number of more abstract discourses (the sociology of neighbourhoods in the late twentieth century, soap operas as a genre). In an everyday conversation these little theoretical flashes would normally go unnoticed, but in the framework of an educational discourse they serve as nodal points through which entry into more abstract discourses becomes possible.

It is now possible to address some of the issues raised in Gardener's research which, while emphasizing the importance of discussion, also recognizes the need for transitions into other modes of discourse. This is only possible through an increased understanding of the nature and organization of oral discourse and the kinds of situated theorizing that can go in casual conversation. This situated theorizing can be made the basis for a more explicit introduction of theoretical discourses: how would a sociologist talk/write about these issues, how would a literary theorist or semiotician deal with the presentation of neighbourliness in Coronation Street or other soaps?

Activity

Imagine that you as a teacher were going to move this small group discussion into writing. What kinds of written genres do you see as potentially underlying the above discussion?

FATHERS AND SONS AT WORK

In the next extract, a group of teenage Moroccan boys are discussing issues raised by a reading of a story by a teenage Bangladeshi, Mahabur Rahman (Rahman 1975), in which a young boy working in his father's clothing factory gets into trouble with his father when he surreptitiously tries to make a jacket in which to go to a party.

T: so if you were a father
S1: yeah
T: with a son
S1: yeah
T: how would you treat him
S1: well all these fathers here all these boys here these young boys if when they going grow up they going to treat their children like not like these fathers now they hard innit I mean they not all of them but
S2: yes I know what you mean
S1: rigid I mean
S2 very strict very strict very stiff
S1: like we we know what it's like we we know like we say
S3: listen listen don't say that because
S1: we want to do
S3: they had you dad had the same experience when he was young
S4: no
S1: that was look those days those days no cinema no nothing all right those days only
S4: when you grow up right you'll be
S2: does your father let you go to the cinema
S1: yeah this is it
S4: listen I'll tell you something
S2: does your father let you go to the cinema
S4: listen listen

The organization of this transaction starts with a clearly nominated topic from the teacher, so to that extent there is a significant degree of teacher control in the shaping of the interaction, but the way it develops has its own dynamic and seems largely independent of the teacher. Student 1 responds by articulating a point of view which can be glossed as:

> These boys growing up now will treat their sons differently (i.e., less harshly) than their fathers did.

Student 2 seems to be playing a back-up role to Student 1, agreeing with his point of view and trying to gloss Student 1's search for the right word to describe the father:

> hard . . . rigid . . . very strict . . . very stiff

Student 3 comes into the discussion with another point of view, which can be reconstructed as:

> Your dad went through exactly the same experience when he was young (i.e., of having a harsh father) so, if that didn't make him less strict with you, it is unlikely to make you less strict with your children

Students 1 and 2 then dispute this position, while Student 4 tries to gain space in the discussion for his contribution and matters become somewhat heated.

While the previous extract seemed to present a discussion that was accomplished in a highly cooperative way (in terms of the tenor of the relationship between participants), this extract seems to be best interpreted in terms of competition for communicative space, with allies and competitors pitted against one another. Student 4 bids for space with

> when you grow up right you'll be

and is cut across by Student 2:

> does your father let you go to the cinema

with support from Student 1:

> yeah this is it

Student 4 tries to gain the floor again with

> listen I'll tell you something

while student 2 recycles his question (a powerful strategy for holding a place in the interaction, as any listener to parliamentary question time will confirm):

does your father let you go to the cinema

The extract ends with Student 4 still trying to gain the floor.

The tenor of the interaction in these two extracts illustrates two crucial poles in conversational organization: *cooperation* and *conflict*. Of the two, we have to assume, with Habermas (1979), on both logical and ideological grounds, that cooperation is the most basic, since even to dispute with words one must invoke the basic cooperative mechanisms of gaining and giving attention, otherwise you are disputing with yourself! While not being chosen to illustrate this particular point, it is interesting to note that the first extract, an adult, all-women group, exhibited the cooperative conversational behaviour, while the teenage males exhibited the conflict behaviour. This is in keeping with a wide range of sociolinguistic findings on gender differences in communicative interaction (cf. Cameron 1985).

Activity

Summarize in writing the arguments put forward about the relationships between father and son in the above text. Now compare your summary with the ways in which the participants in discussion organized what they had to say.

Look back to the material on similarities and differences between spoken and written language. How do the two texts, the original discussion and your summary of it, illustrate differences between spoken and written language?

BILINGUAL CODE-SWITCHING IN THE CLASSROOM

In a case study of bilingual code-switching in a language class-room, Chau (1991) analyses how a group of Cantonese speakers make purposeful use of their L1 to negotiate meaning in learning tasks (see Figure 4.2).

The example from Chau's data shows a group of students working on a literacy task. They are reading in English, but using both English and Cantonese to clarify aspects of the task: information, word meaning and metalinguistic terms such as 'abbreviation'. The only participant to select English throughout is yk; the other three participants select between Cantonese and English, with Mary showing a preference for Cantonese (out of

Transcription 9

This group of learners were matching newspaper ads on accommodation (cut out in strips) with floor plans (given on a cardboard). Each learner could read the ads individually and then decide which floor plan to match it with.

This is an all-Chinese group of 4 Cantonese speakers.
The seating arrangement is illustrated below.

1 yk   : Two-bedroom . . . two-bedroom . . . [reading to herself]
2 Mary   : [to kl] 房，睡房，第一那个不就是有一个房嘛。
             (Room is bedroom . . . the first one has one bedroom.)
3 yk   : Altogether . . . altogether . . .
4 Mary   : [to kl] 哪！这里就是有一个房啦！
             (Look, here . . . there's one bedroom.)
5 yk   : here?
6 Mary   : [to kl] 只一个房…
             (one bedroom only . . .)
7 sy   : 这个简写…
             (This is abbreviation . . .)
8 kl   : Three-beds . . . 三个房的 house.
             (Three-beds . . . three-bedroom house.)
9 yk   : here. [putting the ad on the relevant floor plan]
10 sy   : 这里，这里没有家私。
             (Here, there's no furniture here.)
11 kl   : 总之这两个是有一个房啦！
             (These two have one bedroom.)
12   : 2-bedroom . . .
13 yk   : 2-bedroom? Here . . . 2-bedroom.
14 kl   : 2-bedroom.
15 yk   : here.
16 kl   : 2-bedroom.
17 yk   : 2-bedroom . . . here.
             [picked up another ad]
18   : Modern . . . modern . . . the modern [referring to floor
19   : plan b] . . . sofa . . . maybe . . . maybe sofa . . .
20 sy   : lux . . . lux . . . luxury [reading an ad to herself]
21 Mary   : 这个有家私！
             (This one has furniture!)
22 sy   : 有家私，又近一点。
             (With furniture, and it's closer.)
23 Mary   : 这个有家私。

Figure 4.2

Figure 4.2 continued

```
                (This one has furniture.)
24  yk     : Here.
25  Mary   : No.
26  kl     : 有家私的，在这里。
                (With furniture, it is here.)
27  Mary   : [to sy] 有家私嘛！
                (This one has furniture!)
28  sy     : [to Mary, pointing to another floor plan]
                这个没有。
                (This one has none.)
29  yk     : How many . . . how many bedrooms?
30  Mary   : [to kl] 这个是家私，即是这里很多呀。
                (This is furniture . . . it means there are many items.)
31  sy     : Two.
32  Mary   : Two.
33  yk     : Here . . . here . . . two.
34  Mary   : 有家私啦！
                (This one has furniture.)
35  kl     : 家私（？）钱。
                (Furniture . . . [inaudible] . . . money.)
36  yk     : Here . . . maybe sofa . . . em . . . 3-bedroom . . .
37  sy     : 3-bedroom . . .

[tape 6 side 1 #258 – 286]
```

eight turns at speaking, seven are in Cantonese and one is in English), sy showing out of four turns, three turns in Cantonese, and one in English and kl showing out of five turns, three turns in Cantonese and two turns in English.

One of the anxieties of monolingual teachers about code-switching in the classroom is that students will not remain on task and that the teacher's control over the development of interaction is lost. Chau's data show that students can use their L1 in purposeful ways to negotiate meaning in language tasks, in this case involving reading in English.

THE INTERACTION OF SPOKEN AND WRITTEN LANGUAGE IN THE LITERACY EVENT

The above examples of oral interaction in the classroom emphasize the grounding of written work in spoken language and link back to material in Chapter 2, which demonstrated the interaction of spoken and written language in literacy practices outside the classroom. You will recall that, in writing of the literacy event, Heath suggests that 'literacy events have social interactional rules which regulate the type and amount of *talk* about what is written, and define ways in which *oral language* reinforces, denies, extends, or sets aside the written material'. In that chapter, we characterized the relationship between speech and writing in terms of interactions in contexts of use. We also noted that there is a limit to what ethnographic observation can tell us about literacy events, unless it is accompanied by a close-grained analysis of the discourse that constitutes them.

In *Ways with Words*, Heath writes that 'in almost every situation in Trackton in which a piece of writing is integral to the nature of participants' interaction and their interpretation of meaning, talk is a necessary component'. She goes on to point out that 'for Trackton adults, reading is a social activity; when something is read in Trackton, it almost always provokes narratives, jokes, sidetracking talk and active negotiation of the meaning of written texts among listeners'. She describes the way in which the evening newspaper is read:

> The evening newspaper is read on the front porch for most months
> of the year. The obituaries on the back page are usually read
> first, followed by employment listing, advertisements for grocery
> and department store sales, and captions beneath pictures and
> headlines. An obituary is read for some trace of an acquaintance
> with either the deceased, his relatives, place of birth, church, or
> school; active discussion follows about who the individual was
> and who he might have known. Circulars or letters to individuals
> regarding the neighbourhood center and its recreational or medical
> services are read aloud and their meanings jointly negotiated
> by those who have had experience with such activities or know
> about the forms to be filled out to be eligible for such services.
> Neighbours share stories of what they did or what happened to
> them in similar circumstances.
>
> (Heath 1983: 196)

She describes how Lillie Mae, a Trackton resident, receives an official letter about a day-care project and how neighbours are drawn into a discussion that lasts nearly an hour, pooling their experience of such projects, discussing the pros and cons. Reading leads naturally to narrative and the pooling of experience. 'Lillie Mae, reading aloud, decoded the written text, but her friends and neighbours interpreted the text's meaning through their own experiences' (Heath 1983:197).

These examples give ample evidence of the mix of the oral and the literate in situated interactions around text. Lillie Mae's aloud reading is accompanied by the oral interpretations of her friends and neighbours. This is what we will call *mode-switching*. One of the problems in deepening our analysis at this point is the nature of the data: ethnographic data tend towards summarizing and generalizing interactions; rarely does it present the reader with transcripts of situated interactions, from which information about the fine grain of detailed interactional patterns can be derived. We know what Lillie Mae and her friends and neighbours were engaged in, but we don't know exactly *how* they were engaged in it: were they indeed code-switching between different varieties of English? We can guess that they may have been, but the ethnographic vignette does not yield sufficient linguistic detail for the sociolinguistic analysis of strips of discourse. It seems to me that, at the point in which good ethnographic descriptions of literacy practices can be achieved, the role of linguistic analysis must be to pinpoint the communicative resources available to speakers/readers/writers and provide good descriptions of the social interactional rules that constitute the literacy event and its embedding in specific social contexts.

The ethnographic vignette can tell us that there is an interaction between spoken and written language in the literacy event, but it can't tell us how that interaction is organized: in order to get at the interactional rules that Heath talks about, we have to examine the ways in which literacy events are constructed in discourse, which implies obtaining tape-recorded or video-recorded data of discourse.

In this chapter we have characterized the relationship between speech and writing in linguistic terms. The question arises: how can we use linguistically based knowledge about the organization of spoken and written language to deepen our understanding of the ways that speech and writing interact in context? In this section, we will be using data from a literacy event in a multilingual context (the 'Letter from the DHSS' introduced in Chapter 2), to characterize some aspects of the interaction between spoken and written language in linguistic terms. We will be looking at *code-switching*, a term familiar from the literature on bilingualism and two other constructs, already referred to informally in the course of this chapter, which are derived from the code-switching construct: *mode-switching* and *register-switching*. Murray (1988) looks at mode- and medium-switching in the literary practices involved in the use of the computer as a medium of communication. These constructs are briefly defined as follows:

Code-switching

> Conversational code-switching can be defined as the juxtaposition within the same speech exchange of passages of speech belonging to two different grammatical systems or subsystems.
>
> (Gumperz 1982: 59)

Mode-switching

> Mode-switching can be defined as the juxtaposition within the same speech exchange of different linguistic modes (i.e., spoken and written).

Register-switching

> Register-switching can be defined as the juxtaposition within the same speech exchange of different registers (i.e., technical/non-technical).

In the next extracts I will look at some real-time strips of interaction from the 'literacy-event-in-progress' which was introduced in Chapter 2 to see how discourse analysis can complement the dimensions of ethnographic and oral history enquiry into literacy practices.

In Extract (a) I read the letter which Menana has received from the Department of Health and Social Security and tell her the gist of it. In Extract (b), Menana successfully challenges my suggestion that she should take the letter to a Moroccan worker at the Citizens' Advice Bureau, and I agree to write a letter of appeal for her. In Extract (c) I attempt to reconstruct the story of what actually happened, in order to write the letter of appeal. In Extract (d) I read back the reply that I have written.

A letter from the Department of Health and Social Security: extracts from the data

M = Menana; T = Touria; I = Interviewer

EXTRACT (a) *PARAPHRASING THE DHSS LETTER FOR MENANA*
HER RESPONSE TO IT
MY STRATEGY FOR RESPONDING: GO AND SEE SOUAD
    I: department of health and social security
    M: yeah what's happen
    I: supplementary benefit . . . oh dear . . .
    M: what's happen Mike
    I: it says they've give you too much supplementary benefit too
    much money
    M: social security no much give it to me because I'm pay the rent
    twenty six pounds twenty four pounds for the rent still to me
    twenty onlo give me this . . .
    T: /snu 'andhum/(*What's wrong?*)
    I: it says they've given you ninety six pounds too much
    M: nooh never give me ninety six . . . give me every week
    I: yeah
    M: the book I'm give him the book straight
    I: it says they wanted you to give the book back when you started
    work
    M: yeah I'm give him the book back when me start work . . .
    straight . . .
    I: mmm . . . do you know what I think you ought to do
    M: yeah
    I: is a problem like this is a bit difficult you know is a difficult
    problem you ought to erm do you know Soud who works in the
    office there
    T: yeah Souad
    M: yeah Souad yeah
    I: if you go and see her and then ask her to write a letter cos you
    have to you have to write a letter to say this is wrong
    M: s a wrong
    T: mm
    I: it's called an appeal you have to make an appeal . . . let me just
    tell you I'll tell you exactly what the letter says it says dear madam
    I'm sorry to tell you that you have been paid ninety six pounds
    too much because of you didn't give the book back when you
    started work
    M: yeah I'm give him straight
    I: straight away

M: yeah
T: yes
I: it says you can (. . .)
M: no I'm give him straight the book
T: straight on when she (. . .) she give him straight on
M: (. . .)give him straight away the lady take with me cut the book
I: straight away
T: yes
M: yeah straight away
I: because they says that you didn't they say here that you didn't do it
M: nooh do it straight first week call first week after give him me collect the money friday I'm give him monday
T: monday (. . .)
M: no no no no take the money monday I'm leave the money in the book I'm give him
T: because she off monday and she start work
M: yeah
T: she start work
M: no
T: (. . .) she get first week for her work the first week is friday
M: yeah
T: she get her money and then (. . .)
M: (. . .)
T: and monday she go straight away she don't go to post office to take money she go straight on to give him his book because she have money now

The first phase of this extract involves my silent reading of the letter, with the oral accompaniment of reading out loud two key phrases from the letter, 'Department of Health and Social Security', followed by 'Supplementary Benefit' = 'oh dear'. The function of this is to alert Menana to the type of news she should expect from the letter and inform her of where the letter is from and what it concerns. The formula here is

SILENT READING OF TEXT + OUT-LOUD READING AS COMMENT
OR GLOSS

The out-loud reading keys Menana in to the bad news to come.

My third utterance is an example of a different kind of switching, which we call *register-switching*. I switch from the register of official letters 'supplementary benefit' to a simplified paraphrase: 'too much money'. My understanding of that particular switch is that it involved a kind of amplification of the initial utterance, designed to make absolutely clear to Menana the implication of being given too much Supplementary Benefit. The switch is from the technical to the everyday ('Supplementary Benefit' is, of course, a term which is also in everyday use, so it may well be that the register switch employed here was redundant, but there clearly is a switch here, motivated by the interaction around the text).

Further on in the interaction, we find a register switch in the opposite direction, from the everyday paraphrase equivalent of a technical term to the term itself:

> you have to write a letter to say this is wrong it's called an appeal
> you have to make an appeal

Here we start with the simplified form and then switch to the technical expression.

The interaction is punctuated by utterances in which I, the interviewer, provide paraphrases of what the letter says, carefully attributing them (it says . . .) at each point. In the final utterance in this extract, I provide a paraphrase of the whole letter, preceded by the phrase:

> I'll tell you exactly what the letter says

Throughout this strip of interaction I, as reader, am providing paraphrase equivalents of the original text, carefully attributed, so that it is clear that the accusation is contained in the letter and is not one that I am personally responsible for.

We can understand the function of IT SAYS + PARAPHRASE on the analogy of direct and indirect speech. Direct speech claims to report the utterance, or in this case text, both in its surface form and in its content. Indirect speech, however, always involves the reporting not of surface form but of propositional content. The utterance 'I'll tell you exactly what the letter says', followed by a telling that patently isn't an exact reading but a paraphrase, seems in some ways problematic. We can perhaps suggest that the utterance 'I'll tell you exactly' can be glossed as 'this paraphrase will give you exactly the propositional content of the letter, what it *means*'. We begin to see that an interaction which, at first glance seemed like a fairly simple mix of 'the oral' and 'the literate', contains in fact some rather complex shifts and switches of footing in the ways that the text is related orally. It is not far-fetched to see in the interpretative paraphrase which I provide of the text something akin to cross-linguistic interpretation, except in this case it is a question of mode (spoken/written) and register (technical/non-technical).

(b) *MENANA CHALLENGES MY STRATEGY AND I OFFER TO WRITE A RESPONSE FOR HER MYSELF*

> I: well what you should do you have to write a letter saying
> M: this letter look (. . .) send me this letter look this (. . .)
> I: I think it's much better Menana if you take erm take this to see Souad because she understands all the problems
> T: Yes
> I: and what you'll have to do is write a letter saying I returned
> M: what this write letter this letter (. . .) fill this form small
> I: yeah
> T: (. . .)
> M: what she tell him/que quiere decir *(What does that say?)*
> I: pues . . . (. . .) do you want me to write the letter
> M: yeah please
> I: can you tell me I'll start the letter and you can tell me
> M: /empieza a trabajar el dia cinco de abril/ *(I start work on the 5th of April)*

In the earlier part of this interaction strip, I am trying to suggest to Menana the form that her response should take, without committing myself to actually writing it, since my opinion is that she should take it to the CAB so that someone experienced in these matters can deal with it. What Menana is doing throughout the interaction is challenging my advice in a very explicit way, by drawing my attention to the fact, which had escaped me, that there was a section on the form to complete if you wished to appeal. The letter, if such it be, can be written on the form in the space provided. In the middle of this, we find an example of Menana code-switching from English to Spanish in a way much closer to the type of code-switching described by Gumperz, specifically the type he calls *reiteration*:

> Frequently a message in one code is repeated in the other code, either literally or in somewhat modified form. In some cases such repetition may serve to clarify what is said, but often they simply amplify or emphasize a message.
>
> (Gumperz 1982: 78)

It is at this point that I give in and offer to write the letter myself.

(c) *RECONSTRUCTING THE STORY OF WHAT ACTUALLY HAPPENED*

    I: where where did you give /dónde eh dónde trajiste el libro este/
    (where did you take the book?)
    M: social security
    I: /dónde en westbourne grove/ *(Where? In Westbourne Grove?)*
    T: yeah westbourne grove
    M: yeah westbourne grove . . . no no this westbourne grove
    here no no
    I: /el otro/ *(the other one)*
    M: /el otro/ *(the other one)*
    I: /cómo se llama/ *(what's it called?)*
    M: /no sé como se llama/ (I don't know what it's called)
    T: /maši dyel hinaya/ *(not the one round here?)*
    M: nooh the rounjit baker street
    I: lisson grove
    M: yeah this one nearly in baker street
    I: yeah
    M: yeah . . . look the letter where she come from

Once I have agreed to write the letter, an extended stretch of oral interaction is dedicated to getting clear the actual event sequence, the location of events, prior to writing the response to the DHSS letter. This has similarities to a jointly reconstructed story, although its purpose is not just to tell the story, but to serve as information for drafting a response. The story genre is embedded in the letter genre. We note that the oral interaction, which elicits 'the facts', is conducted in English, Spanish and Moroccan Arabic.

(d) *READING THE LETTER BACK TO MENANA AND HER EVALUATION OF THE INCIDENT*

    I: /espera un momentito que yo voy a yo voy a/ *(wait a moment I'm going to I'm going to)*
    M: /bueno/ *(OK)*
    I: /le voy a leer/ *(I'm going to read)* I wish to appeal against your demand of ninety six pound ninety six I returned the book to the office in lisson grove on the 13th of april I started work on the 5th of april I cashed the cheque for the week of the fifth
    M: yeah
    I: because I did not have the money to pay me rent
    M: yeah
    I: to buy food for myself and my daughter
    M: that's it
    I: I did not cash it after that

M: nothing no eat one penny him
I: uh
M: no eat one /no deja a mi/ (*I didn't keep*) one penny s crazy/locos/(*mad*)

After the process of reconstructing the event sequence, I read the letter back to Menana. The reading is embedded in oral interaction in Spanish; indeed, the phrase which introduces the reading back:

lo voy a leer

is in Spanish, followed immediately by a switch into English. This is the category of code-switching which Gumperz calls *quotational*: 'In many instances the code switched passages are clearly identifiable either as direct quotations or as reported speech' (Gumperz 1982: 75–6). This quotational code-switching is very different form the quoting clauses we noted in Extract (a), which were followed by a verbal paraphrase of the text of the letter. The format in Extract (a) was

IT SAYS + PARAPHRASE

The paraphrase involved a kind of translating of the formal technical language of the letter into a more informal, everyday language:

too much supplementary benefit = too much money

as well as translating back from the everyday to the technical:

you have to write a letter to say it's wrong

it's called an appeal you have to make an appeal

The paraphrasing activity in Extract (a) seems to involve *making texts talk*, providing a reading that is in itself a switch from literate to oral, what we have called a mode-switch.

In contrast the out-loud reading of the reply to the DHSS in Extract (d) gives a clearer example of both code-switching and mode-switching at work. The initial clause is in Spanish, but the text read out is in English. 'Le voy a leer' is an oral marker for a strip of 'reading' and a clear instance of mode-switch.

Activity

There are many other communicative contexts where the researcher would find mode-switching and register-switching occurring typically.

A lecture might typically involve the lecturer reading out loud portions of a prepared lecture, extemporizing other sections (that is, mode-switching), and register-switching to define technical terms. In a meeting, a motion to be voted on will be constructed orally, then read back once it is agreed upon. There will be many subtle mode-shifts and switches in this process.

Tape-record a communicative event (for example a lecture), transcribe part of it and try to establish if there are features of mode-switching and register-switching going on, and what that tells you about the interactional organization of the event, including the power relations between participants.

Can mode-switching and register-switching feature in written language, or is it more typically a feature of spoken language?

CONCLUSION

While seeing 'literacy' as a socio-political construct, I have nevertheless argued that it needs to be underpinned by a linguistic theory of (spoken and written) language. Such a theory of language must be contextual, in that it recognizes that language is both embedded in social contexts and in turn constructs those contexts. For example, the language of bureaucracy, such as the Librarian's response to Billy, the letter written to Ms Sylvia concerning the Tillegra Dam, the minister's speech in the ni-Vanuatu village, the letter that Menana received from the DHSS, all construct a particular kind of conceptual space. We have illustrated the discussion with examples of spoken and written language occurring in the public settings of the library and the literacy classroom, as well as in the private, domestic domain of the home.

SUGGESTIONS FOR FURTHER READING

Biber, D. (1988) *Variation across Speech and Writing*, Cambridge: Cambridge University Press.

Halliday, M.A.K. (1985b) *Spoken and Written Language*, Geelong, Victoria: Deakin University Press.

Kress, G. (1989) *Linguistic Processes in Sociocultural Practice*, Oxford: Oxford University Press.

Stubbs, M. (1986) *Educational Linguistics*, Oxford: Blackwell.

Tannen, D. (ed.) (1982) *Spoken and Written Language: Exploring Orality and Literacy*, Norwood, NJ: Ablex.

FIVE

Reading as situated social practice

WHAT CAN A MISREADING TELL US ABOUT THE READING PROCESS?

I am sitting in the bus on the way to work one morning when a poster on a lamppost by the bus stop catches my attention as the bus draws to a halt. Out of the corner of my eye I read the following words:

bag leg hold traps

With a certain amount of puzzlement I look back to the poster, trying to make sense of the message I have 'read'. On second reading, I realize that I had in fact misread the first word, 'ban' as 'bag' (perhaps transposing the final /g/ from 'leg'). I am now in a position to work out a meaning to what on first reading was a jumble of isolated words. The sentence reads:

ban leg hold traps

and I can now work out a grammatical structure to the word list of my first attempt at reading (VERB + Nominal Group), and simultaneously work out that the text of the poster is exhorting the reader to support an activity (banning whatever leg hold traps are). By this time the surrounding text of the poster is beginning to fill in the gaps in my understanding of the original. I catch the word 'demonstration' and a date. The force of the original sentence, read in isolation from the surrounding text, is fleshed out as additional information becomes available to me both from the surrounding text (co-text) and from my own knowledge about the socio-political context in which the reading is embedded.

This additional information is not just verbal. A black and white image in the centre of the poster provides me with a visual representation of a 'leg hold trap' to flesh out my representation

Figure 5.1

of what should be banned. (For an analysis of the interaction of the visual and verbal in text, see Kress and van Leeuwen 1990.)

My own knowledge about the current socio-political context suggests that the use of leg hold traps referred to would be intended for trapping animals, not humans. This leads me to be able to read off an ideological position from the poster: that it comes from an Animal Rights perspective.

I can now 'read' the poster, not just as a sequence of letters and words in an order that I cannot process, nor even as a grammatical sentence to which I can assign a pragmatic force, but as a text which is the articulation of a political stance and an exhortation to the reader to participate in that stance.

This example, originally based on a mis-reading of /g/ for /n/ which has to be repaired by a second reading and contextualization of the reading, results in a series of stages to the 'reading' of the text.

The reader started with a string of words, then, when confronted by a combination he couldn't make sense of, shifted from the word level to the phonological level to correct the mis-reading. Having corrected the mis-reading, the reader is then in a position to work out the grammatical organization of the text in isolation. Having worked out the grammar, the reader is now in a position to work out the pragmatic intention of the text: the effect the writer is trying to produce in the reader. A further reading of the text in its visual co-text and by bringing in contextual information based on the reader's world knowledge enables the reading to be enriched and the full purport of the message to be identified.

The above example is an account of a mis-reading and how it was corrected. So what do we conclude from this example? That reading typically progresses from decoding sound/symbol correspondences to words and grammar to pragmatic force and other higher types of textual organization? The peculiarity of this example is that it lays bare the mechanisms of reading in an orderly, slow-motion fashion, the way a theoretical model-builder might wish to see them. The example displays the range of linguistic and contextual components that a theory of reading and what readers do would have to account for. But does it describe how readers 'typically' read? Is there in fact such a thing as 'typical' reading, or is reading dependent on the kind of text being read, the purposes for reading and other contextual factors?

Compare using a telephone directory with reading a novel. The user of a telephone directory must be familiar with the way in which lists of names are organized alphabetically and, indeed, with the more general principles of alphabetical order. She must be able to identify roughly where in the book the name she is seeking is likely to occur, again making use of knowledge of alphabetical order. It would be a waste of time, for instance, to turn page after page from page 1 onward, in search of the right page. Having identified the page on which the name she is seeking is likely to be located, she must scan down the columns until she has identified a surname, initial and address. At this point she is in a position to find out the telephone number.

The whole process is a series of more and more finely tuned applications of the understanding of alphabetical order. For the fluent reader, this is commonplace and barely worth reflecting upon. A non-fluent reader may indeed end up leafing through page after page of the directory, trying to locate the right page.

Reading a novel involves engaging with the full complexity of the grammatical and textual organization of continuous prose, and, because of this, reading a novel is likely to be a very different kind of activity from reading a telephone directory, where the trick is to select out as quickly as possible what you don't need to read in order to get to what you want to read. The novel, on the other hand, invites the reader to a 'full' reading.

There are, of course, always possible alternative readings. Some readers may choose to browse through telephone directories or read novels selectively for specific information; in the case of a student of literature preparing an essay, for example. Yet the range of possible readings is never completely open: the text itself constrains to a greater or lesser extent the range of its possible readings.

Discussion point

What other kinds of social knowledge, apart from the principles of alphabetic ordering, are involved in reading different kinds of telephone directory?

A trade directory like the Yellow Pages lists businesses and services in alphabetical order, yet requires considerable social knowledge to be used effectively. Suppose for example,

(a) your car has broken down;
(b) the body-work of your car needs repairing;
(c) you want to buy a radio;

how do you know which part of the directory to turn to? Jot down your guess as to how each service will be listed, then check your guess with a Yellow Pages directory.

Readers themselves may also differ in the way they approach reading a text, because of their own inclinations and reading strategies or their level of skill as a reader.

The example at the beginning of the chapter shows that errors and mis-readings can be a valuable source of insight into the process of reading. Communication breakdown and conversational difficulty provide valuable information about the organizing principles that make ordinary conversation possible, providing information about the social constitution of communicative practices that is just not accessible when conversation is proceeding smoothly. Breakdowns in reading can provide similar information about the components of fluent reading. In the above example, the mis-reading at the phonological level led the reader to walk through a number of stages in the reading process in a rather orderly fashion and more slowly than would be the case in an unproblematic reading, where the reader would draw on different aspects of text organization virtually simultaneously, in ways that would be difficult to discern.

In addition to the engagement with features of textual organization, the reader must have access to the ways that text is embedded in socio-political context which must be interpreted pragmatically in order for the reader to get meaning from the text. In my reading of the poster, I had to bring my socio-cultural knowledge into play in order to understand its message.

In an often-quoted phrase, Freire argues that 'reading the world precedes reading the word'. Text is literally unreadable without the availability of contextual information, in the shape of the reader's background knowledge of the socio-political context and orders of discourse. Readers *interact* with texts to produce readings.

An adequate theory of reading therefore needs to take account of the different aspects of text organization (phonological, lexico-grammatical, textual) as well as the role of background knowledge and interpretation. Their interaction must be borne in mind in evaluating the controversies on reading, which will be examined in the following section.

TOP-DOWN, BOTTOM-UP AND INTERACTIVE MODELS OF READING

The traditional approach to the teaching of reading followed the order of combining smaller linguistic elements to make up larger units. Sound–letter correspondences were first learned, then combined into syllables and words, which were further combined into sentences and thence into texts. This is what is commonly referred to as a 'bottom-up' approach to reading, starting from smaller linguistic units and combining them to make progressively larger linguistic units.

In contrast, top down approaches to reading emphasize the interaction of the reader with whole texts, reading for meaning and the significance of context in reading. We will look at some top-down models of reading and reading development later in this chapter, but first we will examine some examples of bottom-up approaches.

Davies (1973) quotes from the method advocated by the Elizabethan reading teacher Edmund Coote (1596, cited in Davies 1973):

> The teacher begins with the vowels and, 'after two or three days, when he is skilful in them,' the pupil is taught 'to call all the other letters, consonants'. So he goes on 'with the other words of art as they stand in the margin [but] never troubling his memory with a new word before he be perfect in the old,' e.g.

```
a  e  i  o  u          a  e  i  o  u
Ba be bi bo bu         Ab eb ib ob ub
Da de di do du         Ad ed id od ud
Fa fe etc              Af ef etc
```

> The pupil is now given exercises which he is required to read distinctly three times before he may go on to the next.

> > If we do ill: fie on us all
> > Ah is it so: is he my foe?
> > Woe be to me, if I do so.

> > Up go on: lo I see a pie
> > So it is, if I do lie
> > Woe is me, or I die
> > Ye see in me, no lie to be.

Progressive pedagogical orthodoxy might conclude that such an approach to teaching reading must necessarily be associated with uncritical, domesticating literacies. In fact, as the next example shows, this is by no means the case.

Bottom-up approaches to reading instruction are favoured in languages where there is a fairly systematic sound-symbol relationship. Take, for example, Freire's pedagogy, which, while emphasizing higher-order socio-political factors, through a process of cultural criticism in the development of the curriculum focused on generative words (Freire 1973).

For example, one of the seventeen generative words selected around which to organize the curriculum in the state of Rio de Janeiro in Brazil was

FAVELA (slum)

The procedure used was to divide the word into syllables:

FA-VE-LA

then to draw out the 'phonemic families' of each syllable:

FA-FE-FI-FO-FU
VA-VE-VI-VO-VU
LA-LE-LI-LO-LU

These syllables are then recombined to form words, which are recombined to form sentences and short texts, which illuminate critically the world as problematized in the Freirean method. It is interesting to find a combination of a traditional bottom-up pedagogy with an emphasis on problematizing the socio-cultural order. The lesson is, perhaps, that the traditional/progressive dichotomy may be rather a worn one and that what counts as 'good practice in teaching reading' may be the result of ideological perspectives which are quite contextually specific.   In the next section we will look at the situated nature of the ideologies, values and practices of reading, through revisiting the case study of Moroccan educational practices from Chapter 1.

THE ROLE OF MEMORY AND RECITATION IN MOROCCAN EDUCATIONAL PRACTICES

In the case study introduced in Chapter 1, we looked at the role of memorization and recitation in Moroccan educational practices, in particular the Qur'anic schooling. It was pointed out that memorization of the Qur'an was achieved by rote learning, the younger children memorizing first the shorter 'surahs' and moving on to the longer ones and that the Arabic word for 'read', 'qara'a' also carried the meaning of 'recite by heart'. The pedagogical emphasis here is on faultless reproduction of a sacred text, rather than on a full understanding of the text, which is of a conceptual and linguistic complexity that is anyway out of the range of young children, the learning cycle associated with memorizing the Qur'an involves reciting after a model, copying, learning by heart and being tested. Nine-year-old Driss described the process:

> And after that we have to say Qur'an and I feared that. But then I just learnt. You have to learn Qur'an. And I didn't know any of it, just a bit of it. And then I kept it in my mind and learnt it. And the next day when we came he said we had to say it again at the end of time. And I said it that time. And then the day after that I didn't say it. 'Cos I'd said it to my mother's nephew and it was all right. And

now I know it. I know, let me see, one, two, three, four, five, six, seven, I know seven verses.

An interesting conclusion from the ethnographic stage of the Morocco Literacy Project was that memorization by rote was a pervasive feature throughout the education system, up to university level.

> . . . although many contemporary Muslim educators trained in Western pedagogical methods consider rote memorization to be a debilitating remnant of an archaic system of instruction, memorization has been witnessed throughout the higher levels of modern Moroccan school systems extending into the university, to be a central pedagogical principle and acquisition strategy . . .
>   To acquire a text – here secular classroom notes, not the sacred Qur'an – students repeat it aloud over and over, or, less frequently, read and re-read it silently. Rote memorization of public school materials also occurs outside the house during the annual examination season in the late spring. At this time, students can be seen in serious concentration as they promenade singly in public gardens or stroll near street lamps in the evenings, eyes revited to their open notebooks, lips mouthing the text.
>
> (Wagner, Messick and Spratt 1986)

In the next sections in this chapter, we will be looking at the psycholinguistic approach to reading and the concept of reading for meaning. From a reading for meaning perspective it might seem that reading as the memorization and recitation of a text might not even count as reading and is certainly not likely to be listed in any list of 'good reading strategies'. Yet in the Moroccan context they are clearly valued and culturally central strategies.

I will argue that, from a critical perspective, it is important to recognize that accepted wisdom on the good reader and good reading strategies are themselves socially produced, that there is a tendency to naturalize accepted wisdom in an ethnocentric way, as the only possible way to learn/teach reading. It is important to revisit the dominant accepted wisdoms in areas like reading theory and pedagogy in the light of a situated approach to what counts as reading.

PSYCHOLINGUISTIC MODELS OF READING

For the last twenty years, the most influential account of reading has been informed by psycholinguistic research and is particularly associated with the work of Frank Smith (1982) and the Goodmans (Goodman *et al.* 1987; Goodman 1985). This approach emphasizes the interaction of reader with text, reading for meaning, reading as a 'psycholinguistic guessing game' in which the reader uses the 'world in the head', which includes world knowledge of the kind referred to by Freire, along with knowledge of linguistic organisation for prediction in reading text.

The Goodmans were responsible for developing an important approach to researching the reading process which they called 'miscue analysis' (cf. Goodman *et al.* 1987). Miscue analysis involves documenting and analysing the aloud-reading of a given subject, noting all the instances when what is read varies in some way from the text on the page. Miscues can involve substitutions, omissions, insertions and repetitions, and can be grapho-phonic, syntactic or semantic.

In the example which began this chapter, I misread, albeit silently, 'bag' for 'ban'. In the Goodmans' terms this is a graphophonic miscue involving substitution of /g/ for /n/. If I had misread 'stop' for 'ban' as in:

stop leg hold traps

this would have been a semantic substitution, substituting a word that is roughly synonymous to the word on the poster.

The value of this approach is in the emphasis on what readers do, on how they read and the close observation of practice as a means of theory-building. Its limitation is that it stays within the psycholinguistic sphere of reader interacting with text, and does not bring into play the contextually determined factors of literacy practice in general which have been presented in earlier chapters in this book and which lead to the emphasis on 'reading as situated social practice'.

If we try and reconstruct the 'ideal reader' presupposed by the psycholinguistic model of reading, in much the same way as attempts have been made to identify the characteristics of 'the good language learner' (cf. Rubin and others), we might want to posit characteristics such as

The good reader is an active reader

The good reader is a risk taker

The good reader predicts

The good reader is able to activate background knowledge for
   predicting

The good reader relies on linguistic knowledge for predicting

The good reader reads for meaning

This would mean, for example, that the Qur'anic reader was not
a good reader, since rote memorization would not count as active
reading for meaning. What 'counts' as reading may differ from
culture to culture and from context to context.

We need to ask whether the idealized reader/learner who
emerges from the psycholinguistic model is in fact constructed
through specific cultural expectations and whether the model of
reading that emerges is not a rather homogeneous one, oversim-
plifying the potential diversity of literacy practices.

The importance of the psycholinguistic approach to reading is
that it bases its data on the interaction of real readers with text,
and thus opens the way for theories of reading that are more
accountable to context. The drawback of the approach is that it
tends to reify one kind of reading and construct an idealized reader
who may be quite culture-specific; that is, constructed through
cultural and ideological presuppositions. While emphasizing the
importance of whole text, it fails to include the level of textual
organization in its model, thus ignoring the variety and diversity
of text types.

REAL TEXTS/READING FOR MEANING

The psycholinguistic model of reading, with its emphasis on
reading for meaning, the role of prediction in reading and whole
text has been the dominant paradigm in reading theory over the
past twenty years. It incorporates a whole range of theoretical
advances in linguistics and cognitive psychology that had been
taking place in the late sixties and early seventies; in particular,
in the areas of semantics and pragmatics. Smith emphasized the
importance of what goes on behind the eyes in the reading process,
the world in the head, whose knowledge is constantly drawn on in
any linguistic process.

Like many educational innovations, the psycholinguistic approach
starts out as a critique of methods then current, in this case
the skills-based reading programmes arranged round the graded

introduction of phonic word patterns. Goodman *et al.* (1987) contrast their holistic model of reading development with two other models: a subskills or phonics approach, which corresponds closely to the traditional model, and a skills model, which advocates a mix of phonics, grammar/vocabulary and meaning-based comprehension activities, carefully graded.

One of the logical outcomes of the first two models is that the texts used tend to be artificial, either specially written or simplified for the pedagogic purpose. In other words, the text is driven by its pedagogic purpose, rather than any of the commonplace, everyday, real-life purposes for reading.

The whole language approach emphasizes real texts and real uses of reading, so the material used in teaching reading is drawn from a needs analysis related to the student's interests and ambitions. For example, a student learning to drive may have a series of lessons based on learning to read the 'rules of the road' (see Figure 5.2 on pages 176–7).

Reading material may be drawn from newspapers and magazines or texts authored by students. The emphasis is on authentic reading for real purposes.

Within this approach to reading development, the expectations of the reader can be cued by activities designed to make explicit their expectations of text. Ulrike Meinhof describes such a procedure for preparing students to read foreign language texts. She lists four strategies:

- *Strategy No. 1: Activating situational knowledge* What kind of information do learners have about a particular situation type that a text encodes – for example, an article in the foreign affairs section of a national newspaper, a restaurant menu, a cookery book, a romantic story in a weekly magazine?
- *Strategy No. 2: Predicting the text* The readers predict the kinds of meanings likely to be encoded in a range of texts. Meinhof uses a range of newspaper texts on the same or similar topics, and the readers brainstorm a range of possible positions that might be taken in the text, given what they know of the topic and the publications selected from.
- *Strategy No. 3: Checking the predictions against the text.*
- *Strategy No. 4: Identifying areas of the text not predicted or falsely predicted.*

The emphasis in this sequence of activities is on activating the world in the head, the types of linguistic and situational knowledge used in reading. Meinhof uses a specifically linguistic framework to organize the activity, but there are also similarities with the concept of *schema*, used in cognitive psychology to denote a higher-order type of mental representation used in organizing knowledge.

Two examples of 'real' reading texts: a cake recipe and a DIY repair tip

In Figure 5.3a, reading the recipe would activate a schema based on the reader's knowledge and expectations of the processes and procedures of cookery. This knowledge would be of different sorts:

- real-world knowledge of how cooking is done, the implements, ingredients and settings required;
- mathematical knowledge to calculate the ingredients, set the oven at the right temperature, choose the right size of cake tin;
- linguistic knowledge of how recipes are organized as a genre, specialist or technical language – for example, here the verbs used to describe actions involved in cooking (mash, mix, cream, beat, fold);
- ability to relate the procedural event sequence of the recipe to the real world activity of cake making. Take for example the stage of making the cake filling, which involves four distinct steps:

  1 whipping cream;
  2 mashing a banana;
  3 mixing lemon juice into the mashed banana;
  4 stirring the banana into the cream.

Reading the recipe involves linguistic and practical knowledge.

Now look at the DIY tip example. What kinds of knowledge schemata are involved in reading it? What kinds of linguistic knowledge are involved? Would you be able to carry out the DIY repair yourself based on these instructions? What is wooden dowel, for example? Where would you get hold of it? What is 'a wood-worker's brace' and an 'auger bit'? What kinds of mathematical knowledge are required?

Road rules you must know

- Signs
- Road markings
- Lanes
- Intersections
- Turning
- Parking

Signs

Signs are displayed on roads to warn you of possible dangers and to give you general and safety information.

They tell you what the rules are and what the road conditions are like.

This chapter looks at

- Regulatory signs
- Warning signs
- Temporary signs
- Freeway signs

Regulatory Signs

Regulatory signs tell you about laws that **must** be obeyed. They tell you about things you must or must not do. Except for stop and give way signs, most regulatory signs are shaped like rectangles. They are usually black on a white background, sometimes with red as well. Some parking signs are green on white.

Figure 5.2 Two pages from the *NSW Road Users' Handbook*

Some of the most important regulatory signs are shown here.

KEEP LEFT

Keep left of this sign

NO ENTRY

No traffic may enter

ALL TRAFFIC

All traffic must follow the direction of the arrow

RIGHT LANE MUST TURN RIGHT

All traffic in the right lane must turn right

FORM 1 LANE

Traffic must merge into a single lane

TWO WAY

There is now traffic going both ways in this road

Warning Signs

A warning sign tells you that there may be dangers ahead. They are usually black on a yellow background and are mostly diamond shaped. Pictures, diagrams and symbols are used to alert you to danger. Some of the most important warning signs are shown here.

If you see one of these signs, be alert. You may need to slow down or stop to avoid an accident.

Dip in the road ahead

Road is slippery when wet

Side road junction

Beware of slow moving vehicles entering traffic

Figure 5.2 continued

Golden Banana Cake

Sweet ripe bananas keep this cake deliciously moist

Cost: £2.50
Preparation: 25 min
(plus cooling)
Cooking: 25 to 30 min
Freeze: up to 6 months
(unfilled)

2 ripe bananas

3 tbsp (45ml) natural
  yogurt

4 oz (100g) margarine

10 oz (275g) golden
  granulated sugar

2 (size 3) eggs, beaten

12 oz (350g) self-
  raising flour, sieved

¾ tsp (3.75ml)
  bicarbonate of soda

1 tsp (5ml) vanilla
  essence

¼ pt (150ml) double
  cream

1 small ripe banana

1 tsp (5ml) lemon juice

Banana slices

1 Set oven 350°F, 180°C (Mark 4).
   Grease and line two 8 in (20.5cm)
   sandwich tins.

2 Mash 2 bananas and mix in yogurt.
   Cream margarine and sugar
   together, then gradually beat in the
   eggs.

3 Fold in flour and bicarbonate of
   soda. Stir in yogurt mixture and the
   vanilla essence.

4 Divide mixture between the two
   tins, levelling tops.

5 Bake for 25 to 30 minutes until risen
   and golden brown. Turn out and
   cool on a wire rack.

6 For the filling, whip cream until
   thick. Mash 1 banana and mix with
   lemon juice to stop discolouration.

7 Stir banana into cream and use to
   sandwich cakes together.

8 Decorate with banana slices, dipped
   in lemon juice, just before serving.

Cook's tip

This recipe also makes a delicious pud-
ding the children will love – omit the
cream and banana filing and serve with
custard

Figure 5.3a

Activity

Try and visualize the circumstances in which these texts might be
read for practical purposes, rather than just for interest. Jot down
a little scenario sketching when, where, by whom and in what
circumstances these texts might be read.

The emphasis here is on higher-order features of text-processing,
involving schemata, inferencing and the interaction of background

---

DOOR TROUBLE

Frequent tugging of doors often leads to the handle plates coming loose. Mr Conn from Farnham in Surrey passed on this tip for re-fixing the damaged plates.

- Take off the handle plates on both sides of the door
- Bore holes through the door face using a wood-worker's brace and auger bit
- Repeat the operation on the other side of the door.

Accuracy is easy to achieve because if both door handles are of the same size and type, then the old screw centres will be exactly in line with each other. The next stage is to:

- Cut four lengths of wooden dowel, each length should be slightly shorter than the thickness of the door and the same diameter as the holes
- Drill a $\frac{1}{16}$ in hole about $\frac{1}{4}$ in deep in the centre of each dowel end and insert the dowels in the previously bored holes.

All that needs to be done now is to re-fix the plates using the existing screws. The result – a perfect repair at considerably less than the cost of a new door.

Figure 5.3b

knowledge, both linguistic and socio-cultural, in working with text. However, what goes on behind the eyes in the reading process is not just background knowledge related to the immediate context of situation of the text that is being read: it involves the intervention of higher-level readings of social structure and ideological positions in text. It is not impossible, for example, that the reader might have read the above examples of cake-making and DIY with the implicit assumption that the cake-maker would be a woman and the DIY fixer would be a man.

Activity

Look back over your scenario of who might read the above texts for practical purposes – where, when and in what circumstances. Did you make a gendered interpretation of who might be doing what? Do you think there are ways in which the texts themselves suggest an ideal reader male or female? In the DIY magazine from which the DIY hint is taken the photos accompanying the articles tend to show men doing the 'difficult', 'technical' work like plumbing. The one article which features a woman working in accompanying photographs is about assembling pre-fabricated furniture, less difficult, less technical. The main cover illustration features a photo from this article. In other illustrations, women are shown 'at leisure', enjoying the home improvement. In the letters page as it so happens, there are two letters from women DIY enthusiasts, accusing the magazine of carrying advertising material on DIY that assumed that all DIY enthusiasts were men.

We have shown how the reader makes use of both the features of the text as well as their knowledge of socio-cultural practices to read off the meanings in the text. In fact, the best way to characterize the reading process is not as 'top-down' or 'bottom-up', but as *interactive*: the different linguistic levels (phonic/graphic, lexico-grammatical and textual) interact with one another and with other kinds of cultural knowledge to produce readings of texts (cf. Carrell, Devine and Eskey 1988).

So far, we have seen a move from a traditional pedagogy to a pedagogy associated with a concept of reading for meaning, real text, whole text, active participation in learning and learner-centred curricula. In the next sections of this chapter we will look at two critiques of a 'whole language' approach to reading. The first is centred on arguments for a sub-skills approach to reading instruction, 'phonemic awareness', and the second is a more general critique of whole language perspectives, which will suggest how the phonemic awareness position can be incorporated into a broader theory of reading.

PHONEMIC AWARENESS

Recent studies in psychology (cf. Stanovich 1980) have argued that Goodman, Smith and others are mistaken in attributing such importance to guessing, prediction and reliance on context in the reading process. These studies argue in contrast that there is a strong relationship between reading comprehension and the learner's ability to recognize and decode words and particularly on the role of 'phonological processes' in assisting word-decoding.

One of the difficulties involved in assessing the relative merits of the arguments is that both types of research are based on very different research paradigms. The research quoted by Stanovich is based on psychological experiment, while the arguments in

Goodman, Smith and others are based on observation of actual readers engaging with actual texts, using the miscue analysis methodology, as well as data about how particular readers 'read' or interpret reading, what kinds of meta-models in the head influence their reading practices.

Proponents of the phonemic awareness approach do in fact relate theory to practice, and the solution they come up with are programmes of 'phonemic awareness training', by which learner readers can develop the sub-skills in manipulating the sound components of spoken and written language.

From the perspective of language as well as of pedagogic practice, there are a number of difficulties in the phonemic awareness approach in its pure form. Linguistically, it has been made clear that the spelling patterns of English encode not just information about the sound system of English, but also visual information, morphological relationships (for example, the relationship between 'electric' and 'electricity' where the second 'c' is represented by /k/ in 'electric' and /z/ in 'electricity'. Sound–symbol correspondences will never account for the whole lexical stock of English (cf., for example, Stubbs 1986).

A small example of the difficulties of one of the procedures advocated in phonemic awareness training will suffice. In blending, which involves the synthesis of sound units to form words, there is the difficulty that certain consonants cannot occur in isolation, but are always accompanied by a minimal schwa vowel in an isolated context.

Try, for example, saying /b/ and /t/ and combining them into the word 'bat'; /b/ in isolation is in fact realized as /bə/, /t/ in isolation is realized as /tə/. The initial sound of 'shop' however /s/ can be said in isolation without the appended schwa.

Despite these practical and theoretical difficulties, it is foolish to ignore the level of sound–symbol correspondences at the phonological level entirely. Phonemic awareness can be incorporated into a more general framework of language awareness and critical language awareness (cf., for example, Hawkins 1984; Carter 1991; Fairclough 1992a) which argues that it is important for the learner not just to be able to do but to be aware of what they are doing.

Based on a comprehensive model of language as text/process/practice, phonemic awareness fits in as part of a whole framework of language awareness which would involve:

AWARENESS OF LANGUAGE AS SOCIAL PRACTICE

In the case of the cookery recipe and the DIY hints above, this would involve an awareness of the ways in which society creates roles for men and women and reinforces them in discourse.

AWARENESS OF LANGUAGE AS SOCIAL PROCESS

This would involve an awareness of the social purposes of the two texts: both of them 'how-to-do-it' procedural texts.

AWARENESS OF TEXT ORGANIZATION

This would involve an awareness of the organization of procedural texts schematically.

AWARENESS OF LEXICO-GRAMMATICAL ORGANIZATION

This would involve an awareness of the typical grammar of such procedural 'how-to-do-it' texts and the special terms for each technical field.

AWARENESS OF GRAPHO-PHONOLOGICAL ORGANIZATION

Both texts contain a number of words in the following graphophonic patterns:

-ea-

leads
repeat
easy
each
grease
cream
beat

-ee-

deep
needs
sweet
keep
freeze

-tion

operation
discolouration

Conscious access to information of this sort may be unnecessary for the fluent reader, unless he or she is trying to correct a misreading, as in the example which started this chapter, but for the learner reader may be of considerable importance.

A theory of reading which is linguistically accountable needs to include all these interacting linguistic systems. Rather than seeing phonemic awareness as in opposition to higher-order types of linguistic awareness, we need to see how phonemic awareness fits into the language awareness framework. In a case study of a reading lesson later in this chapter, I will show how grapho-phonic information can become a focus for disputed readings of a text.

Despite the polemics of the proponents of various methods of teaching reading, the recognition of the significance of phonemic awareness in the reading process seems so basic that it is hard to understand how it needed to be reinvented. However, in the next section I will look at the strong model of the psycholinguistic basis for reading and how it combines with a whole language perspective and will suggest why the de-emphasizing of the phonemic level came about.

THE PSYCHOLINGUISTICS OF READING AND WHOLE LANGUAGE

The proponents of phonemic awareness training are easily coopted into the powerful 'Back to Basics' trend in literacy education, which would broadly argue that a generation of teachers have failed to impart the basic skills of the three Rs to generations of schoolchildren, and that this pedagogical failure will be set to rights by a return to the basics of instruction, involving skills-based teaching and regular testing.

Despite the emphasis in the psycholinguistic model on the three levels of language – grapho-phonic, syntactic and semantic – there is a distinct tendency within the model to favour the higher-order skills and to de-emphasize the grapho-phonic level.

Smith wrote in 1978 of 'the fallacy of phonics', in a chapter which is entitled 'Shallows and depths of language'. He argued for the primacy of 'deep meaning' over the shallowness of grapho-phonemic form. The form of the word and the word sequence on the page is what confronts the eye, it is what is in front of the eye, whereas his argument is in favour of what is behind the eye:

the higher-order kinds of knowledge about language and context which inform inferencing and prediction.

However, part of the knowledge behind the eye is precisely the grapho-phonemic patterns of English and the way these interact with lexical and grammatical information to enable readings to take place. So it is artificial to cut off the most visible, if still somewhat abstract, level of linguistic organization as a strong reading for meaning approach does.

The strong version of the psycholinguistic model of reading asserts that if the reader is reading for meaning and is capable of the informed guesswork of prediction or inferencing, then the elements of the building blocks will be falling into place automatically as the reader reads: to become a good reader you need to read; progress in reading is practice-driven.

Underlying this strong version of reading for meaning is another assumption: that learning is a natural process, and providing the reading teacher creates the conditions of a print-rich environment, with relevant and interesting reading materials and the means for the learner reader to access them, then reading will develop naturally, in the same ways in which spoken language is supposed to do.

This approach underplays the significance of explicit instruction and emphasizes creating the conditions for learning. In that it is a learner-centred approach, it attempts to account for how learning takes place, while de-emphasizing the contextualizing factors of instruction and social situation. The conditions for learning are autonomy and playfulness. Investigating how learning takes place is typically conducted through what Goodman calls 'kid watching', observing and gathering data in the actual settings where reading instruction takes place, gathering the perceptions of participants (their worlds in the head).

It is important not to underestimate the achievements of this approach to the investigation of reading, which makes possible, as we shall see, the investigation of reading as situated social practice. Yet some of the underlying assumptions of this approach can be criticized.

Perhaps the first point is that of 'natural' language development. It has been argued that language development is not natural but socially constructed in interaction, in specific social practices and contexts. There is an extensive literature now on the ways in which the practices of early schooling introduce the learner into modes of discourse organization; for example, the relative decontextualization of information, typical of the school curriculum. The work of Cook-Gumperz and her associates (1986) is an example of this (as are some of the readings in Baker and Luke 1991). So-called 'natural' language learning turns out to be highly constructed.

The second argument against some of the pedagogical practices associated with the strong form of the reading for meaning approach is that it privileges those learner readers who are already members, by birth, of literate speech communities. By not making the basis, particularly the textual basis, of practice explicit, those who are not in the club of shared meanings are systematically disadvantaged.

While the basis of pragmatic theory is the possibility of shared meaning or interpretation, room has to be made for a pragmatics of difference, of different interpretations/readings of the same text, of differential access to the meanings required to work with that text. The success of Meinhof's materials, quoted above, presupposes some degree of cultural commonality between the English learner readers of German and the German texts, or it would be simply impossible to predict.

The third critique relates to the developments in our understanding of discourse organization over the last decade. Whole language, psycholinguistic models of reading do not sufficiently distinguish between the different types of text. Whole text is something of an empty category, with no systematic way of accounting for the internal organization of text at the lexico-grammatical and phonological level.

This critique can perhaps begin to account for the relative neglect of the grapho-phonic level: with attention focused on whole texts, but no analytic devices available to understand the layers of textual organization, there was no obvious relevance in the micro-structure of text, since broader meaning categories were systematically privileged.

A fourth critique relates to the systematic relationship between text and context. Within the whole language, psycholinguistic approach to reading, the knowledge behind the eyes which facilitates prediction is very local, involving just enough meaning to make sense of what the text presupposes locally and does not draw in the higher order socio-cultural dimensions like ideological perspective which are essential to a critical theory of reading.

The situated context of instruction tends to go no further than the classroom setting, ignoring the ways in which broader socio-cultural categories can impinge on the immediate context of situation. In Hallidayan terms, the theory implies a context of situation but not a context of culture.

In the next section, when we examine reading as situated social practice, we will be looking at ways of theorizing the gaps identified in the psycholinguistic model; in other words, developing the model in ways that are more accountable to what Luke calls 'the political economy of reading' (1991).

READING AS SITUATED SOCIAL PRACTICE

We have seen how the psycholinguistic model shifted reading theory away from the investigation of reading behaviours in experimental contexts, towards the study of real readers working with real texts. However, the psycholinguistic approach tends to emphasize the world in the head and the text/reader nexus at the expense of the social contexts in which readers and texts operate and readings are produced. The psycholinguistic model draws on the immediate context of situation but does not provide a theory of reading as social practice. Also, it lacks a theory of text, seen as the ability to account for the interactions of the different levels of organization of the text and its embedding in social context. So the psycholinguistic model shifts perspective and opens a door into a space which it does not have the theoretical devices, both linguistic and social contextual, to explore fully.

What does it mean, then, to talk about reading as situated social practice? Thinking of reading as situated social practice involves a shift away from what reading *is* towards what reading *does*, from objectifying reading (Heap 1991), to looking at the settings and contexts in which reading occurs, what counts as reading, who does it and what reading does. This is the dimension of practice.

It involves documenting the range of types of texts available in particular contexts, the purposes for reading and the ideas and constructions that participants have about reading. The psycholinguistic model shifts attention towards reading as doing, but uses it to construct a theory of what reading is. In situated approaches, the attempt is to maintain the focus on reading as doing and emphasize the diversity and specificity of reading practices.

Take, for example, investigating reading practices in a work-place. The text dimension will involve gathering samples of the reading texts in use in the workplace (notices, pay-sheets, health and safety information, items on the staff noticeboard and so on). A textual analysis will show up distinctive ways that the texts are organized. It will also be important to document the ways in which the reading texts are used: health and safety information that is not read, since the information is passed on orally, plays a rather different role in the communicative economy of the workplace than health and safety information that is read. Ethnographic method suggests a necessary distrust of the 'official position' and a need to look below the surface at the gap between what is said to be going on and what is actually going on. Investigating reading as situated social practice will involve examining the gap between the official version and what actually is going on.

Investigating reading as situated social practice will necessarily bring in spoken language. If a group of workers pore over their pay-slips and try to work out how their bonus is calculated, that reading is being done in ways that are highly embedded in spoken language (cf. Heath's example of the joint reading of the newspaper in Chapter 3).

Investigating reading as situated social practice will necessarily involve consulting the perceptions of participants (asking, in addition to *how* and *in what circumstances, what is held to be going on*). Again there may be a gap between what one participant perceives as going on and what other participants may hold to be the case. The methodology for investigating reading in contexts like the workplace must therefore include the gathering of text samples, observation of the ways in which texts are being used, observations of the ways in which different participants construct what is going on for themselves and others.

In the classroom context, if you are investigating reading from a situated perspective, you will need to gather samples of the reading texts used, how they are used, noting differences between the official version and the actual practice as well as consulting participants about their perceptions of what is going on. Work on the micro-ethnography of classroom interactions – for example, Green and Wallat (1981) and Bloome (1989) – are relevant here.

In her case study of bilingual code-switching in a language class-room, Chau (1991) noted the uses of the bilingual English-Chinese, Chinese-English dictionary as well as audio-taped instances of

Chinese students negotiating understandings of word meanings orally. She also gathered data from participants as to their attitude towards such use of the first language in the second-language classroom and texts in the form of students' worksheets with annotations in Chinese. Different kinds of data provide 'thick' documentation of what is going on in the classroom and the roles that reading plays.

Investigating reading in the classroom as situated social practice, if it is to be accountable both textually and on the level of practice, necessarily involves some form of analysis of spoken classroom discourse, in addition to the more established methods of ethnographic investigation such as participant observation. It involves an analysis of the typical written texts circulating in the classroom and the documentation, either directly or indirectly, of participants' constructions of what is going on.

LINGUISTIC ORGANIZATION OF WRITTEN TEXTS

Considerable advances in our understanding of the organization of text, albeit mainly in the areas of schooled literacies, have taken place over the last decade or so. There have been studies of scientific writing (Martin 1991), writing in the social sciences (Cope and Kalantzis 1990), historical discourse (Eggins *et al.* 1987) which have emphasized the distinctive kinds of textual organization in the different genres or discourse types.

The pedagogical implications of this research have, so far, been mainly in the area of writing, and we shall look at them in more detail in Chapter 6. For the purposes of understanding the linguistic and semiotic organization of reading texts, we need to take into account features like:

- cohesion devices (cf. Halliday and Hasan 1976, as in pronoun anaphora, substitution and ellipsis, lexical cohesion);
- schematic structure or the staging of the text (for example the sequencing of steps in a procedure manual or a recipe book);
- choices of lexis and grammar (e.g., the language of economy in a newspaper article on the budget; nominalization: 'the introduction of expenditure cuts', as a nominalization of the simple sentence types 'Expenditure cuts were introduced' or 'X introduced expenditure cuts');
- selections of tense and mood (e.g., present/future tense with

extensive hedging in economic or weather forecasting, cf. Makaya and Bloor 1987);
- the intended relationship set up between text and reader;
- ideological positions, either explicit or implicit;
- the relationship between written text and other semiotic information (pictures, diagrams, graphs);
- typographic features, layout, and so on.

If we focus on reading for meaning and assume the role of different levels of linguistic organization in providing input based on prior knowledge, then we need some framework or checklist of the different types of text organization features the reader may be able to hook predictions onto. It therefore follows that the reader can only predict on the basis of what is already familiar. If the discourse type in question is unfamiliar and demanding in some of the ways laid out in the checklist above – for example, in heavy use of nominalization or a Latin- or Greek-based technical lexis (cf. Corson 1985) – or if the schematic structure is in some way unfamiliar, then the reader won't have familiar types of text organization to predict from.

Activity

Look back at the DIY and recipe texts above. How would you rate them, as a reader, in terms of familiarity and language difficulty, in terms of lexis, grammar and schematic organization? Can you think of any other contexts where similar procedural 'how-to-do-it' texts would typically occur?

CULTURAL PRESUPPOSITIONS OF WRITTEN TEXTS

If the readability of texts depends in part on their linguistic organization, it is also dependent on the sort of cultural knowledge that the writer assumes or expects the reader to bring to the text. The DIY and recipe texts assume a certain familiarity with the procedures involved in cooking and home repairs. They are indexed to the community of those who can and want to cook and who can and want to make home improvements. On a broader cross-cultural level a powerful theme in children's stories of many different cultural groups is the anthropomorphization of animals, who take on human characteristics and behave in human ways. This finds its way into many early reading materials for young children. What is culturally presupposed here is that animals can be portrayed as behaving like humans and, to the young early reader who shares this convention, a story about animals behaving in this way cues her into a familiar story world. The child may be able to relate this early reading text back to oral story-telling at home and in pre-school contexts, which again would powerfully cue her into the reading text.

Take, on the other hand, a child who did not share the cultural convention of making animals behave like humans and therefore did not come to the reading text with the same set of presuppositions. The kinds of predictions she would be able to make about the text would be constrained.

In the prediction activity of Meinhof, described above, prediction across languages is made possible by certain cultural congruence between German and English, or possibly a set of globalized international concerns: pollution, the environment. In cross-linguistic, cross-cultural contexts, these kind of congruences can not be assumed, but may have to be constructed *in situ* as a framework for informed, critical reading.

To put it another way, texts are not just situated, they situate themselves by the kind of previous knowledge assumed for the reader to work with them and produce readings. Texts construct their own pragmatic space, and part of access to texts is access to their pragmatic space.

By now, the attentive critical reader may be thinking, 'Well, if you are not objectifying the reader and the reading process you are objectifying the text as an object in and for itself. How does that square with an emphasis on situated social practice?' The answer to this query lies in the need to relate the reader's construction or reconstruction of the text through interpretative work to the ways in which the text structures itself. An approach to the understanding of reading that emphasized the practical, interpretative work of the reader and ignored the ways in which the text constrains and shapes these interpretations (structured and structuring) would be inadequate. There is a need to understand the dialectical relationship between interpretation and structure (cf. Ricoeur 1981) in developing a situated account of reading practices.

In this account of the kinds of cultural presupposition and interpretation needed to make sense of a text, we approach Freire's 'reading the world' from a slightly different angle. Reading the text presupposes the ability to bring to the text readings of the world, to fill in gaps, make what Eco (1979) calls 'inferential walks'. It is in this sense that the text is situated and situates itself.

Another sense in which written text is situated is in relationship to spoken language, when text reading or readings involved the embedding of the written material in oral discourse. Heath shows us how much a feature of everyday uses of literacy this is, and it is no less a feature of the classroom, where texts are read and readings constructed. In the next section of this chapter we will look at the embedding of reading in classroom discourse.

ORAL CONSTRUCTION OF THE READING LESSON

Studying the practices and procedures of reading pedagogy requires that we inspect actual instances of reading-in-a-classroom, and theorise from these, rather than from prescriptions or idealisations. Transcripts of recordings of classroom discourse are treated here as texts that can be read and re-read for evidence of how participants construct forms of classroom reading and how they assemble social relations and social order.

(Baker 1991: 164)

Case Study 1: Workplace literacy – emergency procedures

In the first extract we look at some data from a workplace language and literacy class (Chang 1992). The teacher is trying to elicit from the group their understanding of the procedures involved in the case of a serious accident at work. The discourse is therefore procedural and bears a similar relationship to the 'real sequence of events' in the case of a serious accident, as the written work procedure of 'what to do in the case of an accident at work'. Indeed, what the teacher is doing pedagogically is building up the field using spoken language, prior to a joint reading of part of the procedure.

(Ange = Angela, a teacher; Tran, She(rrif), Abdul and Dan(iel) = students)

ANGE: Hold on . . . hold on . . . what if Sherrif had an accident . . .
TRAN: If Sherrif accident (ANGE: A major accident what would you do?) I must stop the machine first and after talk with Charlie fix up, Charlie fix up.
SHE: No no no major injury not like little cut, can't walk maybe fell down.
ANGE: Maybe he's unconscious.

SHE: Maybe I can't control myself.
ANGE: Maybe a heart attack.
TRAN: Talk leading hand.
ANGE: Talk with your leading hand!
ABDUL: If you get a really bad accident you can't talk with leading hand must go to . . .
SHE: Straight away sister.
ABDUL: Go to first aid.
ANGE: Would you go to first aid or would you ring first aid?
TRAN: Go to first aid.
ABDUL: If you . . .
ANGE: What would you do Abdul, would you ring or go?
ABDUL: No if very bad accident you can't walk only. I ring up the operator whatever somebody can uh help or ring up to first aid to come over to help us.
ANGE: Yeah what's the telephone number for the health centre?
SHE: I don't know.
ABDUL: Triple 2?
DAN: Double O Double O.
ANGE: Alcan Health Centre?
DAN: Double O double O emergency.
TRAN: Double O double O.
ANGE: Is it?
DAN: It's on the box.
SHE: I was know.
ANGE: Well that's good to know, I'll ring up.
ABDUL: I think triple double 2 double 2.
ANGE: I know we'll have a look at the book *(confusion)* I'm going to ring up the Health Centre and ask them it's not clear to me.
DAN: It's on the box there, I look yesterday.
ABDUL: I don't know, I never check.
ANGE: What does it say on top of that Tran?
TRAN: PLANT EMERGENCY (Abdul/ EMERGENCY) EMERGENCY PRO-GENCY (ANGE: PROCEDURES) PROCEDURES (group echoes: PROCEDURES).
ANGE: 'Procedures' means what, Sherrif?
SHE: Inside all everything have.
ANGE: No 'procedures' means what you must do 'emergency procedures' means what you must do in an emergency. OK the next word, can you read it?
ABDUL: EMERGENCY TELEPHONE NUMBER.
ANGE: Good good Abdul. What's the emergency number for the Health Centre again, Tran?
TRAN: 29 44.

DAN: No Health Centre.
ANGE: Health Centre.
TRAN: Health Centre. – 28 42.
ANGE: 28 42.

The first part of this extract involves building up the local back-ground procedural knowledge orally; the second involves a jointly constructed classroom reading event, which illustrates in the classoom context the interrelatedness of spoken and written language in literacy practices. The teacher prompts particular students to read out loud, and we hear other group members participating by repeating and echoing what has been read. The teacher quizzes students about the meaning of words that have been read:

'procedures' means what, Sherrif?

and questions a particular student about the emergency phone number for the Health Centre:

what's the emergency number for the Health Centre again, Tran?

When Tran fails to give the correct response, another student prompts him, the teacher prompts and he revises his first attempt.

Activity

Based on the information in the above transcript, can you write a procedure, outlining what should be done in the case of an accident in that particular workplace?

Case Study 2: Would you work with your father? Literacy in an FE classroom

The second case study is from a class based on a reading of a short story by a Bengali teenager (Figure 5.4, page 194) with a group of teenage Moroccan boys on a work experience course at a local technical college in West London. All of these boys had migrated with their families from Morocco as children, attended school in England and were now moving into a new phase of their education in technical college. Almost without exception their ambition was to work as a mechanic in a garage.

The passage chosen by the teacher had a number of themes which intersected with the life experience of these students. First, the experience of working in a small business, where all

An Asian boy gave an insight into a family factory, where the son-worker is carefully watched by his foreman-father:

Dress Factory

Alal and Abdul work with their father and mother. They lived at 88 Settles Street, and they make ladies dresses. They have a dress factory of their own. Alal's father works very hard and he wants his sons to work hard too. Alal is 17 years old and Abdul is 19 years old, they don't want to work hard. When they don't work hard, their father gets angry with them. But Alal doesn't want to work all day. Alal is a good tailor, he wants to make smart clothes for himself. Sometimes he makes shirts and trousers for himself.

One day Alal wants to make a jacket for himself. So he went to the market and bought jacket clothes, and went back to his home and he cuts it. Then he hid it behind some green dresses because he doesn't want his father to see it. Alal's father is angry when he doesn't work all day. Alal is making the jacket today because he is going to a party this evening. He wants to wear the jacket at the party. Alal's father is at the door, he is looking at Alal.

'Alal,' his father says.
'Yes Dad,' says Alal, and he puts the jacket under the table.
'What are you doing, Alal?'
'I am machining Dad,' says Alal.
'What are you machining?' asks Alal's father.
'I am machining the green dress,' says Alal.
'I can't see the green dresses,' says Alal's father.
'Brr, brr, brr, brr,' the telephone is ringing. Alal's father goes out.
'Whew! says Alal, 'that was very close. I think the jacket will be ready for the party.' Then Alal is finished his machining and he is making the buttonholes and sewing on the buttons. His father comes in. He puts a green dress on top of the jacket.

'Alal,' says his father.
'Yes Dad,' says Alal.
'What are you doing?' asks his father.
'I'm making buttonholes Dad,' says Alal.
'These dresses don't have buttonholes, Alal.'
'I am not making buttonholes, I am sewing on buttons,' says Alal.
'Then why ...'
Abdul comes in and says, 'There is a man at the door Dad, he wants to see you.' Alal's father goes out.

'Whew!' says Alal. 'That was very, very close. The jacket will be ready for the party now.'

Now the jacket is ready and Alal is pressing it and he is talking to Abdul.
'Look at my jacket. It's ready for the party this evening. I made it today.'
'Alal,' says Alal's father. He is standing at the door.
'Oh! Yes Dad,' says Alal.
'What are you doing, Alal?'
'I am pressing, Dad.'

Figure 5.4

Figure 5.4 continued

> 'What are you pressing, Alal?'
> 'I'm pressing a dress, Dad.'
> 'The dresses are green, not purple.'
> 'Well, I'm pressing my jacket, Dad. You see Dad, I'm going to a party this evening.'
>   'A party! You are not going to a party this evening Alal. When you don't work all day, you got to work all evening.'
>   Poor Alal!
>   Alal is not going to the party but his jacket goes to the party. Alal gives it to Abdul and Abdul wears it to the party.
>
> *Mahbubar Rahman, 13*

these youths might well be doing work experience placements. Secondly, in that it raised in interesting ways the relationship between fathers and sons in traditional Muslim families. These were the continuities between the text and the life experience of the readers. The discontinuities lay in such things as that the factory was a dress factory, rather than the garage that would be the ideal of this particular group of youths.

In Chapter 4 we talked about some of the typical patterns of classroom discourse and the unequal distribution of power between participants, with the teacher responsible for framing activities, nominating who has the right to talk, organizing the classroom work, for example, through questioning strategies and the students participating within the frame set up by the teacher. (T = Teacher; Hi = Hisham)

> T: OK who's going to start reading . . . who's going to start reading?
> Hi: me me sir
> T: Hassan all right could you start from the bottom start start from the bottom here right

The teacher's question here is revealed not as a genuine request for volunteers, but as a kind of rhetorical organizer, like talking out loud. He retains the right to nominate the reader in spite of vigorous bidding from Hi.

Although the transcription of the class gives evidence of the fairly persistent efforts of the teacher to control turn-taking, nominate who is to read and move the lesson along, there are other agenda in play, most notably a strong drift away from the focus on the lesson towards peer interaction, into which the teacher intervenes quite strenuously, sometimes effectively, sometimes not. The lesson gives a somewhat unruly appearance and moves in cycles from an orderly focus on task to a hubbub of conversation in Moroccan Arabic and English, at which point the teacher intervenes to bring the group back to task. Despite the unruliness of much of the interaction, when task orientation is achieved, participation is intense. These youths, newly out of secondary school, carry over some of the conventions of school – for example, addressing the teacher as 'Sir' in some cases, particularly when responding to a query or request from the teacher. In other cases they use 'mate' or 'man', which gives some indication of the variability or uncertainty of the tenor of relations in the class case studied.

We will illustrate the case study from two phases of the lesson: first, the out-loud reading round the class of the text; secondly, the discussion of the text, prompted by the teacher's questioning. It will become clear that, within the conventional frame of the teacher's shaping of the lesson, different agenda are in play and the teacher is not always able to sustain the authoritative version of the text or even the kinds of readings that his questioning proposes.

Phase one: out-loud reading

EXTRACT 1   ABDUL'S TURN AT READING
(T = teacher; A = Abdul, H = Hassan, Hi = Hisham)
Capitals = Material read aloud

T: Abdul
A: Yes, please . . . WOMEN
H: Naah
A: WORKS I mean ONE DAY that's all
H: ALLAL IS SEVENTEEN YEARS
A: Shutup ALAL IS SEVENTEEN YEARS OLD AND A BROTHER'S
T: AND (points)
A: ABDUL Abdul that's me ABDUL IS NINETEEN YEARS OLD THEY DON'T WANT TO WORK HARD WHEN THEY DON'T WORK HARD THEY FATHER GETS ANGRY WITH THEM BUT ah A-LAL ALAL DOESN'T WANT TO WORK ALL DAY
Hi: Aʕlal
A: ALAL IS A GOOD
Hi: La Aʕlal (Moroccan Arabic = No Aʕlal)
A: That's it English innit
Hi: La Iʕlala

(LAUGHTER)
A: Listen man g g go n repair your teeth man body worker come to my garage repair your fucking teeth what happen
Hi: Aʕlal . . . boy
A: ALAL IS GOOD well that's ALAL IS A GOOD TAILOR TAILOR
T: Tailor yeah
A: HE WANT TO MAKE SMART CLOTHES FOR HIMSELF SOMETIMES HE MAKES SHIRTS AND TROUSERS FOR HIMSELF ONE DAY ALAL WANT TO MAKE A JACKET FOR HIMSELF SO HE WENT TO A MARKET AND BOUGHT JACKET CLOTHES AND WENT BACK TO HIS HOME AND HE CUT IT
T: OK.

Abdul responds to reading his own name in the text:

Abdul that's me

and a dispute arises between Abdul and Hisham about the correct pronunciation of the name Allal. Muslim names such as Abdallah, Allal, Aisha, all start in Arabic with the phoneme /ʕ/ for which there is no equivalent in English. These names are therefore written in English orthography with a beginning 'A'. Abdul reads the name with an English pronunciation, Hisham corrects him, stressing the phoneme /ʕ/ of the Arabic.

What we have here is a disputed reading on the grapho-phonemic level, but there is an underlying ideological issue: is it right to pronounce Muslim names the English way? Abdul is clearly of the opinion that it is:

that's it English innit?

While Hisham insists that the /ʕ/ should be pronounced. The teacher, perhaps recognizing the underlying ideological issue, does not intervene to provide an authoritative account of how the name should be pronounced and the argument smoulders on throughout the reading of the text.

EXTRACT 2   READING ONOMATOPOEIC WORDS
In the following extracts, Hi disputes the reading of two onomato-poeic words in the text:

(a)
    T: (nominating Hassan to read) Hassan
    H: I CAN SEE THE GREEN DRESS SAID ALLAL FATHER what is that (. . .)

T: What do you think
?: Brr Brr
T: BRR BRR
H: OK
T: What's it the telephone is ringing
Hi: Aah that's not the way tring tring
H: I HOPE I DON'T (. . .) What's that again
T: Whew
Hi: That's not Whew sir is it that's wow wow says Allal
H: Whew says Allal that was really close

(b)
T: (Nominating Hisham to read) OK Hisham carry on
(. . .)
Hi: I'M NOT MAKING BUTTONHOLES I'M SEWING ON BUTTONS
SAYS ALLAL THEN WHY ABDUL COMES IN AND SAYS THERE'S
A MAN AT THE DOOR DAD HE WANTS TO SEE YOU ALLAL
FATHER GOES OUT WHO
T: WHEW
Hi: You think that's WHEW sir
T: That's the way they write it
??: Where is it where is it
Hi: WHEW
T: WHEW
Hi: WHEW SAYS ALLAL

In Extract 1 there was a dispute between Hisham and Abdul as
to the correct way to pronounce the Muslim name Abdul, in
which the teacher did not intervene. In the two extracts above
we find another dispute about two onomatopoeic words, this time
between Hisham and the teacher. In the first instance, Hisham
provides an alternative onomatopoeic word for the ring of the
telephone (tring tring) [based on French?]. The teacher doesn't
respond and the aloud-reading continues.

In the second instance, Hisham disputes the sound represented
by WHEW, both in commenting on it during Hassan's aloud
reading and in his own. He provides an alternative version, 'Wow
says Allal'. Again the teacher lets this pass, but on the second
occasion when it comes up, during Hisham's aloud-reading,
the teacher insists on the conventional reading of WHEW and
the reading proceeds, Hisham having accepted the conventional
reading.

The power relations in this classroom allow Hisham to challenge the dominant reading of the text, albeit on the grapho-phonemic (the sounding out of WHEW) and lexical levels (BRR BRR or TRING TRING for the phone ringing), although the teacher ultimately insists on the conventional reading of WHEW, thus maintaining the authority of the text and the authoritativeness of his reading. His choice of pronoun in:

that's the way they write it

instead of, for example, 'that's the way we write it' has the effect of both distancing ('not me, them') and adding authority to the reading ('it's you against them').

There are structural similarities between these two instances and the interaction round the pronunciation of the name Allal. All three involve a contradiction of the reading proposed by another participant, followed by an alternative version.

In the dispute over the pronunciation of Allal, the contradiction is carried out in Moroccan Arabic, and turning as it does on the socio-cultural embedding of the name this is perhaps natural. The ideological argument underlying this is to do with the stance of Muslims whose socio-cultural practice is embedded in a dominant culture which does not support those values. Is it a case of 'When in Rome . . .' ('that's it English innit') or the maintenance of cultural linguistic values through pronouncing the 'ain? Hisham is here introducing the possibility of other authorities and other authoritative readings than the authority of the text in English.

The question of which onomatopoeia should represent the phone ringing reflects the multi-lingual nature of Hisham as a reader. A speaker of Moroccan Arabic, having some education in French in Morocco, he has access to the onomatopoeic potential of three languages. Hisham's access to this multi-lingual potential in some way authorizes his dispute with the text.

The reading of WHEW is not so much a dispute with the text, as with the teacher's reading of it:

You think that's WHEW sir

This provokes the teacher's use of the authoritative and dis-tant third-person plural pronoun. During Hassan's aloud-reading, Hisham demonstrates that the authority for his alternative reading of WHEW is his fluency in English. His version, 'wow says Allal', is a legitimate idiomatic alternative to the word on the page.

The above examples show how even grapho-phonemic and

lexical material can become the focus of disputed readings of texts, bringing questions of *authority* and *legitimacy* in readings into play: there is a potential for more than one authority and more than one authoritative reading.

Phase two: discussion

In the next examples we will look at the idea that there can be variant or conflicting readings of the text at more obviously critical interpretative levels in the course of a discussion about the similarity between the family workplace described with the Moroccan context and in particular the relationship between the father and the sons who work together.

EXTRACT 3
(T = , B = , A = , ? =)

> T: OK this description it's about a Bengali family right they own a factory do you think that's similar to a Moroccan family the way the father the father treats the son?
> B: The Moroccans would never make a business
> A: Why not?
> ?: That's you maybe can't make business.
> ?: You.
> B: Listen the Moroccans ain't organized
> A: We wouldn't need to organized
> B: Listen I'm Moroccan you guys are Moroccan
> A: There is no business in Morocco then
> B: There is
> A: There is no garages
> ?: There is
> A: So shuttup

The students respond, not to the specific focus of the teacher's question, but to something presupposed by it: the idea of Moroccans having businesses. The question of whether the Moroccan community in London was able to organize itself to achieve a range of purposes, including that of setting up and running small businesses, was a key issue within the community in the early 1980s when this lesson was recorded. Their response is to this issue rather than the one precisely framed by the teacher.

It is clear from the interaction that this is an in-group discussion, sparked by the reading text and the teacher's questions but not responding to them in the way predicted by the teacher:

Listen I'm a Moroccan you guys are Moroccan

The teacher suggests an outsider interpretative reading of the text, while the students begin to read it in the context of their own concerns as community members. The teacher is inviting a 'compare and contrast' response, but what the students compare and contrast is something not expected by the teacher: the relative viability of their community to succeed in small business enterprise. They are tuning into an adult discourse of their community, reading the original text, on the interpretative level in a way that is quite different from the teacher's reading.

EXTRACT 4
(T = , A = , Hi = , B = , ? =)

T: So what were you saying Abdul
A: I said like this man in Morocco he got garage
Hi: Not all of them
A: He got he got his er like his he got his brothers working with him his children his his like his brother in law something like that
Hi: Ha this is eh no listen when a very poor family they got a small shop they usually (. . .) so they won't pay other people.
B: That's it
Hi: The money they make the profit the profit they going to make to give to other people said my son will working with me and er all property is his if I die it's his so why don't he work with me
T: So in fact this is quite like the Moroccan family if you had a family business
B: Yes it's quite quite similar yeah
T: What about the behaviour of the father towards the son I mean the son
?: It's worse
T: The father is like this with the son yeah he won't let him go out would that happen in Morocco?
?: No you get a lot
Hi: Yes of course
?: No this time is all different
Hi: This thing you said it's all happened I mean happens
A: But some (you will) like you open nine o'clock you n your dad go to work in the garage and the time you close down about five o'clock close the garage

Hi: You talking about
A: And the son will go somewhere and the father will go to the
house
Hi: You're talking about this bad behaviour, yeah
T: No I'm trying to make a comparison between this family right
who've got a factory and the relationship between a father and a
son and I want to ask you say for instance in Morocco whether that
would be the same thing yeah

In the first section of this extract the students are relating their
reading of the text to their own knowledge and experience in
Morocco.

Both A and Hi present typical scenarios of a small business in
Morocco as part of their argument:

A'S SCENARIO

$(A = , Hi = , B =)$

A: I said like this man in Morocco he got garage
Hi: Not all of them
A: He got he got his er like his he got his brothers working with
him his children his his like his brother in law something like that

HI'S SCENARIO

Hi: Ha this is eh no listen when a very poor family they got a small
shop they usually (. . .) so they won't pay other people
B: That's it
Hi: The money they make the profit the profit they going to make
to give to other people said my son will working with me and er all
property is his if I die it's his so why don't he work with me

They are fleshing out what is presupposed in a situation where
sons work with their father in the family business. To be able to
conceptualize in a relatively full way the implications of fathers
and sons working together in a family business is an essential
precondition for a full reading of the text. It provides the 'context
of culture' which makes sense of the text. The students are reading
the text through contextualizing it in terms of their own experience
and, in discussion, articulate this experience in different ways.

After the teacher's question:

what about the behaviour of the father towards the son

two contrasting responses emerge, polarized around Abdul and
Hisham's contributions. Abdul produces a contrasting version, in

which father and son work together, but the authority of the father does not impinge on the son's autonomy:

and the son will go somewhere and the father will go to the house

Hisham appears to go along with the drift that the teacher is developing in the discussion of the text:

this thing you said it's all happened I mean happens

At this stage, Hisham makes a powerful summarizing intervention, which shows that the socio-cultural presuppositions on which he is basing his readings of the text are very different from the teacher's:

You're talking about this bad behaviour, yeah

Why is this a powerful intervention and what differences does it show between the interpretative ground that the teacher is working from and Hisham's own?

Labov and Fanshel (1977) point out in their analysis of therapeutic discourse that a powerful strategy used by the therapist is to make statements which summarize in declarative form knowledge, experience, motives that legitimately lie within the domain of the interlocutor. Consider the difference between the above and a question:

(a)   Are you talking about this bad behaviour?
(b)   What are you talking about?

in which the interlocutor is progressively more free to define the communicative space in which he or she is operating, in the case of (a) by choosing yes/no, in the case of (b) by leaving the interlocutor maximally free to define what is going on communicatively.

Hisham uses statement + checking question to summarize his understanding of where the interpretative focus of the discussion is, perhaps attempting a contrast with the way in which Abdul is developing the discussion.

'Bad behaviour' is, however, precisely what the teacher is not talking about from his cultural point of reference, and Hisham's utterance prompts a lengthy reformulation of the purpose of the discussion, 'trying to make a comparison'.

These two turns throw up a striking difference between Hisham's and the teacher's interpretative position, which illustrates how two people, apparently talking/reading about 'the same thing', can in fact be miles apart. Hisham appears to be interpreting the whole story within a moral frame of good/bad behaviour, while the teacher is taking a deliberately judgement-free position, perhaps informed by sympathy with the son over the 'oppressive' father figure. In other words, the teacher is making a highly culture-specific and culture-laden interpretation of the text, based on his own construction of father/son relationships, his own politics. The text is being read in quite a different way by Hisham.

This chapter is entitled 'Reading as situated social practice', but it could equally well go under the title 'there are no context-free readings'. In the above case study, context involves the immediate context of situation of the reading classroom, but it also involves the objective social positions of participants, where they are coming from, which defines their stance in relationship to the text. The way in which the teacher constructed the lesson can ultimately be seen as informed by a particular set of ideological positions by no means shared with other participants. On a number of occasions, the students take up issues, related to the text, which are specifically 'Moroccan' and in-group.

These issues can be addressed from another angle by asking what kinds of cultural and social knowledge are required to make this text readable, what is culturally presupposed in it.

The final question is what kind of theory of reading can allow for a possible diversity of readings, and it is to this question that we now turn.

TOWARDS A CRITICAL THEORY OF LITERACY

In the psycholinguistic approach to reading, Smith emphasized that reading goes on behind the eyes. A great deal of this chapter has been concerned with giving detail to the question of what kinds of knowledge, what kind of worlds in the head are involved in producing readings from texts.

I emphasize the plurality of readings rather than a single, authoritative reading to emphasize that texts can invite or be subject to more than one reading, that all texts are to a greater or lesser extent 'open', in terms of the way that Eco writes about 'open' and 'closed' texts (Eco 1979). In the last case study, it became clear that different participants in the reading event were working from very different interpretative positions and therefore producing different readings.

The psycholinguistic model is content to stay with the interaction between the text (the words on the page) and the orderings of knowledge behind the eyes. The project of this book is to take the discussion further from two interrelated perspectives. The first takes us back to the text and asks: what kind of higher-level orderings of textual organization are available to the reader in the process of reading? The second relates to the social world within which these cognitive orderings are produced. We thus emphasize reading as both social process and social practice.

WHAT? HOW? AND WHY? WHO? – DIMENSIONS OF CRITICAL READING

Freebody and Luke (1990: 7) argue that learning to read involves adopting four related roles:

1 code breaker ('how do I crack this?');
2 text participant ('what does this mean?');
3 text user ('what do I do within this here and now?');
4 text analyst ('what does all this do to me?').

In terms of the model of language underlying this book, (1) and (2) of their framework correspond to the dimension of language-as-text, (3) to the dimension of language-as-social-process, and (4) to the dimension of language-as-social-practice. Each of these dimensions can be seen as posing an underlying question. The dimension of language-as-text poses the question *What?* – what resources for making meaning are available to the writer/reader? The dimension of language-as-social-process poses the question *How?* – how does the writer/reader strategically employ these resources in the construction of text? The dimension of language-as-social-practice poses the question *Why?* – what purpose does this text serve, where is it coming from?

Why? questions are the underpinning of critical or resistant readings: readings which do not just accept the words on the page as given, authoritative in their own right, but question where that authority is derived from. Take, for example, the census form. This form is used to gather a wide range of information on a household-to-household basis, some questions being fairly uncontroversial, others – for example, the gathering of statistical data on ethnicity – being quite controversial. When the form arrives through the letterbox, the *What?* question, related to the dimension of text, might be: what is this form and what demands is it going to make of me? The *How?* question, related to the dimension of social process, might be: how am I going to read this and how am I going to gather the material to respond? The *Why?* questions might be: why has this form come through my letterbox, what/whose purpose does it serve, why should such and such a question be asked? A critical or resistant reading of the census form would not just accept that the questions contained in the form are given, not to be challenged.

A critical or resistant reading tries to work out what the writer is trying to do to the reader, where the text is aiming to place the reader. It asks what is assumed as given in a text and what ideological positions are either covertly or overtly constructed by the text.

Part of the underlying assumptions of the census form are that it is necessary and reasonable to gather the range of information requested in the form. The form may also typically assume a certain kind of grouping, say the family, as 'normal'. A critical reading asks:

- where is this text coming from?
- what is it trying to do to me?
- am I going to accept this and work with it?
- am I going to reject it?
- am I going to try to work with it on a modified basis?

CONCLUSION

The approach to reading in this chapter has emphasized the interaction of linguistic and other kinds of social knowledge in the interpretation of texts. To that extent it is a linguistic-pragmatic account of reading, in that it emphasizes first the dimension of text organization and secondly the social processes involved in text construction and interpretation, involving the interaction of linguistic knowledge, with interpretative work and background knowledge schemata. The dimension of text as social practice and therefore reading as social practice brings into play the crucial role of critical reading.

The dominant psycholinguistic approach to reading is criticized because of its primary focus on reading as process. A richer theory of text organization is needed for an adequate account of reading, as well as the inclusion of the dimension of reading as social practice, thus critical reading. The psycholinguistic approach focuses on the processes going on in the reader. It needs to be complemented by an increased awareness of the linguistic organization of written text and an increased emphasis on the critical, resistant dimension of reading.

So the emphasis on reading as situated social practice can be summarized as follows:

- Reading is *situated*, because of its dependence on the interaction of linguistic knowledge, background knowledge and interpretative work.
- Reading is *social* not just in the obvious sense that it is frequently accomplished socially, or even through an analysis of the social purposes of reading, but also because, even in the stereotypical case of solitary reader engaging with text, the activity of reading routinely implicates the social – indeed, reading strictly cannot take place without the implication of socially derived knowledge.
- Reading is social practice because the activity of reading presupposes reading the social world and introduces the potential for critical, resistant readings, not simply uncritical accommodations to the givens of text.

SUGGESTIONS FOR FURTHER READING

Baker, C. and Luke, A. (eds) (1991) 'Towards a Critical Sociology of Reading Pedagogy'. Papers of the XII World Congress on Reading, Philadelphia: John Benjamins.

Carrell, P., Devine, J. and Eskey, D. (eds) (1988) *Interactive Approaches to Second Language Reading*, Cambridge: Cambridge University Press.

Cook-Gumperz, J. (ed.) (1986) *The Social Construction of Literacy*, Cambridge: Cambridge University Press.

Kress. G. and van Leeuwen, T. (1990) *Reading Images*, Geelong: Deakin University Press.

SIX

Writing as situated social practice

The topic of 'writing' can be approached from a number of different angles. First, we can identify *writing as text* and study aspects of the organization of written text. This is an emphasis on writing as product. Secondly, we can study *writing as process* and examine the factors involved in the production or construction of written text. Thirdly, we can focus on *the writer* and try to understand the subjectivity involved in writing. Research on writing as *social practice* will investigate the ways in which writing and the writer are implicated in discourses, ideologies and institutional practices. Research on writing tends to take different emphases, depending on theoretical perspective or the academic discipline in which it is located – linguistics for writing as text, psycholinguistics or psychology for writing as process, critical theory to understand the subjectivity of the writer and his or her implication in social practices.

When we focus on text, the concepts of *purpose* and *audience* immediately become relevant. Who is the writing written for and why? Purpose and audience become issues in the second layer of the model of language presented in Chapter 1, when we think about writing as a social process. Looking at writing from the point of view of its purpose and intended audience brings in the range of types of writing, often referred to as *genres*, and the accompanying contexts for writing. Over time and because of the different kinds of social purposes they serve, different types of writing gather prestige and status. It is an interesting question whether the power and status of one written genre (say, expository prose) over another (say narrative) is *intrinsic*, in that there is something intrinsically more powerful in expository writing as a means of communication, or *ascribed*, in that the power of particular kinds of writing has become entrenched because of the social institutions whose interests are served. Debates on the function of legal language would be an example of this. One of the goals of a critical literacy is clearly to distinguish between intrinsic and ascribed power: the gap between language used in an economical, purposeful way to communicate, and language used to mystify and confuse.

Considering the power of written genres as institutions, as well as the ideological differences that emerge when the critical reader/writer starts to question the source and legitimacy of that power, brings us to the outer layer of the language model, that of language as social practice. To understand writing as situated social practice involves taking into account:

- the subjectivity of the writer;
- the writing process;
- the purpose and audience of the text;
- the text as product;
- the power of the written genre of which the text is an exemplar; and
- the source or legitimacy of that power.

Writing research tends to privilege one or other of these elements at the expense of the rest. In this chapter I will try to show how all these dimensions need to be accounted for to make up an integrated theory of writing as situated social practice.

PUTTING WRITING IN CONTEXT

Activity

Think back over the last twenty-four hours and make a note of all the kinds of writing you have done. List all the kinds of writing that you come up with and try to work out the purpose and audience for each. You might use a format like this:

USE OF WRITING   PURPOSE   AUDIENCE

Suppose, for example, one of the uses of writing you record is 'taking a phone message': what is the purpose of the phone message and who is it for?

When you have worked through the uses of writing which you have noted, try and apply the 'domain' construct from Chapter 2. Can you group your uses of writing into different domains; related to your daily life, for example, home, work, dealing with bureaucracy?

Do you find that the domains overlap in any way? Are there any interesting differences between writing in the different domains? If you are bilingual, for example, you may find that you write in different languages depending on factors like purpose, audience and domain.

When you have documented your own uses of writing, try this approach out with a friend or colleague. What can you say about their uses of writing?

If you wanted to take this process a stage further, you might try and gather examples of these kinds of writing, in which case you would end up with a range of texts representative of the uses of writing collected above: phone messages at work, phone messages at home, reports and work procedures, notes to a child's teacher, shopping lists, cheques made out and signed, essays, study assignments, postcards written.

Each use of writing would correspond to some role or other of the writer, some social purpose or other. In many cases, as we saw in Chapter 2, the writing would be a collaborative activity. Take, for example, the kinds of writing involved in conducting a formal meeting or drafting the form of words for a motion or a work procedure. The final written product may be the result of many stages of discussion, oral formulation and reformulation, drafting and redrafting. In collaborative writing, the process of writing is laid bare: the observer or reflective participant can trace the stages in which a written text is arrived at, the processes of negotiation. But as we shall see when we look at writing as process in more detail, the individual writer may typically go through many such stages before the finished text.

The following activity from the work domain illustrates the findings of a more systematic attempt to document uses of writing in a range of workplaces.

Activity

In a study of texts in the workplaces of the Australian textile, clothing and footwear industries, Helen Joyce (1991) found the following kinds of writing required in the workplaces surveyed.

In 100% of the workplaces surveyed:

• signing name and writing bundy number.

In 60% of the workplaces surveyed:

- writing descriptions of quality/machine problems;
- copying code onto tickets/forms.

The observation and documentation of uses of writing in context described so far provides us with a way of researching the *what* of literacy but not necessarily to get at the *how*, which is the process dimension. There are two issues in the process dimension:

1   what processes does the 'fluent' writer go through in constructing text;
2   secondly what are the acquisition processes that the learner/ apprentice writer goes through?

These are interesting and important questions, at the heart of much 'writer-centred' writing research. However, before addressing them it is important to look in more depth at the *what* of texts and contexts for writing. This involves examining the focus of current 'text-centred' writing research.

FROM USES OF WRITING TO THE ORGANIZATION OF WRITTEN TEXT

Activity

For this activity it is best to work with another person, but if you are working on your own, you should carry out both part (a) and part (b).

(a) Write a procedure describing the steps involved in changing a tyre.
(b) Write a story describing an occasion when you had to change a tyre.

Now compare the difference between your two texts in the light of the discussion that follows.

The procedure written for (a) might look something like this:

Step one Make sure handbrake is on.
Step two Locate the jack and the spare tyre.
And so on . . .
or
First you make sure the handbrake is on.
Then you locate the jack and the spare tyre.
And so on . . .

The story written for (b) might start something like this:

I was driving along the highway early one morning minding my own business, when I suddenly noticed the steering wheel pulling and a familar bumping of the front inside wheel. 'Oh no, a flat tyre,' I said to myself. Fortunately the road was empty so I pulled over onto the verge and got out to survey the damage.

And so on . . .

What are the similarities and differences in the language used in (a) and (b), and how do these relate to the purpose and audience of the text? We notice in (a), for example, that the verb choices are either imperative:

make sure . . . locate

or else rely on a generalized pronoun 'you', with a tense choice which again generalizes the action referred to. Any time you change a tyre, you do the following. The selection of the imperative form against the you + present-tense verb also has implications; the former is likely to be read as more formal or distant, while the generalized 'you' shifts the text towards informality and is likely to be read as more 'user-friendly'.

Another feature of the procedure as written text is that it follows very closely the sequence of actions in real time to which it refers. If you imagine a video of the procedure of changing a tyre, you would see a series of actions in which a driver gets out of the car, opens the boot, locates the spare tyre and the jack and then proceeds to change the tyre.

The procedure of tyre-changing also relates to an everyday activity commonplace to car owners. If the reader is not a car owner or not 'mechanical', then it may not seem so obvious. A procedure can be defined as a text which describes how to perform a series of actions so as to achieve an outcome (which is as much as to say that procedures have to have something like a narrative point). *Relevance* is a pragmatic feature in procedural texts: the writer should not exhaustively describe every minute step and stage of the action sequence (getting out of the car, inserting the key in the boot, opening the boot, removing material in the boot prior to locating the spare wheel) because this would introduce irrelevant material. Procedural texts, like narratives, involve the writer in complex selections from activity in the world.

So what is the purpose and audience of the procedure? The purpose can be defined as providing information as to the correct manner of performing a task, including the sequence of operations involved. The audience, very broadly, is anyone who needs or wants to be informed about how to carry out the task. We have seen how the choice of imperative or you + verb can shift the relationship of writer and reader, to create a more accessible and 'user-friendly' tone. Procedural texts generally refer to sequences of operations which are repeatable over and over again, hence the tense choice of the general present.

Procedures referring to a sequence of actions with an outcome can also describe things like scientific experiments or a complex work process, like, for example, carrying out a literacy skills audit in a workplace. These procedures may be in themselves somehow more complex than everyday procedures, like tyre-changing (though we all have stereotypes of brilliant people who can't boil an egg, so this isn't always the case).

What about the story version of tyre-changing in (b)? First we need to take into account the typical schematic staging of a narrative:

ABSTRACT = What is this going to be about?
ORIENTATION = Who, where and in what circumstances did this happen?
COMPLICATING ACTION = What actually happened?
EVALUATION = What was so newsworthy about what happened?
RESOLUTION = What was the outcome?
CODA = How does this link back into current discourse time?

The narrative fragment above orientates the narrative (an empty highway, early in the morning, the storyteller driving on his or her own). The complication: 'I suddenly noticed the steering wheel pulling and the familiar bumping . . .I pulled over and got out . . .'

One similarity between the narrative and the procedure schematically is in the temporal sequence of each which tends to go first A then B and then C and so on. What is different is that in a narrative text, the temporal sequence happens once and once only, and this is of course reflected in tense choice.

Another difference is in the way in which narrative typically dramatizes the events described through the reactions and thought processes of the participants, as a form of internal evaluation of the significance of the events described. The following all contribute in some way to the dramatization of the subjective reaction of the protagonist:

minding my own business

I suddenly noticed
familiar
'Oh no, a flat tyre,' I said to myself.
fortunately
survey the damage

All of these items in different ways incorporate the subjective responses of the protagonist to the flat tyre.

A key difference between narrative and procedure is that subjectivity has little or no place in a procedural description, whereas it is a central feature in narrative. The success of a narrative is primarily judged on the way it can enact its newsworthiness stylistically; the success of a procedural text is primarily judged firstly by the clarity with which it communicates the necessary information (as text) and secondly by its correspondence with the real world sequence of operations to which it corresponds. A procedure describing how to change a tyre may be well formed linguistically, but if it omits an essential operation it is still a bad procedure.

As a development from the narrative activity, it is interesting to see what happens when the purpose/audience variables are shifted. Suppose the above was a written statement required for legal purposes describing the changing of the tyre, for example in making a legal claim. What features of the narrative would be different? A shift in the social purpose of a genre will always result in some shift in the way it is organized.

TEXT-CENTRED THEORIES OF WRITING

Recent developments in discourse analysis and pragmatics have made it possible to analyse and understand the organization of written text in a way that was not accessible to sentence-level grammar. I have argued throughout this book that a theory of text is a key component of a theory of literacy as situated social practice. Without it, we are stuck on the descriptive level of 'uses of literacy', without having any principled way of describing the product of these uses of literacy, in this case written texts. The significance of these advances in linguistic knowledge is that they make possible the explicit teaching of text organization in a way that was not possible before.

There is a fair degree of congruence between procedures and narratives in the spoken and written mode, so there are obvious transfers between spoken and written to be made in working with texts of this kind. It is in other genres like expository writing, where the principles of textual organization do not refer in a simple manner to a set of referents in the 'real' world (the operations involved in changing a tyre, the event sequence of a story) that these new understandings of text organization will be most revealing.

Take, for example, the following:

1   Criteria for the assessment of the competency in tyre-changing can be located in Section 4 of the training manual (page 35).
2   Competency in tyre-changing is assessed for preference by a practical demonstration of competency. This may be accompanied by either oral or written questioning.
3   Competencies achieved should be recorded on the form provided.

Typical of this expository, report-type writing are the elision of the human agent, the foregrounding of complex nominal groupings ('Criteria for the assessment of the competency in tyre-changing') which can be unpacked in the following ways:

- X changes tyres.
- X is competent in changing tyres.
- Y assesses X for competency in changing tyres.
- There are criteria for the assessment of competency in tyre-changing.
- Z draws up criteria so that Y can assess X for competency in tyre-changing.

And so on. These invented examples demonstrate what Halliday has called the lexical density of the written mode. All of the above are packed into the density of the nominal group, while that grammar is relatively straightforward:

A can be located in B

It is in texts like the above that debates on plain English come into play (remember the earlier discussion about intrinsic and ascribed power in discourse). A number of writers, particularly Kress (1985) and Martin (1989) argue that the language of expository prose must be seen as a kind of technology for communicating abstract, technical information in an economical way. For these theorists, there is something intrinsically or functionally powerful about expository genres, in terms of what they can do. It follows from this stance that technical registers are justified as part of the technology of a particular discourse.

If contextual writing research emphasizes the range and diversity of uses of writing, text-centred literacy research explores the internal organization of the texts which are thus identified. Take, for example, the case of researching the writing practices of a workplace, as Helen Joyce did in the material quoted on page 210. The researcher would need to identify the range of writing practices in the workplace and from that gather a representative sample of texts. In order to gain some insight into the linguistic demands of these workplace texts, a further stage of analysis is necessary in order to understand the textual organization of these text types. From this an understanding of the relative demands of the writing tasks of that workplace can be worked out, having done what is in effect a writing task analysis.

A recurrent theme of this book is the complementarity and interrelationship between linguistically based and socially contexted approaches to understanding literacy. Text-centred literacy research requires ethnographic research of literacy in context in order to come up with information as to which kinds of writing are criterial in which contexts.

PHONE MESSAGES: MOVING FROM ORAL TO WRITTEN

As we saw in the previous section, a genre can vary depending on factors like setting, purpose and audience. Take, for example, a telephone message. Telephone messages are likely to feature in at least the home and the work domains. The purpose of the telephone message may be similar in both domains, but other factors may vary. For example, in the workplace there may be a usual pro forma for recording telephone messages. At home it may be just a scrap of paper or whatever is convenient to write on. In other words, there may be a tendency at work to greater formality in taking and recording phone messages.

The following examples of phone messages taken in my workplace will help us to work out the characteristics of the phone message as a genre. They will also help us to examine the bridge between writing as text and writing as process, and to begin to ask what kinds of evidence can throw light on writing as process.

TELEPHONE MESSAGE

Received by ....

For M .... M. Baynham .... Date 22.5.90

From .... Kate Howell .... cannot

.... make tonight. Pls call her

.... to arrange for appointment.

....

....

....

Please Ring No:

Time ....   W 432 2152

H 451 3239

Figure 6.1a

TELEPHONE MESSAGE

Received by ....

For M .... M. Baynham .... Date 24/5/90

From .... Kate Howell had

.... appointment this afternoon,

.... she can't now make it.

....

....

....

Please Ring No:

Time ....

Figure 6.1b

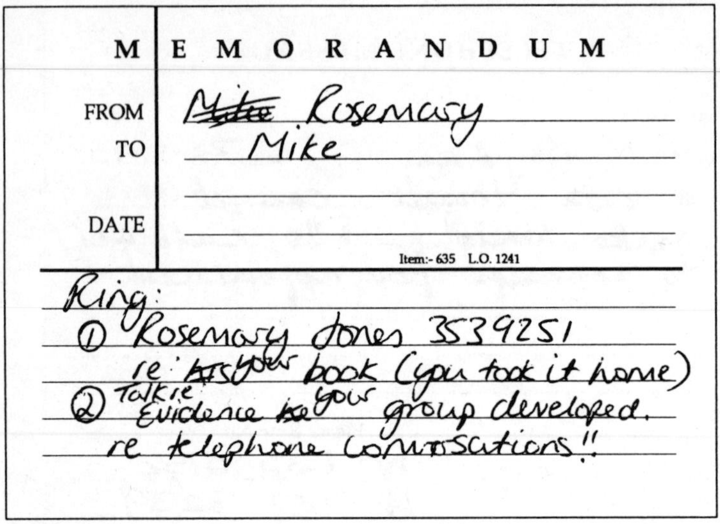
MEMORANDUM

FROM ~~Mike~~ Rosemary

TO Mike

DATE

Item:- 635 L.O. 1241

Ring:

① Rosemary Jones 3539251
re: ~~ATS~~ your book (you took it home)

② Talk re
Evidence ~~to~~ your group developed.
re telephone conversations!!

Figure 6.1c

From these examples we can begin to see the demands of taking phone messages as a writing task. First, it involves converting a message in the spoken mode into writing. Reconstructing the original communication on which the phone message is based involves reconstructing the I/you polarity of the original conversation:

> I AM PHONING YOU TO ASK YOU TO PASS ON A MESSAGE TO HIM/HER

Recording the message in written mode, as would passing it on orally, involves pragmatic work shifting the deixis of the pronouns. What is HIM/HER in the original message frame of the telephone conversation, becomes YOU in the new I/YOU polarity set up between the message-taker and the recipient of the message. Similarly, when the message-leaver makes I references within the I/YOU polarity of the original telephone conversation, these have to be converted into HE/SHE references within the new message frame.

This is clearly related to the mechanisms of indirect speech reporting, in which the reporter usually has to do pragmatic work on shifting pronoun reference in order to report a clause indirectly.

We can illustrate this by reconstructing what might be the original reference of messages (1a), which might go something like this:

> This is Kate Howell speaking. I'd like to leave a message for
> Mike Baynham. Could you tell him that I can't make our meeting
> tonight and could you ask him to phone me to arrange another
> appointment.

or

> I'd like to leave a message for Mike Baynham. Could you tell him
> that Kate Howell can't make the meeting tonight and ask him to
> phone me to make another appointment.

Both of the above would be possible reconstructions of the original
conversation on which the message (1a) is based. The following might
be a possibility for message (1b):

> This is Kate Howell speaking. I'd like to leave a message for Mike
> Baynham. I had an appointment with him this afternoon and I'm
> afraid I can't now make it.

In addition to the shifting of pronoun reference, derived from the
mechanisms of speech-reporting, there are interesting differences
between these two messages in their degree of explicitness.
Message (1a) explicitly fills out a piece of relevant background
information:

> Kate Howell had appointment this afternoon

In contrast, in the following:

> Kate Howell cannot make tonight

it is left to the recipient to reconstruct pragmatically what not
making tonight refers to.

There are also grammatical characteristics of the telephone
message genre, which can be fairly easily explained by the
hasty circumstances in which phone messages are usually taken:
a tendency towards a telegraphic omission of function words, as
can be seen from the examples above.

Example (1c) provides more of a window into the process of
message-taking in that the message-taker has corrected the original
version of the message, in ways that illustrate some components of
the planning process in message-taking.

First, the pronoun reference of HIS, which refers from within the deictic frame of the original conversation is changed to YOUR, within the I/YOU polarity of the written phone message. Secondly, the correction of 'He' to 'Your group' makes more explicit what the referent is. The message involves other kinds of assumed information. What is the referent of 'your book', for example? What is the significance of '(you took it home)'? It might appear quite normal for a book belonging to an individual to be taken home by that individual.

What is assumed in this message is that the message-receiver will understand what book is being referred to and what is the significance of its being taken home.

To understand this message fully it is necessary to know the implicit narrative underlying the message, which is that the message-receiver had been at a consultation meeting on a literacy assessment project, which had involved completing a book of questions and had forgotten to hand it in at the end of the meeting. R.J., the project worker, was phoning to ask for it to be sent on and to talk about discussions that had been held in the group about the literacy demands of telephone message-taking. 'Your book' in this context does not mean 'book belonging to you', but 'book belonging to us which you completed'.

We also note the typical telegraphic grammar of telephone message-taking.

Through analysing these examples of telephone messages we have been able to say something about writing as text, but we have increasingly been drawn into saying things about writing as process. For example, the shifting of pronoun reference in writing the telephone message based on the original oral message demands pragmatic work of the message-taker who is having to convert pronoun reference into the new discourse frame of the written message. In addition, we noted textually that there was considerable reliance on implicit knowledge in the phone messages, making them fairly context-bound. Assessing what background knowledge the reader of the message needs to know and what will be available to him or her from context also moves us from text to writing process, in other words, in the direction of the writer.

Activity

(a) Collect examples of written telephone messages. Try to record the actual form of words as well as your written message. If the

message is relatively short, this should be possible. When you
have a few examples of these data, try and work out what shifts
were involved in transforming the spoken to the written message.
(b) Now collect some examples of messages left on answerphones.
In what ways are these oral messages different from the written
telephone messages?

Another important issue, as we start to talk about writing process,
is what is the nature of the evidence that can be brought forward
to cast light onto the process of writing? How can we know what
is going on in the writer? This will be the focus of the next section
of this chapter. We will be looking at the writing process both in
'fluent' writers and learner writers.

UNDERSTANDING WRITING AS PROCESS

Understanding writing as process brings us into the second layer
of the language model presented in Chapter 1. It is worth pointing
out once again that writing-as-text and writing-as-process are two
aspects of the same thing and that the approach to understanding
writing-as-text necessarily implies the dimension of writing-as-
process. It is for this reason that we include factors like purpose,
audience and setting in text analysis.

To put it another way, the emphasis in writing-as-text is on the
options that are systematically available to the writers of given
'literacy communities', the emphasis in writing-as-process is on
the ways in which writers select from the options available to them
and on the decision-making processes involved in constructing
written texts.

Text-centred writing research, which involves the collection
and analysis of written texts, in order to understand better
their internal organization and structure, provides evidence of
the targets of literacy processes. Advances in discourse analysis
are beginning to enable us to understand in great detail what the
features of text organization are, and this provides important input
into literacy teaching processes.

One of the crucial advances in knowledge about writing involves
just the diversity of kinds or genres of writing that we have been
discussing. Instead of seeing writing as a monolithic whole, we can
begin to develop a theory of difference in writing, emphasizing the
difference in writing purposes and the resultant text structures. So

if we are to start to characterize the knowledge and skills of the fluent writer, we need to emphasize a dimension of metalinguistic awareness, the critical language awareness which was discussed in the last chapter.

If language awareness, and in particular the awareness of different text types, gives the writer an understanding of where the goal posts are, the pragmatics of text – in particular, the relationship between given and new information, what needs to be made explicit and what can be left to the reader to fill in – is another important dimension. In the examples of telephone messages, we saw that some quite significant pieces of information were assumed to be recoverable from the message recipient's contextual knowledge. In the narrative of changing a tyre we saw the importance of orientation in narrative writing as well as the importance of stylistic choice in the evaluative component of the narrative. We saw how the narrative has space for the subjectivity of participants in ways that the procedure did not.

A major source of incoherence in texts is when the writer does not effectively assess the kinds of background information that must be available to the reader to interact with the text. An instance of this from spoken language is when a speaker insists on telling the plot of a film or television programme at length with a confusion of pronouns referring to the different characters:

> And then he picks up his gun and takes a shot at the other guy,
> while his friend is escaping over the garden wall of his house.

One of the processes involved in organizing writing is just this fine-tuned assessment of what the reader needs or is likely to know in order to process the text. In doing so, the writer draws on pragmatic knowledge, the ability to decentre, as Donaldson (1984) puts it, and reconstruct the potential readership.

There are occasions when pragmatic knowledge enables a written text to be read successfully even when the information contained within it is incomplete in some way. The following is a note which was left on my desk at work some years ago:

ALI   MSR MAIK AM SORE

NO CAM TOD

This message is incomplete in a number of ways, in terms of its spelling (SORE = SORRY, CAM = COME, MSR = MR, AM = I'M, TOD = TODAY), for example; its grammar (what does NO CAM TOD refer to? does it mean 'Don't come today' or 'I can't come today'?). Yet, in context, I was able to make perfect sense of it. The context was that I had made an appointment to visit Ali Lazizi, a shift worker in a hotel, to give him an English lesson. The purpose of the message was cancel the arrangement. How, for example, did I derive 'SORRY' from the evidence of 'SORE'? Having once identified the overall purpose of the message, which was cancelling an appointment, apologizing becomes something that might be conventionally expected. So the overall purpose of the text provides a structure of expectation about what it will contain which enables me to read particular words.

Clearly, this pragmatic knowledge interacts with knowledge about text, permitting, for example, a fair degree of inexplicit, context-derived reference in some genres, such as personal messages, while demanding a much higher degree of context-free, explicit reference in others.

Activity

> Look back over the tyre-changing texts. Can you find examples
> of places where you relied on implicit knowledge, derivable from
> context in these two texts? What strategies did you use for ensuring
> that the reader had adequate background knowledge to process the
> text? Do you find any difference between the degree of explicitness in
> the procedural description and the narrative?

Evidence of the pragmatic work involved in text construction is recoverable from texts themselves; indeed, the major data source of linguistic pragmatics is the analysis of spoken and written text, so this particular writing process can be investigated textually. What other kinds of evidence of writing processes are available?

The role of errors, slips and reformulations in understanding the processes going on in language use has been crucial and it is clearly a feature of writing research. In telephone message (1c) above, we saw how the correction of 'his' to 'your' opened a window on one aspect of the task of writing telephone messages. This is a case where the process of text construction is revealed in the text, because the writer, for obvious reasons, did not go the extra stage of providing a final fair copy with no corrections or alterations. Such alterations and corrections are valuable evidence of the planning process.

Many kinds of writing, however, demand the final stage of the fair copy. A job application, for example, would be negatively evaluated if it contained crossings-out and reformulations. Similarly, an essay or class assignment will probably go to the fair copy stage. The final stage of a writing process is to sweep the evidence under the carpet.

So another kind of evidence, again based on text, would be the successive stages of drafting and redrafting which produce the finished text.

Case study

Here are two successive versions of a folk story written by an Iranian student, Manejieh. The context of writing was a reading of a short story by Stephen Leacock called 'My Bank Account' in which the narrator timidly tries to open an account with a small amount of money and is treated scornfully by the staff in the bank. Manejieh told the story as topically relevant to a story of humiliation by the 'gatekeepers' in the bank, for reasons that will be apparent.

Version one

> One day Molla-Nasraddin was invited to a party, he went to the party without changing his ordinary clothes, but the receptionist stoped him to go there, and told him he couldn't go while he is wearing ragged clothes, but he rushed backed home and changed his clothes to the best clothes ever he had.
> He came backed to the party everyone bowed at him, and offered him nice place to sit down.
> It was time for dinner, they served best food, but Molla instead of eating the food he was putting the food in his sleeves.
> Everyone was astonished, what was he doing, probably they thought he was mad. Somebody asked him why is feeding his clothes.
> He said I am hear because of my clothes.

The first version of the story was written by Manejieh and read out to the class. The second version of the story was scribed by the teacher on the whiteboard and incorporated revisions and reformulations suggested by the teacher and other students, with significant interventions from the teacher.

Version two

MULLAH NASREDDIN AND THE PARTY

One day Mullah Nasreddin was invited to a party. He went to the party without changing out of his ordinary clothes. When he arrived at the party, the doorman stopped him from going in.

'You can't come in here wearing ragged clothes like that,' he said. So Mullah Nasreddin rushed back home and changed his clothes. He put on the smartest clothes he had. Then he hurried back to the party. Everyone bowed at him when he arrived and offered him a nice place to sit down.

It was time for dinner. They served the best food. But Mullah, instead of eating the food, started putting the food in his sleeves. Everyone was astonished. What was he doing? They thought he was mad.

Then somebody asked him: 'Why are you putting food in your sleeves?'

And Mullah said: 'My clothes have been invited to the party not me. So I'm feeding them.'

Revision and reformulation can involve work at all levels of the text, from spelling and punctuation, through grammar and lexical choice, to features of the discourse organization. What kind of reworking took place between version one and version two of the Mullah Nasreddin story?

Spelling
(few changes)

stoped ——— stopped
hear ——— here

Punctuation
(significant changes)

The text is chunked into shorter units in version two, using full stops instead of commas.

Direct speech is indicated by quotation marks.

Lexical choice
(just one change)

receptionist ——— doorman

Sentence grammar and morphology
(a number of changes)

everyone bowed *at* him —— everyone bowed to him

he rushed *backed* home —— he rushed back home

the receptionist *stoped him to go* there —— the doorman stopped him from going in

but *Molla* instead of eating the food *he* was putting the food in his sleeves —— But Mullah, instead of eating the food, started putting the food in his sleeves.

(The pronoun 'he' copying the proper name 'Molla' is not a typical feature of standard English, though it is common in learner varieties of English and in other languages, for instance Arabic.)

Somebody asked him why is feeding his clothes. —— somebody asked him: 'Why are you putting food in your sleeves?'

Text cohesion

Version two has a rather more diversified range of conjunctions in play. Version one uses only two conjunctions, 'and' and 'but'. In Version two, 'and', 'but', 'then' and 'so' are used.

Discourse organization

Discourse organization involves the stylistic shaping of the schematic structure of the story-line. The choice of direct/indirect speech is one of the stylistic options in organizing the narrative story-line. Version one starts with indirect speech:

the receptionist . . . told him he couldn't go while he is wearing ragged clothes

The next instance is an example of free indirect speech, which dramatizes the thoughts running through the minds of the other guests when Mullah starts spooning food into his sleeves:

what was he doing

followed by an indirectly reported thought:

probably they thought he was mad

and another example of indirectly reported speech:

Somebody asked him why is feeding his clothes

It is only in the punch-line in this version that direct speech occurs:

He said I am hear because of my clothes.

In the second version, a number of the instances of indirect speech have been converted to direct speech, with the effect of foregrounding and dramatizing the utterances. In some senses the grammatical range of Version two is less complex in this respect, though more typical of the conventional expectations of the folk-story genre.

Schematic structure

The schematic structure of Version two is much the same as that of Version one. One difference is in the punch-line, in which the point of the story is highlighted more explicitly, by reorganizing Mullah's utterance to bring out the logical connection between his earlier treatment (being barred from the party because of his shabby clothes, then admitted once he had changed into smarter ones) and his incomprehensible behaviour (spooning food into his sleeves).

Discussion

The overall effect of the original version is significantly reworked on a number of textual levels, resulting in a second version. Is the second version an 'improvement' on the first?

At the time, the participants in the class, Manejieh and myself included, thought so. Other readers have not agreed, arguing that the second version is rather dull and conventional and has interrupted Manejieh's distinctive voice. Were the revisions and changes in the different textual levels equally necessary; for example, the spelling, punctuation, sentence level grammar, as opposed to the text cohesion, discourse organization, schematic structure? What would the effect have been if we had reworked spelling, punctuation, sentence grammar and left the other levels of text organization alone?

Research into drafting and redrafting processes has shown that the writing process is cyclical or recursive, not linear (cf. Zamel 1983, for example).

Clearly, there is a general problem in researching writing

processes (as with other cognitive processes), which is that of knowing what is going on in the mind of the writer. The evidence in the form of text output or various special cases like error correction, reformulation and redrafting is used to create a theory of text construction.

One solution to the problem of knowing exactly which cognitive processes are going on as writers write is what is called the 'think aloud protocol' and was used by Flowers and Hayes (1980, 1981) in their research into writing process. Kelly (1986) describes think aloud protocols as follows:

> In this procedure, as applied to writing, a subject is required to say aloud every thought which arises and to say aloud what he or she writes. These utterances are recorded on tape and at the end of the session the manuscript and the tape are collected. The tapes are transcribed and later coded to identify the type of behaviour manifested. Thus all instances of planning, questioning, hesitating, repeating, re-reading, reformulating, are identified, including such phenomena as silences, comments and sighs. Together with the piece of completed writing the protocols give a rich data base for research. However, it must be acknowledged that much is unaccounted for.
>
> (Kelly 1986:99)

Think aloud protocols attempt to make explicit, albeit in a rather artificial manner, the cognitive work that is going on in planning and executing a written text. The implication here is that the writer is normally working in isolation.

Activity

Kelly outlines the procedure for conducting research on writing process using think aloud protocols. In terms of our discussion of the procedure genre above, write:

(a) a procedure for the researcher outlining the steps and stages involved in think aloud protocol research;
(b) a procedure for the research subject, outlining what they have to do to participate in the activity.

Having done this, try out the think aloud protocol procedure, either to document your own writing processes, or else someone else's on your network.

What do you think are the strengths and limitations of this way of gathering data on writing processes?

Now one of the implications of the research described above, within a cognitive paradigm, is that writing is an individual activity. However, the research on literacy in social context described in Chapter 2 contradicts this stereotype and shows that in many contexts writing is jointly constructed, with perhaps one person scribing and others contributing to the construction of the text. The second version of Manejieh's story was constructed in this way. Outside the classroom , it is possible to think of a range of contexts where texts might be jointly constructed, which generally means constructed using spoken language as a medium. Take, for example, the construction of written testimonies in legal settings, the formulation of a resolution in a formal meeting. In these contexts the process by which a written text is constructed will be explicit in the embedding spoken language.

Coming back to the context of classroom instruction, it will be clear that the joint construction of written texts can provide evidence about the nature of writing processes, since the construction of the written text is done in spoken language. Processes of joint construction provide their own evidence of the ways in which texts are constructed because they are public and relatively explicit, rather than privatizing the writing process.

So far we have examined writing as text and writing as process, while noting that these do not represent a dichotomy, but complementary aspects of the same phenomenon. We have seen how it is important to recognize difference, both at the level of text types and contexts, and that 'writing' is not a homogeneous construct. We have been largely characterizing the writing process in terms of the 'fluent' writer, although in the last example we introduce some of the issues in teaching writing. In the next section we will look in more detail at issues of writing process in the writing classroom.

WRITING DEVELOPMENT: NATURAL OR SOCIALLY CONSTRUCTED?

Approaches to writing pedagogy are likely to be significantly informed by the underlying conceptualization of how learning takes place. In this section, we will review two contrasting positions on how writing (and language more generally) is learned and show how these positions have informed debate about writing pedagogy.

The 'natural' position

This position holds that language in general, and writing more particularly, are best learned by creating learning environments in which the learner has access to the material to be learned in ways which re-create, as closely as possible, the conditions under which a child 'naturally' acquires his or her first language. The argument goes something like this:

> Under normal circumstances all children routinely achieve the enormous intellectual task of acquiring human language more or less independently of context. Children across cultural and social groups seem to acquire language in broadly similar developmental stages, without apparent effort. If children are able to make this enormous leap in apparently unschooled contexts, why does the learning of reading and writing seem to be an effort and a struggle? Surely the way to teach reading and writing is to approximate as closely as possible to the conditions under which the child initially learns language?

Underlying this position are also ideas that schooling as an institution oppresses the natural creativity and learning ability of the child, creating a pedagogical straitjacket which some children will adapt and submit to, while others will rebel against and be crushed by. The answer is to attempt in different ways to re-orientate what happens in the classroom, to try and make contact with the 'natural' creative energy of the learner which is somehow suppressed and oppressed by the demands of schooling as an institution.

This emphasis on tapping the individual creativity of the learner is one theme of the 'natural' approach to learning. Another deals with the kind of learning environment that should be created for learning to take place. If it is the case that learning occurs naturally and the surrounding environment serves as a trigger to that learning, then one of the main tasks of the teacher is to create the conditions under which learning can take place: a safe, non-threatening environment, which is rich in the kind of stimulus necessary to trigger learning. Underlying this condition for learning is an analogy with the language-learning environment of the young child, who is bathed or surrounded in language and, it is argued, has innate abilities to learn language triggered by this environmental stimulus.

So it follows that the literacy classroom should be similarly print-rich and stimulus-rich, that learning should promote the use of literacy within the classroom context in meaningful ways. We can see in this a clear contrast with 'traditional' writing pedagogies going from the bottom up from letters to letter combinations to words (possibly via syllables) to words combined into sentences, to sentences combined into short pedagogical texts and so on. The learner's gratification is indefinitely deferred until he or she has 'mastered the basics' and can set out into applying that mastery in daily uses of writing.

Another key concept in the natural approach to teaching writing is therefore that of *relevance*. Instead of the deferred gratification of the traditional approach, learning takes place through relevant, meaningful tasks. The classroom becomes a print-rich, stimulus-rich environment in which the written word is a natural solution to communication demands created by learning tasks.

An implicit assumption in this approach is that learning will occur as a series of approximations towards the 'end product'. This again is based on an analogy with the developmental approxima-tions through which the child learns his or her first language. If this occurs 'naturally', then the learner can be left to progress through the developmental stages of learning to write, providing enough input is provided, the conditions for learning are right and he or she has plenty of opportunity to practise.

From a theoretical perspective, this model of learning empha-sizes the innate cognitive abilities of the learner, and regards the input from the surrounding environment, while necessary, yet not sufficient to enable learning to take place. It is based on an *innatist* approach to cognitive development, particularly associated with the work of Chomsky and others who significantly influenced language learning theories from the mid-1960s onwards. Chomsky articulates particularly clearly the idea that language is an innate human faculty, part of the biological endowment of humankind, arguing that 'children grow language like birds grow wings'.

From an applied perspective, this approach to language learning has been developed in a particularly explicit way by Krashen (1981) and, in terms of writing pedagogy more particularly, in 'process' writing. Basically, the argument is that if you get the conditions for learning right, learners will learn, that they must be allowed to go through a developmental learning process, that they will reinvent or reconstruct learning stages, arriving, all things being equal, at coherent, well-organized text through a process of drafting, feedback and redrafting, during which the emphasis is on their 'ownership' of the text they are producing.

The emphasis here is on whole text or 'whole language', contrasted with the decontextualized exercise-based approach of traditional writing pedagogy. The 'natural' position on writing development has, however, been criticized from a number of perspectives. For a survey of these debates cf. Reid (1987).

Learning writing is socially constructed

First, the emphasis on the naturalness of language acquisition has been challenged. A number of researchers (Snow and Ferguson 1977; Painter 1989), looking at the early stages of first language acquisition, have shown the significance of the caretaker role in the language acquisition of the child. Language is learned not as an innate, internalized process, but in interaction with others. Studies like *Ways with Words* by Shirley Brice Heath have documented in great detail the ways in which young children are initiated into the communicative practices of their speech communities in ways that are structured and predictable. The analogy between early first language learning and later written language learning falls down because not even early first language learning fulfils the naturalness condition, it is socially constructed in ways that are predictable and open to analysis and understanding.

The second problem with the natural, whole language approach arises if there is no principled way to talk about how whole texts are organized. If the domain of the traditional approach to learning writing is sentence grammar and lexis, and the domain of whole language is whole text, it is therefore necessary to have an understanding of how the whole text is organized.

Now it is only in the last decade or so that advances in the understanding of the organization of discourse have provided analyses of text organization which may be of some help to the learner writer and the teacher of writing. An example of this is the use made of linguistics to build up a writing pedagogy based on the linguistic concept of the 'genre' (cf. Martin and Rothery 1980, 1981). In linguistic terms, the genre approach describes the typical schematic ordering of a range of types of text as well as the typical linguistic features used to realize them.

Another problem that can arise with a whole language approach to the teaching of writing derives from the emphasis on expressive writing and creativity. Studies of writing in primary schools have shown that there may be undue emphasis on writing for expressive purposes, as opposed to writing, for example, to convey factual information (cf. Martin and Rothery 1980, 1981). The discussion of Sue Gardener's work on writing in second-chance education, with the difficulty she identified in shifting students out of narrative into expository mode, is an indication that this may also be an issue in the adult writing classroom. At any rate, studies of the range of uses of writing and writing purposes of the sort discussed in Chapter 2 are necessary input into designing a writing curriculum. Systematic frameworks of types of writing can provide a checklist to ensure that particular text types are not being ignored because of teacher preference, for example.

Another key tenet of the strong version of the natural approach to teaching writing is that the writer initiates and owns the text and any work on the text in the form of conferencing on drafting and redrafting should respect the writer's freedom of expression. The model of learning underpinning this can be described as *creative construction*. The writers construct the text on their own terms in order to say what they mean. In contrast, an approach to teaching writing which emphasizes the organization of different kinds of text and the constraints that these place on the writer works with a metaphor of *access* or *initiation* into the means of text construction: writers need to learn how to write in particular ways. Particularly the more complex kinds of writing won't develop naturally but need to be taught explicitly; for example, prefaced by the reading and analysis of model texts.

This issue raises the question of explicit instruction versus unconscious learning. Within the natural model, learning is seen to be in large part unconscious, on the analogy with first language learning: we learn and use our mother tongue in an unconscious way, without being conscious of its organizing principles. In fact, the terms 'acquisition' and 'learning' are often used to distinguish between unconscious and conscious learning. It may be that writing programmes organized round principles of natural, unconscious learning through doing will restrict the learner writers to particular types of writing, familiar, expressive modes, without giving them access to more complex, abstract ways of writing, which don't develop 'naturally', necessary, for example, to achieve in formal study.

The shift away from concrete familiar uses of written language (such as, for example, writing a story about a familiar, everyday incident or writing out the steps and stages of a recipe) towards more abstract, unfamiliar domains (such as writing up a scientific experiment) may be one way of characterizing the relative difficulty or demands of writing tasks. Writing development can be seen, globally, as an increasing ability to control a range of types of writing of increasing difficulty.

In order to understand what difficulty in writing might mean, apart from in a purely intuitive way, we need to have some organizing framework of the sort described above, which can map the shift from concrete, everyday uses of written language, to more complex, abstract uses of language. Systemic functional linguistics is particularly good at characterizing abstraction in language, using constructs like *congruence/incongruence* and *grammatical metaphor* to describe the ways in which language adapts to refer to entities and processes that are not within the immediate human life world.

A congruent utterance is one in which actions are represented by verbs, things by nouns or nominal groups (cf. Halliday 1985a), typically in the basic transitivity type of X did Y or X did Y to Z:

John donated the money
John donated the money to the Smith family

Incongruence involves a shifting away from the basic transitivity pattern, through the use of devices like nominalization, which allow the possibility of more complexly embedded grammatical organization:

John's donation to the Smith family was acknowledged by a letter informing him that it was tax deductible

One means of shifting around the meaning relations of the congruent sentence is grammatical metaphor. Take the following examples from a primary-school history book (Windrow 1986):

1   Between the 1100s and the late 1400s there were enormous changes in the design of armour.
2   In the mid-1300s the knight began to face two challenges to his mastery of the battlefield: the use of trained foot-soldiers with long-range weapons, and the appearance of the first guns.
3   The 1400s saw commanders making slow progress in forcing their knights to obey a disciplined plan.

One of the necessary resources in writing history is to be able to locate actions and events in their historical period. Examples 1 and 2 do this in a relatively commonplace way with adverbial phrases of time. They are congruent in the sense we have been talking about. Example 3, however, skews the congruence of the typical:

At such and such a time X happened

by making the time component the subject of the verb of seeing/ perception.

Once the possibilities of these metaphorical reworkings of meaning relations have been grasped, the writer then has access to a wider range of stylistic resources in the writing process. We can illustrate this by reworking the history book examples above:

1   The period between the 1100s and the late 1400s saw enormous changes in the design of armour.
2   The mid-1300s saw the knight facing two challenges to his mastery of the battlefield . . .
3   By the 1400s commanders were making slow progress in forcing their knights to obey a disciplined plan.

Grammatical metaphor is a key component of the 'abstract' texture of expository writing and opens up a wider range of possibilities in the organization of text. Halliday writes (1985a: 321):

> Metaphorical modes of expression are characteristic of all adult discourse. There is a great deal of variation among different registers in the degree and kind of metaphor that is encountered; but none will be found entirely without it.

A theory of text that can cast light on the ways in which texts are typically organized not only enables us to focus on the differences between text types, but also to develop some measures of comparison; for example, all other things being equal, this text is more difficult than that one.

It has been pointed out (Christie 1990) that the 'bottom-up' teaching of writing in traditional pedagogies is complemented by the study of rhetoric, which concerns itself with the organization of discourse in contexts of use (mainly public and formal). In medieval taxonomies, grammar was the key of the door which opened onto the further studies (major and minor), including rhetoric. The chief tool of traditional rhetoric was the imitation of models. We have noted above a shift away from texts constructed 'out of the

head' of the writer, towards an emphasis on modelling as a prelude
to text construction. There are a whole range of traditional learning
strategies, imitating models, learning by heart, dictation, which
are out of step with progressive pedagogy because they do not
fit with the construction of the learner as active, in control and
owning what is learned. The emphasis here is on apprenticeship
leading to access into modes of discourse which are not available
'naturally'.

FROM TALK TO WRITING: THE WRITING CURRICULUM

In an earlier chapter I emphasized that writing is not talk written
down and that it has its own principles of organization which in
fact make spoken and written language very different. We have,
however, established above that some kinds of writing (the more
'congruent' types) are in fact closer to spoken language than others.
For example, an oral account of a recipe, if taped and transcribed,
may be similarly organized schematically to a written version.

In starting writing it makes sense to begin from the familiar
and the congruent and to move out from there to the unfamiliar,
incongruent. An established technique for beginning writing is
to do precisely this, basing the initial writing instruction on
the *language experience* of the learner. The procedure for doing
this may vary from context to context, but might broadly look
something like this:

- tutor and student jointly identify some topic of interest to
  the student and generate some ideas for writing through
  discussion;
- the tutor suggests composing a piece of writing based on the
  discussion; if the student is a beginner writer then the tutor
  may scribe a text, which can be later used for reading or writing
  practice;
- the written text may go through a process of drafting and
  redrafting and end up typed or word-processed, for use in
  further literacy work or for publication.

It is worth remembering, however, that, even when the objective
of the tutor is faithfully to transcribe a spoken account word-for-
word, the transfer from spoken to written will necessarily involve
significant restructuring of the spoken.

Case study

The following text was written by Daniel, a Chilean student. The context for writing was a discussion on some reading materials from Cuba. He mentioned in the course of discussion that he had visited Cuba as a child, and the teacher asked him to write in his own words what he remembered of the trip. This is what he wrote:

> In 1969 when I went to Cuba what I remember is that the people were very nice the kids in the street were friendly and in the school too it was very hot (it was in summer about the end of summer) and I saw how the people lived in there. Well the conditions of the country were not very good after only ten years of the revolution. Well when I said the condition of the country were not good I meant housing and that kind of things because they were reconstructing the country.

This text contains many features typical of spoken language, for example the use of 'well' in the last two sentences, the ongoing repetitions, reformulations and elaborations, which convey a sense of thinking out loud:

> it was very hot (it was in summer about the end of summer)

> Well when I said the condition of the country were not good I meant housing

Activity

Using the categories that were employed to analyse the reworking that took place between Versions one and two of Manejieh's story –

  spelling
  punctuation
  sentence level grammar
  morphology
  text cohesion
  discourse organization
  schematic structure

– work through Daniel's text to see how the different levels of text organization contribute to the overall effect. If you find features that are significantly different from the discourse conventions of standard

English, try reworking them to see how the overall effect of the text
is changed.

Here is how Hood describes the introduction of literacy with a
group of beginner learners of English, illiterate in their L1:

> Literacy was introduced in ways that closely related to oral language
> contexts. A gradual process of introducing contexts of use that
> draw the learner away from the highly concrete and familiar would
> constitute the long term planning for such learners. A range of
> written texts (beyond simple recounts or name and address) could
> be introduced. These texts would relate closely to the fields of oral
> language interactions, but would begin to introduce new functions
> of language or new information. For example in the Hmong program
> described above, in the context of discussing crafts, the learners
> could be introduced to the idea of price tags. This could lead
> to the labelling of items for sale and the reading and writing of
> advertisements for sale. Other contexts such as cooking could lead
> to written texts such as product labels or recipes and so on.
>
> (Hood 1990: 59)

The organizing principle for the writing curriculum might be:

> start from the familiar, the concrete, that which is close to the
> lifeworld of the learner, but don't stop there.

To stop there may mean to keep the learner within the familiar
circle of everyday knowledge and experience, without the ability to
move into the incongruent domains where experience is construed
on unfamiliar principles, or where the textual base is not that of
everyday experience at all.

Where the writing curriculum stops is, of course, determined by
the needs and purposes of the learner. A learner whose desired
outcome is to continue his or her education will necessarily have
to come to terms with the discourses of the material they wish
to study. A learner whose desired outcome is work-related, or
who is job-seeking, will need to be extended and helped to deal
with texts related to the workplace. It is at these points that the
writing curriculum stops being an easy matter and can involve
considerable conflict on the part of the learner writer, struggling
to come to terms with dominant discourses, whether to reject,
acquiesce or struggle. This will be the topic of the next section,
which focuses, not on writing as text, or writing as process but on
the *writer*.

THE WRITER, SUBJECTIVITY AND RESISTANCE

Vignette

I am reading some pages of a novel in a further education class with a group of Afro-Caribbean teenagers, all of whom have grown up in England. The novel is by a Guyanese writer. The text is in standard English and the dialogue is in Guyanese creole. One of the teenagers comments contemptuously on the language of the novel (the authorial voice, not the dialogue in Guyanese creole): 'Black people don't use those kind of words.' He has detected a kind of 'whiteness' about the author's choice of language, which sets it apart from his own construction of black language and culture.

In an earlier chapter, we looked at what Gramsci called the 'inventory of traces': the accumulation of experience that creates the subjectivity of the literacy learner and the objective social positions which structure those experiences. For the adult returning to learning, who has been through the school system, those experiences are typically framed by concepts of success and failure, of dominance and powerlessness: failure in terms of the school as institution, and powerlessness in the face of the dominant discourses of schooling, whether it is the way the teacher controls the classroom through spoken language, or the kinds of written texts that make up the curriculum.

As the incident above perhaps shows, other objective social factors like gender, ethnicity and class contribute to the picture. The powerful discourses in society may be powerfully attached to success (as opposed to failure) and dominance (as opposed to powerlessness), but they may be just as powerfully attached to the other social categories: 'this is how white people talk/write', 'this is how men talk/write', 'this is a middle-class way of talking/writing'. This is the 'mainstream' culture that Heath writes about in *Ways with Words* (1983), contrasting it with the black and white-working class communities of Trackton and Roadville.

So what happens when adult learners are confronted with the powerful discourses, the discourses of exclusion; and just as interestingly, when do adult learners and adults in general encounter these discourses?

Typical everyday encounters would be the interview with a doctor, the interview with a social worker, a child's teacher: all professionals, backed up by powerful discourses, acquired as part of their education and training. Combined with the social power of their professional status, and the institutional settings in which such encounters typically take place, we can see clearly how the unequal distribution of power is systematic, both in discourse and social structure.

If, however, an adult is returning to study or training, they will confront these powerful discourses in a different way, in terms of the expectation placed on them to become adept in these ways of writing and talking, in terms of what they are required to read and write and the ways they are expected to participate in spoken interaction. Sue Gardener's study of second-chance education threw up some of the issues which arise when adults are expected to shift away from the more familiar, everyday modes of discourse towards the powerful modes of expository writing.

Ivanič and Roach (1990) quote a powerful metaphor through which Roach tries to explain the shifts involved in learning the discourse conventions of academic writing:

> I might not like the clothes that I wear but I wear them because I haven't got anything else. I use that language because I haven't got anything else. Now if I've got access to get new clothes, different clothes, even though there are clothes on offer I will make distinctions in which ones I'm going to buy...and it's the choice between the words that you use, between the clothes that you buy, says something about you . . .
>
> (Ivanič and Roach 1990: 103)

Acquiring new discourse conventions, particularly those that are socially powerful, raises important questions of identity: am I the same person that I was before I learned to speak/write like this, or has the process changed me? If it has changed me is the change some sort of betrayal of what I was? In adopting the discourse conventions of the powerful, am I becoming identified with the powerful in excluding the powerless?

When we think of powerful discourses and discourse conventions, it is useful to think in terms of 'discourse communities'. Who is on the inside in this particular discourse community – for example, the discourse community of particular kinds of academic writing? How do you get to be on the inside? What are the costs and benefits of being on the inside?

Swales (1990) describes the discourse community as having the following characteristics:

1   A discourse community has a broadly agreed upon set of common public goals
2   A discourse community has mechanisms for intercommunication among its members
3   A discourse community uses its participatory mechanisms primarily to provide information and feedback
4   A discourse community utilizes and hence possesses one or more genres in the communicative furtherance of its aims
5   The discourse community has some specific vocabulary
6   A discourse community has a threshold level of members with a suitable degree of relevant content and discoursal experience.

(adapted from Johns 1990: 28)

Put more briefly, we could say that a discourse community shares a register and a set of institutional practices for communicating through that register.

The idea of a discourse community has been useful in characterizing the demands of academic writing, while emphasizing its institutional nature. How does a novice become initiated or socialized into the ways with words of medicine or nursing or sociology or linguistics? It's not just a question of the language, but also of the accompanying social roles. Clark *et al.* (1990) quote a response to a student's essay from a tutor:

> your argument is undermined at several points by use of the personal pronoun. Avoid the use of 'I' or 'in my opinion' in all formal academic writing: (Name of student) is not a recognized authority or author – or at least not yet.

(Clark *et al.* 1990: 87)

Not all writers are equal within the discourse community: the apprentice writer quotes the views of others, but elides his or her own subjectivity.

So what is the response of the learner writer when confronted with the discourse conventions of a new discourse community? One response is simply to take on the discourse conventions, critically or uncritically, and learn how to be an effective writer in a given discourse community. This is a relatively straightforward response and the benefits may be clear, but the costs may not be so immediately clear. There may be learners for whom the discourse conventions of the new discourse community radically contravene previous discourse and social conventions. This is particularly likely to be the case when there is some degree of social distance between the learner and the discourse community.

The work of Scollon and Scollon provides a clear example of this. They discovered in their research that Athabascan Indian students in Canada were disadvantaged in a number of ways by the discourse conventions of the dominant Anglo culture. One of the cultural norms of Athabascans is against overt display, for example. One of the expectations of essay-writing in the dominant Anglo culture is that knowledge should be displayed. Athabascans are therefore reluctant to engage in this display of knowledge in essay-writing, because of the way in which this contradicts their cultural norms, and hence underperform in these school-related tasks.

So there may be some learner writers for whom learning new discourse conventions involves some sort of betrayal. Learning a new register can be compared here to learning a new language. Will the new register/language supplant the old register/language, or will in fact the new register/language become an addition to the communicative repertoire of the learner?

The concept of additive and subtractive language learning is relevant here: does learning a second language necessarily involve forgetting or giving up a first? We know from studies on bilingualism that there is no necessary relationship between learning a second language and giving up a first one. Similarly, learning another register need not necessarily take the learner permanently into the realm of those who talk/write 'posh' or like white people or whatever. Language users have the ability to switch between a whole range of language varieties. Where the problems seem to arise, however, is when there is some measure of linguistic and/or social distance between one language variety or social group, and where learning the discourse conventions of one may contradict the discourse conventions of another. This is most obvious when there is a relationship of unequal power or oppression between one language variety and another.

Accommodation can be conscious or unconscious, critical or uncritical, and either way is likely to lead to fairly unproblematic learning for the learner writer. The choice is either to learn the discourse conventions of the dominant culture because they are there and 'given', uncritically, or else to learn these conventions critically and strategically as a means of gaining access to powerful discourses and their benefits.

What happens when a writer rejects, partly or completely, the strategy of accommodation? Again there is a dimension of conscious/unconscious, critical/uncritical. If a writer rejects the discourse conventions of a given genre in a critical, conscious way, this could involve deliberately introducing the first-person pronoun into expository prose, or introducing features more typical of spoken language into written text. The following is the reproduction of a paragraph from earlier in this chapter:

> Acquiring new discourse conventions, particularly those that are socially powerful, raises important questions of identity: am I the same person that I was before I learned to speak/write like this, or has the process changed me? If it has changed me, is the change some sort of betrayal of what I was? In adopting the discourse conventions of the powerful, am I becoming identified with the powerful in excluding the powerless?

The strategy used in this paragraph to dramatize rhetorically the 'important questions of identity' is of creating a fictionalized 'I' who can ask himself or herself these important questions. Dramatizing the speech or thought of fictionalized characters is, of course, typical of narrative. It is here used as a rhetorical device to lessen the social distance between writer and reader which is created by the more objectified tone of the expository prose in which it is embedded.

The question that then arises is whether the use of a particular strategy is conscious and critical or whether it is unconscious and uncritical; for example, if the writer is not aware of the demands of the discourse conventions and flouts them unknowingly. Conscious and critical manipulation of discourse conventions, either for stylistic effect, or else as an act of 'resistance', as Giroux (1983) and Chase (1988) call it, presupposes a prior knowledge of what these discourse conventions are. If a writer chooses a more spoken-like style of writing to signal a set of relationships with the reader or as an act of resistance to the dominance of certain discourses, that is one thing. If a writer writes 'as he or she speaks' primarily because he or she is not aware of the options of written language, that is another.

The critical reader, including the teacher of writing, needs to be able to read whether particular choices in discourse are conscious critical choices, or simply due to a lack of awareness of the range of options open to the writer. In bilingual contexts another factor is whether a particular textual feature is a transfer from the discourse conventions of the first language or whether it is a result of not having learnt some aspect of the textual organization of the L2.

CONCLUSION

In this chapter I have argued that an adequate theory of writing needs to take into account the different but complementary dimensions of writing as text, writing as process, the subjectivity of the writer and writing as social practice.

Focusing on writing as social practice necessarily involves the recognition of different and possibly competing ideological perspectives on writing. We have identified a number of these ideological points of cleavage in the course of the chapter. Is writing (and language more generally) acquired naturally, or is the learning of writing socially constructed? Does the learning of writing take place through a process of creative construction, or should a writing pedagogy aim to open up access to the ways that dominant modes of discourse are constructed through writing? What is the relationship between the learner writer's 'voice' and the conventionalized voices of the dominant discourses? What stances can or do writers take in relationship to the dominant discourses: accommodation, rejection, resistance? Once we begin to answer these questions, we will be working towards an adequate theory of writing practices.

SUGGESTIONS FOR FURTHER READING

Barton, D. and Ivanič, R. (1991) *Writing in the Community*, London: Sage.

Christie, F. (ed.) (1990) *Literacy for a Changing World*, Melbourne: ACER.

SEVEN

Researching literacy as social practice

LITERACY AS TEXT/PROCESS/PRACTICE

This book has argued for an emphasis on literacy as social practice, involving both what people do with literacy and what they make of what they do: the values they place on it and the ideologies that surround it.

In order to deal with the multi-dimensional nature of literacy practices, this book has argued for a complementary approach to analysing literacy, drawing on ethnography and social theory and linguistics: that what is needed is both a theory of text and a theory of practice. The model of language which informs this book, derived as it is from the critical linguistics of Kress and Fairclough, emphasizes the interaction of text and practice by presenting three basic dimensions of language in use:

- language as text;
- language as social process;
- language as social practice.

This book has also emphasized the situated nature of literacy practices and thus the crucial role of context in understanding literacy in use. Context here is not just the immediate context of situation in which uses of literacy occur, but the ways in which broader socio-cultural categories impinge on and shape literacy practices, through social power relations, the impact of institutions and ideologies.

It is, however, important to hold onto the fact that it is in the process dimension that the everyday unfolding of social life is played out: institutions and power relations are made and remade through a myriad of instances of social interaction, whether face-to-face or mediated by other forms of communication. In the case of literacy as social process, these myriad of instances are the uses of writing to achieve social purposes, whether it be taking a phone message, writing a report at work, keeping a diary, sending the Christmas cards, writing books, the uses of reading – for example, to look up a name in the telephone directory, read a newspaper or read a novel. Introducing the dimension of literacy as social practice helps to account for the ways in which power relations operate in social process. When Billy asked the librarian for a book about hawks, he was engaged in face-to-face interaction, yet complex power relations were in play. He was engaging with the library as institution and the library as discourse.

So, if ideologies and institutions and discourses routinely impinge on everyday social life, the next question is how do they do so? One of the most important answers to the *how* question is clearly through language. This throws us back to the dimension of language as text: how are the resources of language (spoken and written) mobilized to achieve social purposes? What resources were Billy and the librarian drawing on to negotiate meaning? This leads us to try and understand some of the linguistic and interactional features of conversation. Yet another resource which the librarian (though not Billy) was drawing on is the organization of knowledge in the library (where does ornithology fit? under Zoology), again done through language. More distantly, the bureaucratic structure within which the library sits (the Borough) impinges on Billy's attempt to borrow a book. Again bureaucracies are organized through language.

So understanding literacy practices involves drawing on these interrelated dimensions. Instead of the neat, autonomous model of literacy as a neutral package of skills, the ideological model of literacy emphasizes its variability from context to context, from social practice to social practice (cf. Street 1993). What follows from this is that literacy cannot be taken as a given, a known technology transferable from context to context. Literacy practices remain to be discovered, investigated, researched.

INVISIBLE LITERACIES

This is in a way most obvious in the case of literacy practices that are in some ways submerged or invisible in relation to dominant literacy practices. Shuman (1986, 1993) researches the literacy practices of high-school students and discovers uses of literacy that would be invisible to the teaching staff. Weinstein-Shr (1993) investigates the literacy practices of members of the Hmong community in Philadelphia. Saxena (1994) gives a case study of literacy practices of Punjabi speakers in Southall. Again, these literacy practices are likely to be invisible to members of the dominant culture. As I suggested in Chapter 1, they need to be asserted, made explicit and their implications for education and other aspects of social life explored. This approach to investigating literacy practices serves to counter the universalizing claims of dominant literacy practices. The impact of gender in the production of invisible literacies is documented by feminist researchers such as Rockhill (1993) and Horsman (1990). In all of these contexts, power relations have in different ways created an invisibility around specific sets of literacy practices, set against the visibility of dominant literacy practices.

DOMINANT LITERACY PRACTICES: VISIBLE TO WHOM?

Curiously more difficult to grasp than the need to discover, investigate and research invisible literacies is the fact that dominant literacy practices are not necessarily obvious or visible either, and are in need of being uncovered and made visible. I will describe two ways in which this is so.

First, as the work of Heath and others has shown, different social groups have very different degrees of access to the communicative practices of the dominant culture. Heath's mainstream children make relatively easier transitions into the communicative practices of schooling than children from Trackton or Roadville, whose communicative practices are significantly different. Athabascan learner writers have discourse conventions which run counter to the discourse conventions of Anglo academic writing. Martin and others have argued that there is a 'Secret English' (Martin *et al.* 1988) which is not accessible to members of non-mainstream communities, which needs to be made explicit, made visible as part of a literacy pedagogy. This Secret English is one of the means by which dominant groups achieve and maintain social power.

Secondly, rapid shifts and changes in society produce corresponding shifts and changes in communicative practice generally and literacy practices in particular. The advent of word-processing may radically alter the ways in which writers compose. The advent of the technology that permits teleconferencing radically alters the meeting as a communicative event, since the visual dimension of face-to-face interaction is absent. Changes in work organization mean that materials may be ordered in a storeroom through a computer system with requisitions entered on a keyboard. The dimensions of literacy practices are constantly being re-defined by these changes in social practices. These shifts and changes need to be made visible. Take as a concrete example a literacy teacher in a workplace: in order to teach report writing in that workplace, she must have a good idea of the range of current practices in which report-writing is required. A reorganization or the introduction of a new communication technology – electronic mail, for example – will radically alter the communication demands of report writing, requiring a new phase of research and investigation.

What logically follows from this is the need for ethnographies of dominant literacies, to make explicit what is merely taken as given. In a current research project, Street and others are investigating the writing practices of respondents to the Mass Observation Archive at the University of Sussex. The subjects they are researching are necessarily literate enough to participate in the activity of responding to the Archive's questionnaires and directives. The project asks: what does writing mean to them?

In Heath's work, mainstream literacy practices are somehow taken as the given, while the literacy practices of non-dominant groups remain to be discovered and described. The shift described above means that we should not necessarily assume this is so, that there may be important gaps between the official versions of dominant literacy and actual practices. We need to treat the literacy practices of dominant groups as an important research area in itself.   It follows from this that a research/investigative orientation is an essential component of the understanding of literacy practices, and in the remaining sections of this chapter I will outline the different ways in which this is so, ranging from academically based research to practitioner research, as well as investigative work in literacy classrooms, carried out by students and teachers together. We will review some of the main methods of gathering information about literacy practices, asking what kind of research evidence they provide as well as what kind of ethical/political accountability is involved. The key questions here are:

- what counts as evidence in literacy research?
- how can this evidence be gathered?

Underlying this is an even more fundamental question:

- what counts as research?

DIFFERENT DOMAINS OF LITERACY RESEARCH: WHAT COUNTS AS RESEARCH?

In this chapter section I will argue for broad definitions of what counts as research: not just the research carried out by professional researchers in academic contexts, but also practitioner-led research and small-scale participatory research investigations in classrooms and as part of learning processes. As Cameron writes:

> All in all, I would prefer a broad definition of research, one that recognizes it can be done by people other than professional academics and for different types of audience – if a few hundred academic colleagues scattered over the globe count as the public domain, why not a few dozen people in a particular local community? Any active involvement in finding out something you did not know before must have a claim to the title 'research'. That some instances may prove more valuable, more influential and more lasting than others, I do not dispute. But I would want to insist that a project is not devoid of value because its impact is limited to a narrowly circumscribed time and place.

> (Cameron *et al.* 1992: 124)

Separating out the categories of academic research/practitioner research/small-scale investigations in classrooms and learning groups should not, however, be taken to mean that these categories are entirely separate. Powerful research strategies in areas like literacy should probably work in terms of partnerships between practitioners and researchers, while also involving the research 'subjects' in active ways. New definitions of research should challenge the dominant paradigms of academic disciplines. But since there is often little understanding between the different constituencies (researchers/practitioners/users) as to what the other is trying to do, it is worth dwelling for a while on the differences.

Academically based literacy research

Here professional researchers engage in a variety of types of research, including large-scale funded research, perhaps in multidisciplinary teams to investigate the literacy practices of a community or social group, to answer questions which will in some way create and extend a discipline-related body of knowledge and theory. In many cases the creation of knowledge and the extension of theory will have significant practical results as well. Good research will tend to be well informed about current practical issues and dilemmas in its field of interest. Examples of such research are the Morocco Literacy Project, described in Wagner *et al.* (1986) and Scribner and Cole's research in Liberia (1981), which combined psychological and ethnographic approaches.

Politically and ethically sensitive research will ask questions like: what are the research subjects getting out of the research, are their perspectives being represented fairly, what kind of commitment on the part of the researchers is there to keep the subjects of their research informed about its progress and outcomes? These issues are discussed in detail in Cameron *et al.* (1992). Research projects like the Literacy in the Community project, based at Lancaster University (cf. Barton and Padmore 1991) have tried to develop participatory approaches to literacy research that are 'person-respecting' and have the potential to empower participants in the research, not just to provide portable knowledge for the researchers.

Practitioner-led research

If academic research is to a greater or lesser extent defined by the production and extension of knowledge and theory, constrained by the research cultures of different disciplines in terms of what counts as knowledge and what counts as theory, practitioner-led research is to do with identifying research questions as they arise out of the practical activities of teaching and learning literacy, investigating these questions in ways that will inform, influence and improve practice. This kind of research will have an orientation to action, to refining and improving practice. It will often be conceived as a cyclical process of 'problem-sensing', 'problem-posing', 'problem-answering'. Ivanič and others, for example, have worked on the development of academic writing through research partnerships between learner writers and teachers (Ivanič and Roach 1990). The concerns of practitioner research can and should feed into the fields of academic research, thus creating a linkage between the different domains.

Small-scale investigations in classrooms and learning groups

If we understand research as process as well as product, then there is an important place for small-scale research in classrooms and learning groups. Heath (1983) has described how her students carried out ethnographies of literacy in their own communities, how school students adopted an investigative research approach in their studies. The activity of doing research itself is a complex one, involving different kinds of literacy practices. Take, for example, designing a questionnaire, carrying out an interview and writing up a report of the content of the interview. All of these will involve participants in complex uses of spoken and written language and will serve to expend their communicative range.

Case study
Research in a literacy class

As part of the ongoing evaluation process in a literacy class, students and teacher discuss what the students' preferred methods of learning are, to what extent the ways in which the class is currently organized meet the students' needs. Do they prefer to work individually or in groups? Which of the learning methods in use in the classroom seem to be most effective?

As an extension of this activity, the students in this class might design a questionnaire to find out what the preferred methods of learning are for other students in other classes. This would involve discussion and writing in the preparation of the questions to ask and preparing the interview as a whole: introducing yourself, explaining what the interview is about, making sure the interviewee is comfortable about it, asking questions, drawing the interview to a close. In carrying out the interview, oral skills would be demanded of the interviewer and written skills in recording the answers.

Through doing such an activity, students become actively involved in the evaluation process as well as extending skills in both spoken and written language.

QUALITATIVE OR QUANTITATIVE?

Qualitative research involves working with material that does not lend itself to the statistically based research methods of quantitative research – in other words, data that cannot be easily counted and compared with other similar data. Much ethnographic research and indeed much linguistic research is qualitative in this sense: based on case studies, the analysis of particular instances, or data where strictly comparable instances of the same phenomenon cannot be isolated. Stereotypically quantitative researchers would criticize qualitative research because it is not based on a representative sample, because the research cannot be replicated in other contexts and therefore tested. Qualitative researchers would reply that qualitative research can illuminate issues and problems that are beyond the reach of quantitative methodology. In fact, there is increasing recognition that both qualitative and quantitative approaches are necessary and that, rather than being opposed to each other, they should be seen as complementary.

It is useful to think of research that is *theory-generating* and research that is *theory-testing or theory-refining*. Qualitative research will often generate theory which can be tested or refined by quantitative methods.

An example of this is the work of Biber (1988), who uses a quantitative methodology to test out the constructs developed qualitatively to describe linguistic differences between spoken and written language. He argues that, instead of a one-dimensional representation of the differences between speech and writing, speech and writing can differ on a number of dimensions: he proposes a multi-dimensional model. He bases his conclusions on the analysis of grammatical features that have been claimed by different researchers, using qualitative data, to be typically spoken or typically written.

Biber's work brings quantitative methodology to bear on features of text organization, the language-as-text dimension of our model. Quantitative research can also operate at the macro-social level of literacy surveys, which try to discover, using large-scale sampling and questionnaires, the literacy profiles of members of a given population. Literacy surveys can have a great social impact and quantitative data can significantly influence policy-makers.Wickert (1991) describes the following scenario:

> The deputation: the minister, or his or her minder, has perhaps three minutes of active listening time. He or she wants to know, how much of a problem it is (i.e. how many votes are in it), why should he/she do anything about it (i.e. how many votes are in it) and what is it going to cost? In this context, literacy rates are

'counters in a political game over resources' (Street 1990). Literacy is defined and literacy rates are developed for this purpose.

(Wickert 1991: 6)

Wickert goes on to argue that literacy surveys, to determine literacy rates and thus inform policy, are only as good as the theory of literacy that informs them. In her own study of literacy in Australia, she works from the assumption argued in this book that literacy is not a monolithic entity, that instead there are a diversity of literacies and therefore 'no single measure' is adequate to describe what counts as achievement in them.

Quantitative research is, and will continue to be, important in all areas of literacy research, particularly where it seeks to influence policy-makers, but it is important that it is influenced and informed by adequate theory and that theory may well be developed through qualitative work.

INVESTIGATING LITERACY IN THE WORKPLACE

The workplace as a 'literacy site' provides a kind of microcosm for many of the issues raised in this book. In this section, I will illustrate the ways that a research and investigative approach to understanding literacy practices is part of educational work, rather than part of an academic research project.

So how do you start investigating literacy practices in the workplace? There are a range of research methods possible, all of which involve getting into the 'literacy site', spending time there finding out how literacy is done, how it is seen to be done and how it interrelates with other kinds of social organization.

RESEARCHING THE WORKPLACE

What needs to be avoided is a quick 'raid on the data' approach, in which an outsider spends a few hours on a rapid tour of the worksite, gathering texts, making a few superficial observations about how these texts are being used, possibly speaking to a few workers, and coming out with a hastily put together 'literacy skills audit' which may overemphasize official versions of literacy practices and miss crucial ways in which literacy practices operate as part of the social organization of work.

Time is money, and there are clearly pressures against language and literacy providers endlessly cluttering up the workplace, observing literacy practices and interviewing key operators, but it is also important to hold on to good practice principles of a long lead-up time in setting up programmes, where this kind of investigative work can be carried out, involving both *participation* and *observation*.

Case study
Training for signallers in a state rail authority

In this particular State Rail Authority, those working on the line are undergoing training to upgrade their skills in areas like safety when working on the line. A significant proportion of the workforce have poor spoken language and literacy skills, therefore an effective language and literacy input into these training modules is essential. A prerequisite for trainers is that they should have obtained the ticket for the training module they are teaching, so the language and literacy workers all go through the training modules on which they will be working. This gives them first-hand, inside experience both of the language and literacy demands of the training module, as well as the work skills involved.

This practice enables language and literacy workers, outsiders in this worksite, to become insiders by participating in training, while giving them the opportunity to be observers, using their professional skills to assess the language and literacy demands of the training module and develop strategies for effective training for workers with low spoken language and literacy skills.

ANALYSING WORKPLACE LANGUAGE (SPOKEN AND WRITTEN)

The participant observation methodology can provide important information about the role of literacy in workplace practices, providing detailed notes are taken of the kinds of observations and issues that are noticed by the participant observer. Yet sooner or later, it is necessary to try and find out *how* spoken language and literacy are part of the social organization of work. This involves gathering language data; for example, written texts in the workplace, such as procedures, different kinds of forms, information on pay and conditions, occupational health and safety, to name but a few.

An accident report form, for example, will have both reading and writing demands associated with it. Examples of the accident report forms will form a valuable source of data in understanding one aspect of the spoken language and literacy demands of the worksite. Just as interesting, however, are examples of completed accident report forms, which will provide information both about the language demands of completing the form and about how individual workers are dealing with the literacy task.

Written texts are relatively easy to gather and study, for obvious reasons. They can be collected, photocopied, studied at leisure. However, the role of spoken language is equally crucial. How does a given worker go about completing an accident report form? It may well turn out to be a jointly negotiated literacy event, involving people in different ways as mediators, facilitators, scribes, such as has been described above.

Gathering information about literacy events is more difficult than gathering the written texts that are its output. It is possible to observe and document such literacy events using participant observation, yet to be really useful the spoken language component needs to be gathered, using tape- or video-recording, so that careful, analytic attention can be paid to the spoken language just as it is to the written texts.

Documenting and analysing literacy events involves 'language as social process', getting things done by means of language. What the 'new literacy studies' show us is that literacy tasks are frequently accomplished by the interaction of spoken and written modes.

Language-based data, whether collected written texts, or tape-recorded instances of work practices with literacy components, are 'first-order data'. They provide evidence of what people do with literacy and how literacy operates in the social organization of work. Different kinds of text analysis are a powerful way of demonstrating how literacy practices make possible and support different kinds of social organization and ideological positions. This critical, deconstructive work takes us into the area of 'language as social practice', finding out how literacy practices create and maintain different kinds of social organization, in this case the social organization of work.

As we saw above, literacy practices involve not just doing but the ways in which doing is constructed by participants. For this reason, literacy practices are not discoverable by the external observation of the narrow Taylorist approach, which looks for discrete, observable skills or competencies. Some kind of deconstructive work is necessary which goes beyond what can be observed. Text analysis is a powerful way of doing this.

PARTICIPANTS' ACCOUNTS: A SECONDARY DATA SOURCE

Another, secondary, data source, however, comes from the accounts of participants in the literacy practices in which they talk or write about their own understandings of how literacy is done. Methodologies like 'critical incident analysis' are dependent on this second-order data: not doing, but talking about doing.

This second-order data can, of course, be analysed from a linguistic perspective as text in its own right. How do participants' accounts of literacy practices provide evidence of values and ideological positions on literacy in particular and the social organization of work in general? Take the narrative genre. Stories are generally told to make a point. They evaluate themselves. Unpacking the evaluation and other features of schematic structure and textual organization can provide insight into the ways in which participants are constructing literacy practices in particular and social practices more generally.

By compiling a range of sources of data, a rich, multi-level account of literacy practices can be assembled: the workplace texts, the typical interactions around the production and consumption of these texts, the ways in which these literacy practices form part of the social organization of work. In the following example we will look at the contribution of different kinds of spoken language data to the rich multi-level account of literacy practices.

WHAT COUNTS AS PROGRESS IN A WORKPLACE LITERACY COURSE?

Participants' accounts can provide information of many different sorts in workplace spoken language and literacy programmes. The following extracts, again from Chang (1992), illustrate their use as data for evaluation of progress. In the first stage of the evaluation, near the beginning of the spoken language and literacy programme in which Time participated, he is clearly at a loss to describe in detail the work processes involved in 'checking quality'.

Evaluation stage one

ANGE: In paintline how do you check the quality?
TIME: Oh sometimes we checking up . . . on the . . . uh . . . it's not quite . . . (ANGE: It's not quite what?) it's not quite good, we can . . . uh . . . I don't know how can I say it . . . uh that yeah you can check up where you looking up . . . it's not very uh . . .
ANGE: Do you get many, many pieces that are not so good?
TIME: Well no sometimes.
ANGE: All right, tell me about your family, about how many children.

Time has to appeal directly to the interviewer for assistance:

I don't know how can I say it

and shortly afterwards the interviewer abandons the topic and switches to another.

Evaluation stage two

ANGE: Yeah great, what about safety, Time, do you think you can talk more about the hazards at work, you know the dangers, if there is any dangers?
TIME: Yeah, I think I'm understand the dangers. There's any accident happen, I'm uh understand how to explain and talk to somebody to let them know the problem
ANGE: That's really good, that's important isn't it?
TIME: But the other day I say thanks, I had a day off, sickie last week and when I come with the uh doctor's certificate I ask Steve Hobbs . . . this the form . . . I want to fill and I fill it up and Steve say 'thanks' and I say 'Is that right?' and he say 'Oh yeah' and 'Oh that's the thing I learnt from school'. He's very happy. He say 'Oh, very good'.
ANGE: That's great Time . . . great.

At the second evaluation stage, as Chang points out, Time is able to report positive progress in his spoken and written language development, which he does by means of a little narrative in which he dramatizes an occasion when he successfully used something learned on the course with his supervisor. The narrative provides an opportunity to embed an evaluation of his progress in the reported speech of his supervisor:

He say: 'Oh very good'

WHAT COUNTS AS EVIDENCE IN LITERACY RESEARCH?

The above example of researching literacy practices in the workplace is taking research from a practitioner perspective. In this section we will review the theoretical constructs introduced in Chapter 2 and ask what kind of evidence is needed to investigate them.

Literacy practices

Since the idea of practice contains the two dimensions of what is being done and how participants understand, value and construct ideologies around what is being done, it follows that the necessary evidence for researching literacy practices must produce data to address both these dimensions. The 'what' of literacy practices occurs on observable, empirical occasions where participants make use of written language to achieve social purposes. This is where the idea of the 'literacy event' is important, and we will discuss the research issues in documenting and studying literacy events below.

The other dimension, asking how participants understand, value and construct ideologies around what is being done, clearly points to the collection of first-hand, 'insider' accounts in which subjects talk/write/reflect about their own literacies. Insider accounts can be collected through participant observation, with the researcher recording conversations and reflections in her field notes. Given the constraints of recording and summarizing conversation without tape-recording, this record will necessarily be highly interpreted by the researcher, highly analytical in the terms that Vološinov (1986) uses to describe indirectly reported speech, in which the speech of the reported other is integrated into the speech perspective of the reporter. This will be particularly the case in multi-lingual situations where conversation in one language is summarized in another. The narrative of the subject, the insider account, is recast into the narrative of the researcher and the research process. This kind of data collection is essential in situations where it is not appropriate or possible to use a tape-recorder, but it is clear that researcher accounts of insider accounts will be highly influenced by the researcher's perspective. Are there more direct ways to get access to insider accounts?

Tape-recorded interviews or conversations as well as written accounts both provide data on insider accounts. It is, however, worth remembering that interviews and conversation are jointly constructed by participants, reflecting the agenda of both interviewer and interviewed; there is a kind of intersubjectivity at work.

Tape-recorded data of insider accounts can be used in a number of ways in the research process. They can be analysed for their content, without particular regard for the ways in which the speaker constructs meaning in discourse. Another approach is to use the resources of linguistically based discourse analysis to try and understand how the speaker constructs ideological positions in discourse and asserts values.

Take as an example the data quoted above, when Time describes how he successfully achieves a workplace literacy task and is praised by his supervisor. We saw how Time uses the resources of narrative to dramatize a little incident which illustrates his own sense of having made progress in his English. One of the resources of narrative is to frame speech as being said by different characters, and here he frames a positive evaluation in the words of his supervisor.

I suppose my point here is that what the story is about can be read/interpreted as a kind of evidence of the way that the storyteller constructs ideologies and values – for example, what counts as extraordinary, incomprehensible, unreasonable – that narrative as a genre tends to be heavy with ideology and value. The narrative itself serves as a kind of evidence of the ideologies and values that drive it.

The insider accounts quoted in Chapter 3 are an example of this approach, which values not just *what* a speaker is saying, as summarizing or content analysis does, but also *how* they are saying it, arguing that the how of linguistic organization provides a privileged window into the ways in which a speaker constructs ideology and value in discourse.

Insider accounts of literacy practices such as narrative accounts obtained directly through interviews and the like are not the only way of gaining an understanding of the dimension of literacy practices. Activities and games can yield interesting information about the ways in which people value aspects of spoken and written language. Gardener (1988) describes an interesting activity she used as part of her research into language and second-chance education. She describes it as 'mapping speech relations', and requires participants to draw their inner map of whom they communicate with in what way and for what purpose. An activity which I sometimes use to generate an awareness of the importance of identity and language in teacher education courses that I teach is as follows:

Activity

On sheets of paper I write a brief description of the main language varieties in the current context, for example:

Standard English
Non-standard varieties of English
Languages other than English.

I stick each sheet on a different wall of the room and ask participants to stand up and move around the room till they find a position that most fits their own perception of where they are in relation to the different language varieties.

Invariably people will cluster in different ways, some clustering close to the Standard English sheet, others positioning themselves midway between Standard English and Non-standard English, or a language other than English.

The activity creates a kind of living scattergram of different positions in relation to the language varieties: a bilingual participant who positions himself between his first language and English, a working-class participant whose position mediates between the language acquired in her family and the language of schooling and the dominant culture.

This activity shows how language varieties create a kind of social space and also leads into a discussion of the identities and choices involved in living within this complex, multi-dimensional socio-linguistic space.

LITERACY EVENTS

A literacy event is an empirical, observable occasion when people achieve a literacy purpose, typically through a mix of spoken and written means. I argued in earlier chapters that in order to understand the social construction of literacy events it is not enough to have the summarizing data of the participant observer's field notes; we also need tape-recorded or video-recorded data of the literacy event in progress, in order to be able to analyse linguistically the fine-grained joint construction of meaning.

The ease or difficulty of capturing literacy events in progress is very dependent on the setting or domain where the literacy event is taking place as well as on the relationship between the researcher and the research site. If the researcher is an *insider* – for example, trying to document literacy practices in her own family, extended friendship network or workplace – then negotiating permission to tape-record will be very different than if the researcher is an *outsider*, coming into the research site as a relative stranger, having to negotiate access and permission to undertake research. These issues are usefully addressed in Hammersley and Atkinson (1983). There are, of course, some settings and domains that are easier to gain access to than others: educational settings are relatively easy of access, since the benefits of research may seem obvious, although an increasing awareness of the need for ethical controls over research is currently leading to the setting up of explicit procedures for negotiating permission to carry out research in educational settings. Consider, however, the issues involved in researching literacy practices at the board meetings of a large company, where material might be confidential, of an illegal gambling club, of graffiti artists working on advertising hoardings at night, situations where the presence of a researcher might seem somewhat superfluous.

Activity

Suppose you wanted to do some research into the literacy practices surrounding the leaving and taking of phone messages, either in your workplace or in some other domain: for example, in your own home, or in the homes and work places of your friends.

What sort of data would you need to collect? How would you go about negotiating permission to gather them?

GETTING GOOD SPOKEN LANGUAGE DATA

The ability to analyse the linguistic organization of the literacy event is dependent on being able to get good-quality recordings of the literacy event in progress. In non-experimental settings, all sorts of factors may become issues: in the workplace there may be levels of background noise that make tape-recording virtually impossible; in group situations multiple speakers may make it difficult to work out who is talking when, or produce a background hubbub of conversation that makes transcribing difficult. Some of these problems can be overcome with the right equipment; for example, unidirectional microphones. A good account of the issues involved in gathering linguistic data in context can be found in Stubbs (1983).

TEXT ANALYSIS

I am using text here in the technical linguistic sense, meaning complete chunks of discourse both spoken and written. The problems involved in gathering linguistic data for analysing language-as-text vary considerably depending on whether you are gathering spoken or written texts. In the section on the literacy event, I have described some of the issues involved in collecting spoken data. Analysis of spoken and written data requires a degree of linguistic training, although a useful introductory textbook outlining the various approaches is Stubbs (1983).

CROSS-CHECKING PERCEPTIONS

If, as a researcher, you are successful in gathering data of literacy practices and literacy events, the next problem is how to interpret and make sense of the data: participants' accounts of how they use literacy, tape-recordings of literacy events in progress. An important way of enriching your understanding of the data at this stage is to check back your perceptions with those involved: this is what seems to be happening, this is what you seem to be saying here, am I correct in interpreting it this way? The technical term for this cross-checking is *triangulation*: cross-checking the validity of your interpretations with research participants. It is also a way of giving research 'subjects' increased active involvement in the research process and feeding back some of the understandings gained by the researcher to other participants.

NETWORKS

A person's communication network is the web of relations with other people through which meanings are negotiated and exchanged in spoken and written language (and, of course, potentially through other channels such as visual or paralinguistic means). So how do we document this, what kinds of evidence are relevant? Here again different questions might arise:

1   Who is 'on the network'?
2   How is communication achieved by people on the network?
3   What kind of ideologies and values are implicated?

Answering these questions will involve different kinds of data collection: participant observation as well as interviews (who is 'on the network?'), collection of data on spoken interaction and written texts (how is communication achieved by people on the network?), interviews/conversations to gather insider accounts (what kinds of ideologies and values are implicated?).

Activity

Documenting your own written communication networks

Who do you communicate with through written language? Make a diagram including at least part of your network (which may be quite extensive) similar to the example here.

EXAMPLE (Figure 7.1)
Can you group your network members into specific domains (home, work, other)? Try to include the types of writing exchanged between the nodes of your network. Does your network start to get quite complex and therefore difficult to represent visually? If you are bi- or multi-literate, do your uses of different literacies show up in your network diagram? Are they separated into different domains (say, home or work) or do they overlap?

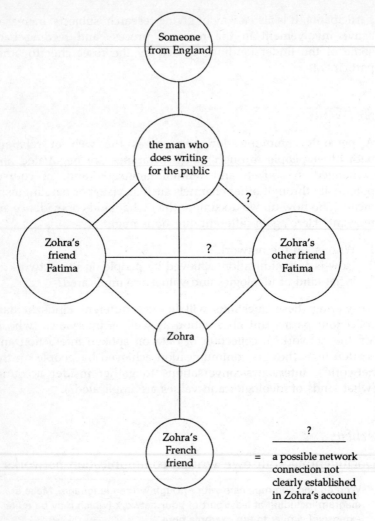

Figure 7.1 Partial network diagram based on Zohra's account of how she obtained her work permit (Pages 60–1)

MEDIATORS OF LITERACY

The questions here are similar to the discussion on networks.

1 Who serves as a mediator for whom?
2 How is the communicative purpose achieved?

3   What values and ideologies surround the activities you observe?

Discussion

What types of evidence and methods of collecting data would help you to answer these questions?

To keep it concrete, try and apply this to occasions when you have made use of a mediator of literacy or been drawn on as a mediator of literacy by someone else.

DOMAINS OF LITERACY

Activity

Look back at the two examples of projects mentioned in Chapter 2 (Wagner *et al.* 1986: Klassen 1991) that used the domain construct (Pages 68–9).

Try and work out the domains in which your own uses of literacy occur. Are the classification of domains you come up with similar to those in Chapter 2? What procedures did you use to classify your uses of literacy into domains of use? What kinds of information did you make use of?

CONCLUSION

This book has argued for the need to understand literacy not as a neutral set of decontextualized skills, but as situated social practice. This shift in perspective presupposes a research/investigative approach to understanding literacy practices. If literacy is not a given, it remains to be discovered.

This chapter has outlined some of the issues involved in researching literacy practices from three perspectives: from the perspective of academic research into literacy; from the perspective of practitioner research; and from the perspective of ongoing investigative activities as part of the literacy curriculum.

The scope of research covered here is rather broader than that covered in conventional academic work, extending to include a range of everyday investigative activities, through which researchers/learners learn to ask questions and try to discover answers. I have argued that an effective approach to literacy research should create research partnerships, not just between researchers in academic disciplines, but also with teachers and students and users of literacy.

The essence of a research orientation is that it asks questions: *what, how, why*? I have argued that asking questions is a key component of critical literacy.

In this book I have tried to show how one of the shifts brought about by the new approaches to studying literacy is that, instead of seeing literacy practices as something given/transparent, obvious to anyone (anyone literate, that is), we need to develop an investigative approach to literacy practices: to find out what literacy does or means in specific contexts, how it is used, how it is seen to be used, exploring the gaps there may be between official public positions and actual day-to-day practices, working out what ideological positions are being articulated, what institutional power bases are being asserted, maintained or challenged. Investigating literacy as situated social practice necessarily involves a critical perspective on literacy, because it uncovers the way in which literacy works with and for other kinds of social practice.

SUGGESTIONS FOR FURTHER READING

Academic research on literacy is written up in a number of journals. Examples of these are:

Discourse and Society
Discourse Processes
Harvard Educational Review
Language and Education
Linguistics and Education

A good introduction to research methods from an ethnographic perspective in Hammersley and Atkinson (1983), Stubbs (1983: chap. 10) gives a good overview of methodological issues in sociolinguistic research. Cameron *et al.* (1992) raise important issues relating to the ethics and politics of research on language, using examples from sociolinguistics, anthropology and cultural studies.

Practitioner research and ongoing accounts of academic research that tries to form participatory links with practitioner perspectives can be found in:

Research and Practice in Adult Literacy (RaPAL) Bulletin

The RaPAL group also produce a bibliography of literacy research which can be obtained from:

RaPAL
Department of Linguistics and English Language
University of Lancaster
Bailrigg
Lancaster LA1 4YT
UK

Bibliography

Anderson, A.B., Teale, W.B. and Estrada, E. (1980) 'Low income children's preschool literacy experience: some naturalistic observations', *The Quarterly Newsletter of the Laboratory of Comparative Human Cognition* **2** (3): 59–65.

Baker, C. (1991) 'Literary Practices and Social Relations in Classroom Reading Events', in C. Baker and A. Luke 1991.

Baker, C. and Luke, A. (eds) (1991) 'Towards a Critical Sociology of Reading Pedagogy'. Papers of the XII World Congress on Reading. Philadelphia: John Benjamins.

Bakhtin, M. (1981) *The Dialogic Imagination*, Austin: University of Texas Press.

Bartlett, F. C. (1932) *Remembering*, Cambridge: Cambridge University Press.

Barton, D. and Ivanič, R. (1988) in J. McCaffrey and B. Street (eds) *Literacy Research in the UK: Adult and School Perspectives*, Lancaster: RaPAL.

Barton, D. and Ivanič, R. (1991) *Writing in the Community*, London: Sage.

Barton, D. and Padmore, S. (1991) 'Roles, networks and values in everyday writing', in D. Barton and R. Ivanic (eds), *Writing in the Community*, London: Sage.

Basso, K.H. (1974) 'The ethnography of writing', in R. Bauman and J. Sherzer (eds) *Explorations in the Ethnography of Speaking*, Cambridge: Cambridge University Press.

Bauman, R. & J. Sherzer (eds) (1974) *Explorations in the Ethnography of Speaking*, Cambridge: Cambridge University Press.

Baynham, M. (1987) 'The oral dimension of a literacy event: a letter from the DHSS', in T. Bloor and J. Norrish (eds) *Written Language*, London: CILT, pp. 98–113.

Baynham, M.J. (1988) 'Narrative and narrativity in the English of a first generation migrant community', Unpublished PhD thesis, University of Reading.

Baynham, M.J. (1993) 'Code-switching and mode-switching: community interpreters and mediators of literacy', in B. Street (ed.) *Cross-cultural*

Approaches To Literacy, Cambridge: Cambridge University Press, pp. 294–314.

Baynham, M.J. and Mace, J. (eds) (1986) 'Doing research: a collection of papers on research and practice in adult literacy', London: Lee Community Education Centre, Goldsmiths' College.

Baynham, M. and Zagzoule, H. (1985) 'The Moroccan community in West London' in *the 25th Anniversary Report of the Notting Hill Social Council*.

Biber, D. (1988) *Variation across speech and writing*, Cambridge: Cambridge University Press.

Billington, R. (1985) 'Our lives . . . our language – student writing', London: ILEA Afro-Caribbean Language and Literacy Project.

Bishop, H. (1989) 'Contradictions in provision for bilingual students aged 15 – 19', Part One *Language Issues*, Vol. 3, No. 2.

Bishop, H. (1990) 'Contradictions in provision for bilingual students aged 15 – 19', Part Two *Language Issues* Vol. 4, No. 1.

Bloome, D. (ed.) (1989) *Classrooms and Literacy*, Norwood, NJ: ABLEX.

Bloor, T. and Norrish, J. (eds) *Written Language*, British Studies in Applied Linguistics, 2, Centre for Information on Language Teaching and Research for British Association for Applied Linguistics.

Boissevain, J. (1978) *Friends of Friends: Networks, Manipulators and Coalitions*, Oxford: Blackwell.

Bourdieu, P. (1979) *Outline of a Theory of Practice*, Cambridge: Cambridge University Press.

Brooks, T. and Roberts, C. (1985) '"No five fingers are all alike": managing change and difference in the multi-ethnic workplace', in C. Brumfit, R. Ellis and J. Levine (eds) *English as a Second Language in the United Kingdom: Linguistic and Educational Contexts*, London: British Council/Pergamon.

Brown, J. and Yule, G. (1983) *Discourse Analysis*, Cambridge: Cambridge University Press.

Burnaby, B. & Bell, J. (undated) *ESL and Adult Literacy: the Canadian situation*, Toronto: Ontario Institute for Studies in Education.

Burton, D. (1980) *Dialogue and Discourse: A Sociolinguistic Approach to Modern Drama and Naturally Occurring Conversation*, London: Routledge & Kegan Paul.

Cameron, D. (1985) *Feminism and Linguistic Theory*, London: Macmillan.

Cameron, D., Frazer, E., Harvey, P., Rampton, M.B.H. and Richardson, K. (1992) *Researching Language: Issues of Power and Method*, London: Routledge & Kegan Paul.

Candlin, C. (1986) 'Explaining moments of conflict in discourse'. Paper given at Linguistics and Politics Conference, University of Lancaster.

Carrell, P., Devine, J. and Eskey, D. (eds) (1988) *Interactive Approaches to Second Language Reading* Cambridge: Cambridge University Press.

Carrell, P.L. and Eisterhold, J.C. (1988) 'Schema theory and ESL reading pedagogy', in P. Carrell, J. Devine and D. Eskey (eds).

Carter, R. (ed.) (1991) *Knowledge about Language and the Curriculum*, London: Hodder & Stoughton.

Cassar-Patty, V. (1991) 'The role of language in teaching maths', *Good Practice in Australian Adult Literacy and Basic Education*, Vol. 11, pp. 1–5.

Cazden, C., John, V.P. and Hymes, D. (1972) *Functions of Language in the Classroom*, New York: Teachers' College Press.

Chang, A. (1992) 'The role of the enterprise based language teacher', Unpublished MA TESOL dissertation, University of Technology, Sydney.

Chase, G. (1988) 'Accommodation, resistance and the politics of student writing'. College Composition and Communication, Vol. 39, No. 1, pp. 13–22.

Chau, E. (1991) 'An Investigation of Learner's Use of their own Language in Classroom Interaction', unpublished MA TESOL dissertation, University of Technology, Sydney.

Christie, F. (ed.) (1990) *Literacy for a Changing World*, Melbourne: ACER.

Clark, R., Fairclough, N., Ivanič, R., McLeod, J., Thomas, J. and Hearrn, P. (1990) Language and Power: British Studies in Applied Linguistics 5. London: BAAL.

Cole, P. and Morgan, J. (eds) (1975) *Syntax and Semantics*, vol. 3, *Speech Acts*, New York: Academic Press.

Cook-Gumperz, J. (ed.) (1986) *The Social Construction of Literacy*, Cambridge: Cambridge University Press.

Coote, E. (1596) *The English Schoolmaster*

Cope, B. (1986) 'Traditional versus progressivist pedagogy', Social Literacy Monograph, 11, Sydney: Common Ground.

Cope, B. and Kalantzis, M. (1990) 'Literacy in the Social Sciences', in F. Christie (ed.) *Literacy for a Changing World*, Melbourne: ACER.

Corson, D. (1985) *The Lexical Bar*, London: Pergamon.

Coulthard, M. (ed.) (1992) *Advances in Spoken Discourse Analysis*, London: Routledge.

Cummins, J. and Swain, M. (1986) *Bilingualism in Education: Aspects of Theory, Research and Practice*, London: Longman.

Davies, W.J. (1973) *Teaching Reading in Early England*, London: Pitman.

Donaldson, M. (1984) *Children's Minds*, London: Flamingo.

Drew, R.A. & Mikulecky, L. (1988) *How to Gather and Develop Job Specific Literacy Materials for Basic Skills Instruction: A Practitioner's Guide*, The Office of Education and Training Resources, School of Education, Indiana University, Bloomington, Ind.

Durie, J. (1991) 'Literacy in the textile, clothing and footwear industries', in P. O'Connor (ed.) *Pitfalls and Possibilities: Women and Workplace Basic Education*, Sydney: Workplace Basic Education Resources Project.

Dwyer, D. (1978) *Self-Images: Male and Female in Morocco*, New York: Columbia University Press.

Eco, U. (1979) *The Role of the Reader: Explorations in the Semiotics of Texts*, London: Hutchinson.

Edwards, J. (1986) *Working Class Adult Education in Liverpool: A Radical Approach*, Manchester: Manchester Monographs.

Edwards, J. (1988) 'Research in adult education: from practice to theory', in J. McCaffrey and B. Street (eds) *Literacy Research in the UK: Adult and School Perspectives*, Lancaster: RaPAL.

Eggins, S., Wignell, P. and Martin, J. (1987) 'The discourse of History: distancing the recoverable past'. Working Papers in Linguistics No. 5. Linguistics Dept: University of Sydney.

Eisenstein, E. (1979) *The Printing Press as an Agent of Change*, 2 Vols, Cambridge: Cambridge University Press.

Elbaja, M. (1979) 'My Life', in *Our Lives*, ILEA English Centre

El Kssmi, Z. (1979) 'Families', in *Our Lives*, ILEA English Centre.

Erickson, F. and Schultz, J. (1982) *The Counsellor as Gatekeeper: Social Interaction in Interviews*, New York: Academic Press.

Fairclough, N. L. (1985) 'Critical and descriptive goals in discourse analysis', *Journal of Pragmatics*, **9**: 739–63.

Fairclough, N.L. (1989) *Language and Power*, London: Longman.

Fairclough, N.L. (ed.) (1992a) *Critical Language Awareness*, London: Longman.

Fairclough, N.L. (1992b) 'Discourse and text: linguistic and intertextual analysis within discourse analysis', *Discourse and Society*, **3** (2): 193–217.

Fingeret, A. (1983) 'Social network: a new perspective on independence and illiterate adults', *Adult Education Quarterly*, **33** (3): 133–4.

Finnegan, R. (1973) 'Literacy versus non-literacy: the great divide', in R. Finnegan and B. Horton (eds) *Modes of Thought*, London: Oxford University Press.

Finnegan, R. (1988) *Literacy and Orality*, Oxford: Blackwell.

Fishman, J. (1972) 'Domains and the relationship between micro- and macro-sociolinguists', in J.J. Gumperz and D. Hymes (eds) *Directions in Sociolinguistics: the ethnography of communication*, New York: Holt, Reinehart and Winston.

Foucault, M. (1972) *The Archaeology of Knowledge*, London: Tavistock.

Foucault, M. (1980) *Power/Knowledge*, Brighton: Harvester.

Freebody, P. and Luke, A. (1990) '"Literacies" programs: debates and demands in cultural context', *Prospect*, **5** (3): 7–16.

Freire, P. (1973) *Pedagogy of the Oppressed*, London: Penguin.

Freire, P. (1985) *The Politics of Education*, London: Macmillan.

Flowers & Hayes (1980) 'The cognition of discovery: defining a rhetorical problem', *College Composition and Communication*, Vol.31, No.1, pp. 21–32.

Flowers & Hayes (1981) 'A cognitive process theory of writing', *College Composition and Communication*, Vol. 3, No. 5, pp. 311–24.

Gardener, S. (1985) 'The development of written language within adult Fresh Start and Return to Learning programmes', ILEA Language and Literacy Unit, Occasional Paper No. 2.

Gardener, S. (1988) 'Language and second chance education', in J. McCaffrey and B. Street (eds) *Literacy Research in the UK: Adult and School Perspectives*, Lancaster: RaPAL.

Gee, J. (1988) 'The legacies of literacy: from Plato through to Harvey Graff', *Harvard Education Review*, **58**, (2): 195–212.

Gee, J. (1990) *Social Linguistics and Literacies: Ideologies in Discourses*, London: Falmer Press.

Geertz, C. (1973) *The Interpretation of Culture*, New York: Basic Books.

Geertz, C., Geertz, H. and Rosen, L. (1979) *Meaning and Order in Moroccan Society*, Cambridge: Cambridge University Press.

Giroux, H. (1983) 'Theory and resistance in education: pedagogy for the opposition'. South Hadley, MA: Bergin Garvey.

Giroux, H. (1988) 'Literacy, critical pedagogy and empowerment', unpublished article.

Goodman, K. (1985) *What's Whole in Whole Language*, Toronto, Ontario: Scholastic.

Goodman, Y., Watson, D. and Burke, C. (1987) *Reading Miscue Inventory: Alternative Procedures*, New York: Richard Owen.

Goody, J. (ed.) (1968) *Literacy in Traditional Societies*, Cambridge: Cambridge University Press.

Goody, J. and Watt, I. (1968) 'The Consequences of Literacy', in J. Goody (ed.) *Literacy in Traditional Societies*, Cambridge: Cambridge University Press.

Graff, H. (1979) *The Literacy Myth: Literacy and Society in the Nineteenth-Century City*, New York: Academic Press.

Graff, H. (1987) *The Legacies of Literacy*, Bloomington, Ind.: Indiana University Press.

Gregory, G. (1991) 'Community Publishing as Self-Education' in D. Barton and R. Ivanič (eds) *Writing in the Community*, London: Sage.

Green, J. and Wallat, C. (1981) *Ethnography and Language in Educational Settings*, Norwood, NJ: Ablex.

Grice, H.P. (1975) 'Logic and conversation', in P. Cole and J. Morgan (eds) 41–58. *Syntax and Semantics*, Vol. 3, *Speech Acts*, New York: Academic Press, p1.

Gumperz, J.J. (1982) *Discourse Strategies*, London: Cambridge University Press.

Habermas, (1979) *Communication and the Evolution of Society*, Boston: Beacon Press.

Halliday, M.A.K. (1985a) *An Introduction to Functional Grammar*, London: Edward Arnold.

Halliday, M.A.K. (1985b) *Spoken and Written Language*, Geelong, Victoria: Deakin University Press.

Halliday, M.A.K. and Hasan R. (1976) *Cohesion in English*, London: Longman.

Hamilton, M. D. Barton & R. Ivanič (eds.) *Worlds of Literacy*, Clevedon: Multilingual Matters.

Hammersley, M. and Atkinson P. (1983) *Ethnography: Principles into Practice*, London: Tavistock.

Hammond, J. (1990) 'Spoken and written language', in F. Christie (ed.) *Literacy for a Changing World*, Melbourne: ACER.

Havelock, E.A. (1978) *The Greek Concept of Justice: From its Shadow in Homer to its Substance in Plato*, Cambridge, Mass.: Harvard University Press.

Hawkins, E. (1984) *Awareness of Language: an introduction*, Cambridge: Cambridge University Press.

Heap, J. (1991) 'A Situated Perspective on What Counts as Reading', in Baker and Luke (1991).

Heath, S.B. (1983) *Ways with Words: Language, Life and Work in Communities and Classrooms*, Cambridge: Cambridge University Press.

Hines, B. (1974) *Kes: A Kestrel for a Knave*, London: Michael Joseph.

Hoggart, R. (1992) *The Uses of Literacy: Aspects of Working Class Life*, Harmondsworth: Penguin.

Hood, S. (1990) 'Second Language Literacy: working with non-literate learners', *Prospect*, **5** (3): 52–61.

Horsman, J. (1990) 'Something in my Mind Besides the Everyday' *Women and Literacy*, Toronto: Women's Press.

Hussein, T. (1981) *An Egyptian Childhood*, London: Heinemann.

Ibn Hisham, A. (1346 A.H.) *Sirat an Nabi*, Cairo.

Inglis, F. (1985) *The Management of Ignorance: Political Theory and the Curriculum*, London: Blackwell.

Ivanič, R. (1986) 'ILEA Afro-Caribbean Language and Literature Project'. *RaPAL*, (Research and Practice in Adult Literature), No. **2** (Winter).

Ivanič, R. and Roach, D. (1990) 'Academic writing: power and disguise', in Clark, R., N. Fairclough, R. Ivanič, N. McLeod, J.Thomas and P. Meara (eds) *Language and Power*, British Studies in Applied Linguistics, **5**, London: British Association for Applied Linguistics/Centre for Information on Language Teaching and Research.

Johns, A.M. (1990) 'L1 composition theories: implications for developing theories of L2 composition', in B. Kroll (ed.) *Second Language Writing*, Cambridge, Cambridge University Press.

Johnson, J. (undated) *The Way Through: 'A Personal Journey through the Maze of Literacy'*, London: Cambridge House Literacy Scheme.

Kalantzis, M., Cope, B. and Slade, D. (1989) *Minority Languages and Dominant Culture*, London: Falmer.

Keller-Cohen, D. (1987) 'Literary Practices in Modern Credit Union', Language in Society, **16**, 7–24.

Kelly, P. (1986) 'How do ESL writers compose?' *Australian Review of Applied Linguistics*, Vol. 9, No. 2, 94–117.

King, S. (1991) 'Writing submissions and reports: submission and report writing for Aboriginal community development', *Education Links*, 39.

Klassen, C. (1991) 'Bilingual Written Language Use by Low-Education Latin American Newcomers', in D. Barton and R. Ivanič (eds) *Writing in the Community*, London: Sage.

Krashen, S. (1981) *Second Language Acquisition and Second Language Learning*, Oxford: Pergamon.

Kress, G. (1988) 'Language as social practice', in G. Kress (ed.) *Communication and Culture*, Sydney: New South Wales University Press.

Kress, G. (1989) *Linguistic Processes in Sociocultural Practice*, Oxford: Oxford University Press.

Kress, G. and Hodge, B. (1979) *Language as Ideology*. London: Routledge and Kegan Paul.

Kress. G. and van Leeuwen, T. (1990) *Reading Images*, Geelong, Victoria: Deakin University Press.

Kristeva, J. (1986) 'Word, dialogue and novel', in T. Moi (ed.) *The Kristeva Reader*, New York: Columbia University Press.

Labov, W. (1972) *Language in the Inner City*, Philadelphia: University of Philadelphia Press.

Labov, W. and Fanshel, D. (1977) *Therapeutic Discourse*, New York: Academic Press.

Lankshear, C. (1987) *Literacy, Schooling and Revolution*, London: Falmer Press.

Leacock, S. (1960) 'My Bank Account' in British and American Short Stories, Longman Simplified English Series, London: Longman.

Levine, K. (1986) *The Social Context of Literacy*, London: Routledge & Kegan Paul.

Levi-Strauss, C. (1976) *Tristes Tropiques*, Harmondsworth: Penguin.

Linguistic Minorities Project (LMP) (1985) *The Other Languages of England*, London: Routledge & Kegan Paul.

Luke, A. (1991) 'The Political Economy of Reading Instruction', in Baker and Luke (1991).

Luria, A. R. (1976) *Cognitive Development: Its Cultural and Social Foundations*, Cambridge, Mass.: Harvard University Press.

Mace, J. (1979) *Working with words*, London: Chameleon.

McAllister, J. and Robson, M. (1984) *Building a Framework*, Cambridge: National Extension College.

McCaffrey, J. and Street, B. (eds) (1988) *Literacy Research in the UK: Adult and School Perspectives*, Lancaster: RaPAL.

McLaughlin, J. (1986) 'Developing writing in English from Mother Tongue Story'. Language Issues, Vol. 1, No. 1.

Makaya and Bloor, (1987) 'Playing safe with predictions: hedging attribution and conditions in economic forecasting, in Bloor and Norrish.

Martin, J.R. (1986) 'Grammaticalising ecology: the politics of baby seals and kangaroos', in T. Threadgold, E.A. Grosz, G. Kress, M.A.K. Halliday (eds) *Semiotics – Ideology – Language*, Sydney: Sydney Studies in Society and Culture, 3: 225–67.

Martin, J. (1989) *Factual Writing: exploring and challenging social reality*, Oxford: Oxford University Press.

Martin, J.R. and Rothery, J. (1980, 1981) Writing Project Reports, 1 and 2, Working Papers in Linguistics, Linguistics Department, University of Sydney.

Martin, J.R., Wignell, P., Eggins, S., & Rothery, J. (1988) 'Secret English: discourse technology in a junior secondary school' in L. Genst, J. Oldenburg & T. Van Leeuwen (eds.) *Language & Socialisation: home and school*. Macquarie University, pp. 143–73.

Martin-Jones, M. (1984) 'The newer minorities: literacy and educational issues', in P. Trudgill (ed.) *Language in the British Isles*, Cambridge: Cambridge University Press.

Masing, H. (1992) 'Literacy practices in a small, rural ni-Vanuatu village', unpublished MA TESOL thesis, University of Technology, Sydney.

Meek, M. (1991) *On Being Literate*, London: Bodley Head.

Meinhof, U. (1987) 'Predicting: aspects of a strategic model of text comprehension', in T. Bloor and J. Norrish (eds) *Written Language*, London: CILT.

Michaels, S. (1986) 'The Teacher's Schema for Sharing Time' in J. Cook-Gumperz (ed.) *The Social Construction of Literacy*, Cambridge: Cambridge University Press.

Milulecky, L. (1987) 'The Status of Literacy in Our Society', in J. Readance and S. Baldwin (eds) *Research in Literacy: Merging Perspectives*, New York: National Reading Conference, 36th Yearbook, pp. 211–35.

Mikulecky, L. (1989) 'Second Chance Basic Skills Education', Project Report, US Department of Labor, Commission on Workforce Quality and Labour Market Efficiency.

Mikulecky, L. (1990) 'Basic skills impediments to communication between management and hourly employees', *Management Communication Quarterly*, 3 (4) (May): 452–73.

Minsky, M. (1975) 'A framework for representing knowledge', in P.H. Winson (ed.) *The Psychology of Computer Vision*, New York: McGraw-Hill.

Moss, W. (1987) *Breaking the Barriers: Access to Learning for Adults*, London: North London Open College Network.

Murray, D.E. (1988) 'The Context of oral and written language: a framework for mode and medium switching' *Language in Society*, **17**, 351–73.

Ong, W.J. (1982) *Orality and Literacy: The Technologizing of the Word*, London: Methuen.

Oxenham, J. (1980) *Literacy: reading, writing and social organization*, London: Routledge & Kegan Paul.

Painter, C. (1989) *Learning the Mother Tongue*, Oxford: Oxford University Press.

Polanyi, L. (1985) *Telling the American Story: A Structural and Cultural Analysis of Conversational Storytelling*, Norwood, NJ: Ablex.

Rahman, M. (1975) 'Dress Factory' in C. Searle (ed.) *Classrooms of Resistance*, London: Writers and Readers Publishing Cooperative.

Reid, I. (ed.) (1987) *The Place of Genre in Learning: current debates*, Geelong Deakin University.

Ricoeur, P. (1981) *Hermeneutics and the Human Sciences*, Cambridge: Cambridge University Press.

Roberts, C. (1989) 'Looking at learning/staff development for a multicultural society: teaching and learning strategies', *Language Issues*.

Robson, M. (1987) *Language, Learning and Race: Developing Communication Skills for a Multicultural Society*, Longman, for the Further Education Unit.

Rockhill, K. (1993) 'Gender, language and the politics of literacy', in B. Street (ed.) *Cross-cultural Approaches to Literacy*, Cambridge: Cambridge University Press, pp 156–75.

Rubin, J. (1975) 'What the Good Language Learner can Teach us'. *TESOL Quarterly*, Vol. 9, 41–51.

Said, E. (1978) *Orientalism*, New York: Pantheon.

Saxena, M. (1994) 'Literacies among the Panjabis in Southall (Britain)', M. Hamilton, D. Barton and R. Ivanič (eds) *Worlds of Literacy*, Clevedon, Avon: Multilingual Matters.

Scheeres, H. (1991) 'Language and literacy in trade classrooms: a teacher education course', *CATALPA Bulletin*, 1 (2) (April).

Scollon, R. and Scollon, S. (1981) *Narrative, Literacy and Face in Interethnic Communication*, New York: Ablex.

Scribner, S. Cole, M. (1981) *The Psychology of Literacy*, Cambridge, Mass.: Harvard University Press.

Shor, I. (1986) *Culture Wars: School and Society in the Cultural Restoration 1969–1984*, New York: Methuen.

Shor, I. (1992) *Empowering Education: Critical Teaching for Social Change*, Chicago: University of Chicago Press.

Shor, I. and Freire, P. (1987) *A Pedagogy for Liberation*, South Hadley, Mass.: Begin/Garvey Press.

Shuman, A. (1986) *Storytelling Rights: The Uses of Oral and Written Texts by Urban Adolescents*, Cambridge: Cambridge University Press.

Shuman, A. (1993) 'Collaborative writing: appropriating power or reproducing authority?' in B. Street (ed.) *Cross-cultural Approaches to Literacy*, Cambridge: Cambridge University Press, pp. 247–71.

Silverman, D. and Torode, B. (1980) *The Material Word: Some theories of language and its limits*, London: Routledge and Kegan Paul.

Sinclair, J. M. and Brazil, D. (1982) *Teacher Talk*, Oxford: Oxford University Press.

Sinclair, J. M. and Coulthard, R.M. (1975) *Towards an Analysis of Discourse*, Oxford: Oxford University Press.

Slade, D. and Norris, L. (1985) *Teaching Casual Conversation*, Sydney: NSW Adult Migrant Education Service.

Smith, F. (1982) *Reading*, Cambridge: Cambridge University Press.

Snow, C. and Ferguson, C.A. (1977) *Talking to Children: language input and acquisition*, Cambridge: Cambridge University Press.

Sonnenburg, J. and Nussbaum, L. (1991) 'Joint adult migrant education service/technical and further education project on literacy and oral communication skills of operators in the textile, clothing and footwear industries', *CATALPA Bulletin*, 1, (2) University of Technology, Sydney, 11–12.

Stanovich, K.E. (1980) 'Towards an interactive-compensatory model of individual differences in the development of reading fluency', *Reading Research Quarterly*, 19(1): 32–71.

Steiner, E (1985) 'The concept of context and the theory of action', in P. Chilton (ed.) *Language and the Nuclear Arms Debate: Nukespeak Today*, London: Frances Pinter.

Street, B.V. (1984) *Literacy in Theory and Practice*, Cambridge: Cambridge University Press.

Street, B.V. (1986) 'Walter Ong on literacy', *Accents*, Journal of the Language Society of the University of Sussex, 1 (1): 1–5.

Street, B.V. (1987) 'Orality and literacy as ideological constructions: some problems in cross-cultural studies', in *From Orality to Literacy and Back . . Culture and History*, 2, University of Copenhagen.

Street, B.V. (1988) 'Literacy practices and literacy myths', in R. Saljo (ed.) *The Written Code and Conceptions of Reality*, Berlin: Springer Verlag.

Street, B.V. (1990) 'Putting literacies on the political agenda', *Open Letter*, 1 (1): 5–12.

Street, B.V. (ed.) (1993) *Cross-cultural Approaches to Literacy*, Cambridge: Cambridge University Press.

Stubbs, M. (1983) *Discourse Analysis: The Sociolinguistic Analysis of Natural Language*, Oxford: Blackwell.

Stubbs, M. (1986) *Educational Linguistics*, Oxford: Blackwell.

Stubbs, M. (1987) 'An educational theory of (written) language', in T.

Bloor and J. Norrish (eds) *Written Language*, British Studies in Applied Linguistics, 2, Centre for Information on Language Teaching and Research for British Association for Applied Linguistics, pp. 3–38.

Swales, J. (1990) *Genre Analysis: English in Academic and Research Settings*, Cambridge: Cambridge University Press.

Szwed, J. (1981) 'The ethnography of literacy', in M. F. Whiteman (ed.) *Writing: The Nature, Development and Teaching of Written Communication*, vol 1, *Variation in Writing: Functional and Linguistic Cultural Differences*, Baltimore, M.D.: Lawrence Erlbaum.

Tannen, D. (ed.) (1982) *Spoken and Written Language: Exploring Orality and Literacy*, Norwood, NJ: Ablex.

Tannen, D. (1989) *Talking Voices: Repetition, Dialogue and Imagery in Conversational Discourse*, Cambridge: Cambridge University Press.

Toolan, M. (1989) 'Analysing conversation in fiction: an example from Joyce's portrait', in R. Carter and P. Simpson (eds) *Language, Discourse and Literature: An Introductory Reader in Discourse Stylistics*, London: Unwin Hyman.

Vološinov, V.N. (1986) *Marxism and the Philosophy of Language*, Cambridge, Mass.:Harvard University Press.

Wagner, D. (1994) *Literacy, Culture and Development: becoming literate in Morocco*, Cambridge: Cambridge University Press.

Wagner, D.A., Messick, B.M. and Spratt, J. (1986) 'Studying literacy in Morocco', in B.B. Schieffelin and P. Gilmore (eds) *The Acquisition of Literacy: Ethnographic Perspectives*, Norwood, New Jersey: Ablex, pp. 233–60.

Weinstein-Shr, G. (1993) 'Literacy and social process: a community in transition', in B. Street (ed.) *Cross-cultural Approaches to Literacy*, Cambridge: Cambridge University Press, pp. 272–93.

Wickert, R. (1989) *No Single Measure: A Survey of Australian Literacy*, Canberra: Department of Employment, Education and Training.

Wickert, R. (1991) 'The door of history has opened . . . adult literacy; beyond facts and figures', *Education Links*, 39:4–7.

Windrow, M. (1986) *The Mediaeval Knight*, London: Franklin Watts.

Zamel, V. (1983) 'The composing processes of advanced ESL students: 6 case studies', *TESOL Quarterly*, Vol. 17, No. 2, pp. 165–87.

Index